THE OPTIMUM HEALTH GUIDE

Eileen Fletcher

THE OPTIMUM HEALTH GUIDE

SPIRE

Copyright © 1993 by Eileen Fletcher
First published in Great Britain 1993
Second impression 1993

Spire is an imprint of Hodder & Stoughton *Publishers*

British Library Cataloguing in Publication Data

A catalogue record for this book is available from the British Library

ISBN 0-340-58041-0

*Printed in Great Britain for Hodder and Stoughton Limited, Mill Road, Dunton Green,
Sevenoaks, Kent by Clays Ltd, St. Ives plc. Typeset by Phoenix Typesetting, Ilkley, West
Yorkshire.*

Hodder and Stoughton Editorial Offices: 47 Bedford Square, London WC1B 3DP.

FOREWORD

There are many factors which help people to realise their full potential in life. It has long been my view that three aspects of nutrition in particular require consideration: the availability of a good diet, the understanding to choose what is best for us, and the example of those whose own natural abilities have been maximised through taking the right nutrients. As Eileen Fletcher shows so well, when all three aspects are present in a family or community then the result is what we call 'health'. Without them, even people in the affluent West can suffer the results of malnutrition and all the common illnesses which this can cause. It is a problem far more widespread than we think.

Drawing together the work of early pioneers of good health such as Robert McCarrison, Weston Price and the doctors who launched the Peckham Experiment, Eileen Fletcher is to be congratulated on her fine achievement in *The Optimum Health Guide*. With many examples from her own experience, she shows how everyone can grow up and learn how to adjust their eating patterns for the better. By doing so we can all avoid the poor habits of a lifetime which damage us so much. Follow her advice and you will live a longer life, raise healthier children and enjoy greater emotional stability.

I commend *The Optimum Health Guide* to you. It recognises that the soil, the plants and animals, and even humankind itself, are all sustained by something greater than ourselves. Eileen Fletcher's is a voice we all need to hear.

Dr Kenneth Barlow
Formerly editor of Nutrition and Health magazine

DEDICATION

To Tracy, Mark, Adrian,
Nicola and Laura with
much love.

ACKNOWLEDGMENTS

My sincerest thanks to J John and to my editor at Hodder and Stoughton, whose encouragement and support made this book possible. Sheila Christopher of Designworks patiently proof-read, corrected and commented upon the manuscript, gave me confidence, and urged me on.

Dr Kenneth Barlow graciously checked my work, made suggestions and gave me encouragement. Dr Walter Yellowlees and Nim Barnes kindly provided papers and information. Dr Peter Dilworth once asked me to write something for him so I'd like to ask, 'Will this do?' Mary Langham of Wholefood Books was a wonderful and ever helpful source of information.

Ian, my husband, kept me up to date with nutritional events and reports, and patiently accepted the domestic chaos while I wrote. With love and gratitude to our precious sons Mark and Adrian who, when they came into our lives, inspired me to begin to learn how best to provide for their health. My sister Maureen has shared my enthusiasm for nutrition, and supported and encouraged me over the years.

My special thanks go to Helen Marley, my administrator, who gives her time so generously. Thanks also to Isobelle Little and Maureen and Mervyn Ricketts who first persuaded me to write a book, had faith in me, and urged me on. I am so grateful to the Toker family for allowing me to tell their stories, and for being such wonderful friends.

What would I have done without Hilary Cook who was always there when I needed her and Nicole Patey who listened? I want to thank Tina Mallinson and Jean Thompson for their friendship and support. To Jill Rigby, whose improved health was a great inspiration to me, I send special love to her and to all her family.

I am grateful to Gillian Broome, Hilary Martin, Suzie Andrews, and Janice Clarke for their contributions, and indebted to Barry Francis and David Morris who were so generous with their time and expertise. And last but certainly not least how can I adequately thank all those, too many to mention by name, who supported me in prayer throughout the writing of the book?

PREFACE

'What do I do and where do I start?' This is the question I've been asked most often whenever I've talked about nutrition. Perhaps the cost of vitamin and mineral tablets for the family had become too expensive and mothers wanted to know how they could improve their family's health on a limited budget. They hadn't realised just how much cheaper than convenience foods a healthy diet can be. It tastes better too!

I've talked to students, trying to get by on a grant, and career people whose biggest problem was shortage of time. I've chatted to young mothers, worried about their children's health, hyperactivity or learning difficulties. And I've spoken to the elderly who had plenty of time to spare, but were living on a barely adequate pension. The one common thread was the call for some *realistic* advice that wouldn't cost the earth.

Some of the people I've talked to had been trying to eat a good diet, either to improve their physical or emotional health, to have more energy, or to lose weight. But their good intentions fell by the wayside when the craving for chocolate or cakes became unbearable. 'How can I be consistent?' they asked. They needed to be persuaded that if they could deal with what was *causing* them to crave stodgy food then the healthy diet would be enjoyable rather than restrictive.

Others told me that they really didn't know why they were suffering from fatigue, headaches, indigestion, or mood swings, for example. 'What is *behind* my health problems?' they asked. They didn't have to live with their symptoms. They could do something about them. By dealing with *underlying* conditions, they were able to get much more out of life.

In this high-speed world people are bombarded with such a welter of information that they need an instantly digestible overview of the subject. 'I don't want to have to plough through too much detail,' people so often said. 'Just tell me what I *need* to know and make it readable!' So I started to produce information leaflets, which was fine until there were so many leaflets that it became obvious that it would be easier to put all the information into one book.

I have begun by dealing with the reasons why health has been declining, in order to throw some light on the cause of so much of the illness around today. Someone once said *'Unless we remember we cannot understand.'* We only need to consider the excellent health and longevity of some of the people of the past who drank full-cream milk and ate butter to realise that some of today's advice on cholesterol reduction, for example, is questionable.

It seems as if there has never been more nutritional information available but people often get confused, in the face of conflicting advice, about what really is beneficial. Alternative therapies abound nowadays and I'm often asked about these too. So the book is my response to the queries that most often crop up about health and alternative medicine, and it is an attempt to provide inexpensive, realistic suggestions for busy people.

However, no book can replace medical diagnosis and care, though good nutrition and lifestyle can accelerate recovery, and even prevent illness. I simply report on the work of nutritionists and doctors past and present. But I, my family, relatives, and many, many friends and acquaintances have made dramatic improvements in both physical and emotional health by putting into practice the subjects I've covered.

Complete health, however, requires more than just good food, so I conclude with a look at the emotional and spiritual aspects of health. There is widespread interest in these areas nowadays and, here again, I have tried to address the queries I most often receive about these subjects. This is the holistic approach, and once you have achieved your optimum health you will never be satisfied with anything less.

Eileen Fletcher
October 1992

CONTENTS

1

HEALTH ON A BUDGET

Tears streamed down my cheeks as I watched a young mother talking on a television documentary about her struggle to feed herself and three small children on £30 a week. There was no sign of self pity as she explained that she could only afford to eat one meal a day and regularly went without food so that her children would have enough to eat. The programme, *Eating Your Heart Out*, was part of ITV's *First Tuesday* series.

Anne Heughan of the Coronary Prevention Group had analysed the diets of various families and found undesirably high levels of fat and sugar in their daily intake of food. On the programme she commented sadly that while many are eating their way to ill health with excessive amounts of the wrong foods, there are still, in this day and age, some who cannot afford to eat enough, let alone to eat healthily.

Tim Lobstein of The Food Commission worked with the National Children's Homes to look at the diets of about 360 low-income families using the centres. The resulting NCH Poverty and Nutrition Survey,[1] published in 1991, reported that one in ten of the children were going without food occasionally, and that nearly half the parents, usually the mothers, were going without food quite often in order to ensure that their children had enough to eat. The survey also found that their diets were not really healthy.

Memories

These disturbing facts of the nineties put me in mind of my own childhood in the forties and fifties. Father worked on the docks in

Liverpool and his wage was barely enough to support a wife and four children. Though I didn't know it at the time, mother often went without food to make sure that we ate. But she could 'make a meal out of next to nothing', as she used to say, and she taught me from a very early age to cook cheap, filling meals.

I have many happy memories of times spent in a warm, steamy kitchen, playing with pastry and talking about the things that were so important to a little girl. Mother had that wonderful gift of being able to listen and to gently draw out those things that were troubling me.

She also had wisdom and a wonderful way of giving advice. 'Eileen,' she would say, 'I'm going to tell you something, but if you can't accept it now then I want you to tuck it away in the back of your mind and perhaps later it will come in useful.' Mum died in 1973 and I'm still fishing those little 'pearls of wisdom' out of the back of my mind!

Sometimes I recall her advice about relationships, or what really matters in life. Right now, though, I'm remembering those very practical lessons she taught me about feeding a family on next to nothing. And I'm thinking about that young mother, and people like her, who are struggling to feed their families on any diet, let alone a healthy one.

You've never had it so good

For many of us old enough to remember Prime Minister Harold Macmillan and his famous comment about our 'never having had it so good', things did get better. Married in the late sixties or early seventies as wages and house prices rose, we found ourselves with mortgages we could fairly easily afford.

We were more concerned with whether we could afford to buy our food from Marks and Spencer, or would have to make do with a cheaper supermarket, than where the next mouthful was coming from. My generation generally had enough to eat and suffered more from the problems of faulty nutrition than the problems of under-nutrition.

Our television screens graphically portray the tragic effects of famine in the Third World. Deforestation, war, and greed all contribute to the poverty that kills millions and leaves many more millions with lowered resistance to disease. Most of my generation had more to eat than ever before but, ironically, an abundance of the wrong foods left us, too, with lowered resistance to disease.

Starvation or under-nutrition is quickly recognised since it kills, either directly, or indirectly, as infectious diseases sweep through communities with little immunity. When the wrong type of food is plentiful, the effects of faulty nutrition are less easily recognised, but the end result is still poor immunity. Eating the wrong food can be just as bad for your health as eating too little food. It simply takes longer for degenerative disease to show itself.

Recession and health

But here in Britain, times are changing yet again. Soaring interest rates in recent years have made thousands homeless while many more thousands are struggling to pay the mortgage on a property they are unable to sell. Unemployment has risen drastically, even in the once prosperous south-east of England, where we now live since we moved from the north-west in 1987.

A massive increase in the size of mortgage we needed to buy a house in this area of the country made us painfully aware of how many people were struggling to pay their bills. Some of these people, like us, once had no more to worry about than where to go for their next holiday or which make of new car to buy.

Students are struggling to pay increasingly high rents on accommodation in addition to their concerns about the effects of cutbacks on equipment and education. Traditionally, they have always had very little money left from their grants for food, but things are getting much worse. While house prices have been rising at an unprecedented rate, the salary level at which parents become ineligible for a student grant for their children has been dropping.

Many of us are finding ourselves having to pay not only an unexpectedly high mortgage, but also an allowance the size of a mortgage for our student offspring. That doesn't leave a lot for food, either for ourselves or for our students.

Forcing change

Professor Philip James, Chairman of the World Health Organisation Committee On Diet And Health commented recently on
two government reports, *Health Of The Nation* and the so-called
COMA Report. The reports warn that, as a nation, we are too fat
and we have too many people with high blood pressure. 'People are
dying unnecessarily from heart disease at a surprisingly young age,'
he said. 'Cancers, diabetes, gall stones, and intestinal problems can
all be linked to diet.'

The reports point out that our food is inappropriate and unhealthy,
and that we should change our diet. They also say that we must have a
plan of action; we must have goals and targets. 'This affects the whole
of government and the whole of society,' said Professor James.

A good deal of responsibility for the present situation lies at
the door of government policies and vested interests that have
influenced agricultural and food production practices for many years.
But those dedicated individuals and organisations who have been
working tirelessly for so long to promote more awareness of the
health risks of many of our foods, have stimulated a consumer
revolution. This has encouraged the British government to legislate
for health, and food manufacturers to begin to produce healthier
products.

Writers and journalists have played a vital role in exposing the
dangers of some food additives, and other forms of pollution in
the food we eat, the water we drink and the air we breathe.
Ecologists have highlighted and campaigned against the potential
health risks of fertilisers, pesticides and other farming practices in
common use.

But when it comes to forcing change, the pound and the vote
are the most powerful weapons of all. Food manufacturers won't
produce what we refuse to buy, and government policies can be
influenced by public outcry, as the poll tax U-turn proved. We've
come a long way in our awareness of the relationship between
food and health since I first became interested in the subject in
1975.

However, Jack Winkler of Action And Advice On Sugars, pointed
out that we should recognise the strategy that the food industry

has pursued throughout the nineteen eighties. 'They are producing what I call healthy alternative products,' he said. 'A low fat, low sugar, nutritionally improved version of a standard food, which they present as the healthy option, and for which they normally charge a premium price. This strategy offers a special health product at a premium price but is of no relevance to the poor. They can't afford to buy it, they don't eat it, and their diet doesn't improve.'

He warned that the real risk of that particular strategy is that we are going to develop a two-tier food market in Britain, with healthy, expensive products for the affluent, and cheap, unhealthy products for the poor. 'That,' said Jack, 'will make the gap in diet-related diseases between the poor and the affluent even wider.'

The cost of health

Publicity about food and health has never been greater. Newspapers, magazines, books and television all promote the same message: 'Our national diet is killing us'. The statistics are frightening. Here in Britain more than 450 people die of heart disease every day! But we are being encouraged to eat a healthy diet at a time when many are becoming worse off.

People are struggling to feed their families, not just in high-rise tenements but in neat detached houses all over the country. Weighed down with the stress of financial problems and job worries, they are now feeling burdened with guilt by publicity about the damage we may be doing to our children's health.

The scale of illness throughout the nation is putting severe strain on the National Health Service and its resources. We have beaten most of the infectious illnesses of the past but replaced them with degenerative illnesses like cancer and heart disease. The Health Service has become a victim of its own success in the area of high-tech surgery. Brilliant but costly organ replacement operations hit the headlines but create higher expectations and even greater financial pressures.

People may be living longer than they did a hundred years ago but that has more to do with our doctors' ability to keep the unhealthy alive than with our capacity to build true health.

Coronary heart disease costs the health service £500 million a year and takes up 5,000 hospital beds a day.

We are already seeing the effects of cutbacks on our dental services, and the pressure is on to take out private insurance to cover dental treatment. No matter what government ministers say to try to reassure us, who can feel confident that the health service will be able to offer suitable treatment for all in the future? Hopefully the government will be able to work a miracle in the health service – but let's not bank on it.

Growing numbers of people, disillusioned with the concept of drugs and surgery, have been turning to alternative medicine. Some pay out hundreds of pounds in fees for a variety of therapies ranging from homeopathy to healing.

Leaving aside the question of the effectiveness of these treatments, the problem is that, though there are an increasing number of alternative health options, again, they are generally only available to those who can afford to pay for them.

Young people

More effort must be put into prevention rather than cure by the government, the medical profession, and by everyone. We cannot rely upon an increasingly burdened health service to undo the harm we have done to our health through poor diet and lifestyle.

Inevitably there will be those in every area of life who prefer to bury their heads in the sand rather than make an effort with diet. Certainly the middle classes have led the consumer revolution. But the selflessness and the determination to give their children the best possible start in life is not just confined to those who have plenty of money to spare. There always have been, and always will be, mothers like mine who, in spite of financial problems, shortage of time, and their own weariness, want to do their very best for their children.

Young people can sometimes be more open to health advice than their parents, and much more prepared to make changes in their lifestyles. Students struggling on a grant may realise that they will be able to concentrate better if they are adequately nourished. But they need to know how to provide themselves with all the nutrients they need at a time when they may still be growing and are busy living life to the full!

The elderly need a good diet but are often unable to afford to buy healthy foods on a low pension. Perhaps they cannot travel to do their shopping and are limited to the foods that are available from their local shops. Many elderly people have small appetites and don't get enough nutrients from the portions they are able to eat, and they may also be confused by conflicting nutritional advice.

What can we do?

The same dedicated individuals and groups who encouraged the consumer revolution will carry on working to try to force changes in agricultural and food manufacturing practices. Ecologists will continue to campaign against pollution and we should do all we can to all support those who are fighting to create a better life for our children.

But what can we do right now to improve our own and our children's health and to increase our chances of enjoying a long and healthy retirement? What can we do when money and time are in short supply? When we are feeling tired, below par and would much rather bury our heads in the pillow or slump in front of the television? When the kids are wearing us out and refusing to eat frozen peas, let alone a wholefood diet?

What can we do when the boss no longer believes we have a right to a lunch hour but expects us to grab a bite while staying at our desks? It's all very well knowing that heart disease and cancer are increasing but what can we do about it, surrounded by all the pressures of our modern lifestyles?

Perhaps because of my own childhood memories, my desire has always been to provide information for mothers who wanted to improve their families' health. In the mid-seventies when there was far less publicity on nutrition than there is nowadays, I would do this by giving a talk at a local church hall, or by producing simple information leaflets.

My greatest satisfaction came from seeing the delight of ordinary mothers like myself when they found that they were able to deal with their children's health problems, ranging from colds and earache to asthma, eczema and behavioural problems.

I've never forgotten those practical lessons that Mum taught me as a child but, as I learned more about the nutritional value of food, I began to substitute inexpensive but nutritious wholefoods for the white flour and white sugar ingredients she used in the days when their harmful effects were not so well known. I also added to our diet inexpensive health food supplements like molasses, brewer's yeast, and wheat germ.

Good health need not be expensive, and nature does have her own 'convenience foods'. I'd hate to have to go back to spending the amount of time cooking and preparing meals that I once thought was necessary. A fruit salad takes very little time to prepare; and give me a crisp, colourful side salad rather than soggy vegetables any day!

For me, the motivation for a healthy lifestyle comes more from the immediate effects I experience than from the hope of long-term benefits. I've proved over and over again that what I eat and do today affects how I will feel tomorrow and the next day.

And I know parents who are aware that they can influence their children's behaviour, concentration and learning skills almost on a daily basis, by what they allow them to eat, and this is confirmed by their children's teachers. The benefits to the whole family of happy, contented children more than make up for the effort and determination needed to coax them on to a healthier diet.

Stuffy offices, computer screens and a workaholic boss aren't conducive to good health. But, if we have no choice but to stay at our desk in the ever more competitive workplace, then the right foods and the best possible use of our free time can help to compensate.

It is a well-known fact that during the war the nation was healthier than at any other time this century. The 'National Loaf', rich in the bran and the germ of the wheat, was produced instead of the white loaf. Sugar, fat and meat were rationed and people were encouraged to 'dig for victory'. The foods that were most plentiful were the vegetables that people grew themselves. Properly grown vegetables, as we shall see later, are excellent health foods.

My experience has convinced me that expensive 'healthy options' ready-made meals and de-additived, de-fatted, reduced-sugar convenience foods, apart from being out of the reach of those on a limited budget, are not the best way to stay healthy.

A much more radical change is needed, and we must look further into the past to see that the healthiest races of people have never been the richest. Admittedly life has become much more complicated now, but there is still a great deal we can learn from those who lived by the land with an intuitive knowledge, passed on from generation to generation.

Life is for living – and cream cakes!

I adore cream cakes, and will continue to do so. When we go back home to the north-west we make straight for a wonderful old style seaside fish and chip restaurant and enjoy every mouthful of crispy battered haddock, perfectly cooked chips and delicious mushy peas, without feeling the tiniest shred of guilt. We have turkey, roast potatoes, and plum pudding at Christmas, and chocolate eggs at Easter.

Life is for living too, and there would be no point in being perfectly healthy if it meant being thoroughly miserable. Good health doesn't mean a life sentence of 'rabbit food' or textured soya protein, and we don't have to give up any of our favourite foods completely. What matters is what we eat day in, day out, not what we have for an occasional treat.

Zinc deficiency is very common and one of its symptoms is a reduction in the sense of taste. This makes food seem bland and uninteresting. People with zinc deficiency tend to need much more salt, sugar and other flavourings. A diet that corrects this deficiency can enable people to get much more enjoyment out of their food, and to rediscover half-forgotten flavours.

Jaded palates and the dietary habits of a lifetime can be re-educated so that foods which once had little appeal become a pleasure rather than an affliction. If my sons eat apple pie in a restaurant, they complain bitterly because it's invariably too sweet.

Foods that have been stripped of the nutrients our bodies need cause us to crave for more and more in an attempt to supply our requirements. Nutritious foods, however, satisfy the demand and enable us to stay slim with less effort.

Many who have tasted the emotional as well as the physical benefits of optimum health have discovered an enthusiasm for life they'd never before known. Nothing would tempt them to go back to their old ways.

Later in the book I'd like to offer some suggestions for a healthy diet and lifestyle that need not cost the earth, take away all the pleasures of life, or tie us to the kitchen sink for evermore. Within the confines of their own circumstances some will be able to do more than others, but even some of the cheapest, simplest tips can bring about marked improvements in health. As my mother used to say, 'Take what you can accept now, then tuck the rest away in the back of your mind and see if it comes in useful later.'

RECOMMENDED READING

Lobstein, T, *When parents go hungry so children can eat* (The Food Magazine July/Sept 1991).

2

HARD TIMES

It was Boxing Day, and our friends Chris and John had invited us over for a meal. Expatriates from Liverpool, like us, they moved south some years ago. Chris's father, Tommy, had made the journey down to Berkshire to stay with them over Christmas.

Reminiscing about his childhood in Liverpool during the terrible depression of the thirties, Tommy told me how his father would often deliberately leave his sandwiches behind when he set off for work in the morning. Money was short, food was scarce, and those 'jam butties' would be eaten by his five children.

For breakfast, Tommy remembers, they had 'pobs': crusts of white bread with sugar and warmed sterilised milk, 'sterry' as it was called then. Jam cost a halfpenny a cup in those days and Tommy would often be sent with a cup to the corner shop, where it was spooned out of a big stone jar. Damson and apple was Tommy's favourite.

The children usually took bread and jam to school for lunch. For tea there might be one egg between two children, eaten with white bread and marge and, in the winter, they would have an Oxo cube dissolved in hot water just before bedtime.

Life was hard for the families who lived in the two-up, two-down terraced houses of Toxteth, where each day would begin with the worry of whether or not father would be lucky enough to be picked out of the work queue. Every morning Tommy's dad would walk the seven miles to the flour mill, hoping that he would be given work.

A steady wage

When Tommy was eleven, however, his father was taken on permanently and, with a guaranteed wage of £2 a week, the family were able to move to a corporation house in Norris Green, to be nearer the mill. 'The difference it made to us was unimaginable,' said Tommy. 'We had a front and back garden, meat paste sandwiches for lunch, an egg each for tea, and shoulder of lamb for Sunday dinner.'

A steady wage meant a bicycle for Tommy's father, and a hand-me-down one for Tommy. In those days Norris Green was surrounded by fields and Tommy only had to walk a hundred yards from his home to find himself in the countryside he'd never seen in his life before. He remembers vividly the thrill of cycling through the lanes and fields, the breeze in his hair and the perfume of wild flowers filling his senses.

The back garden of the house was a good size, and there was enough money coming in to save up for a shed and a greenhouse. Though he'd known nothing about gardening, Tommy's father set to and, by trial and error, succeeded in growing vegetables and keeping hens and ducks. Now at last the family had enough to eat.

Andy and 'E' numbers

We've known Tommy's daughter Chris and her husband John for many years. Ian, my husband, and John, both journalists, had worked together on national newspapers before John had moved into television, and I'd watched their sons grow up. Now we were together again, enjoying another of Chris's wonderful meals.

We were reminiscing about how it had become obvious that their younger boy, Andrew, had a problem with food colourings. 'I would never have dreamed,' said John, 'that there was a connection between what my son ate, and the way that he acted when he was at his most fierce. He would become like some sort of gremlin, sweating, aggressive, erupting like a volcano!'

Andy has fiery red hair, and his sudden and often unprovoked outbursts had simply been attributed to the colour of his hair. When he was just a little boy, I had suggested that the colours which are added to certain foods might be a more important factor in Andy's behaviour.

Dad was unconvinced, Mum a little sceptical but more open, and the boys were quite interested. I bought them a copy of a recently published book which listed and explained the 'E' numbers on food labels.[1]

With the enthusiasm of the young the boys followed Chris round the supermarket, pulling items out of her shopping trolley, checking them against the book, and rejecting those that didn't pass the test. Andy's behaviour changed dramatically. He became calm and consistent, only repeating his previous outbursts after eating foods which contained the guilty colours.

Before long, his parents could tell by his behaviour when he had cheated on his diet. A little gentle probing and it would emerge that a friend had given him some sweets, or that he'd had a binge of his own. Now Andy knows that if he has any significant amount of orange or red colouring he will have a bad week.

Diet and moods

I had felt for a long time that Andy's elder brother, Johnny, was also being affected by his diet. But he didn't react in a sudden and violent way. His was a consistent problem, which showed in his manner and mood.

He was a very bright boy who learned to read before he started school. His teacher had told his parents that he could put in half a day's studying and achieve the same results as the child who had worked for weeks. 'He's just got it!' she had said. Johnny had been among the five brightest children in the top class of his year, achieving excellent grades right through primary school.

Once he'd reached his teens, however, his attitudes and lack of motivation began to cause problems, not only at school but at home. His teachers now said that he had the ability but wouldn't work. Johnny became moody, isolated and unsociable. 'He was always shy,' said Chris, 'but he was much more affectionate when he was younger. He was closer to us then.'

Throughout his teenage years Johnny's relationship with his father became strained, yet occasional glimpses of his true nature revealed a smashing lad, who couldn't understand what was happening. His parents became more and more frustrated with his attitudes. Mum described him as having a 'shorter fuse', and it became obvious that Johnny really believed that he was right and that the grown-ups were over-reacting.

We had often talked about the possibility of food intolerance but, though Johnny and his father had watched Andy's explosive outbursts in response to consuming food colouring, neither seemed willing to consider the possibility that Johnny's problems also had something to do with his diet.

Better school work

John is a very special friend. The strength of that friendship means that we have been able to disagree, sometimes quite fiercely, yet remain very good friends. Our reminiscences over that meal turned, as they often do, into a heated debate. I was insisting, yet again, that diet was an important factor in Johnny's problems, while Johnny's father insisted that the problem was that he'd had too much, too easily in life.

Sometimes I think that the mental effects of dietary problems are the most tragic. If someone has an obvious reaction to allergy or food intolerance, such as eczema, it can easily be recognised. But the problem with a mental reaction is that the effect itself can distort perception. Consequently the individual himself, let alone a relative, may not be able to see that he has a problem.

But this time was different. Things had now become so bad that Johnny himself had realised that something was wrong, and had asked his mother if she would get him a tonic. Chris asked me to come and talk to Johnny and, one evening a few days later, both of the boys, their mum and I sat and talked. Johnny described how he felt.

With his A levels looming he really wanted to work, yet he would go into his room and find that he simply couldn't concentrate. His brain felt as though it had seized up. He was also suffering from constant tiredness. 'I just feel like lying down all the time,' he explained. 'I feel depressed at times and I find that I'm suffering from memory loss. I simply can't remember what I did a day or two ago.'

For a few years Johnny had been having allergic reactions to dogs and cats and he had been becoming more and more tired, and less and less energetic. Now he felt hopeless and completely unable to motivate himself.

The long-term effects of diet

We'll come back to Johnny later. First though, let's look to the past to see if we can find any reasons for some of our present day health problems. Many of our parents and grandparents were born into families who struggled to afford enough to eat. Is there a connection between their diet, and the long-term health of their children and grandchildren?

The diet of the working classes earlier this century has been highlighted by the Medical Research Council (MRC), based at the University of Southampton. Professor David Barker led his team in a search for the reason why people from the north-west of England stand a greater chance of dying from a heart attack than people from the south.

The team had prepared mortality maps which indicated where deaths from various diseases had been recorded for each part of the country. These maps clearly showed the north/south divide for premature deaths from heart disease.

Genetic differences had been ruled out, and the usual explanation for the health divide was the supposed differences in lifestyle between the north and the south. Smoking is slightly more prevalent in the north but, as for diet, the amount of saturated fat is high in both the north and the south; smaller amounts of fruit and fresh vegetables are eaten in the north.

But Professor Barker believes that these differences in adult lifestyle alone are not sufficient to explain why coronary heart disease is more common in the north and west of Britain than in the south. Speaking on a BBC television programme,[2] he explained, 'It was an exploration of this which led us on to ideas that important events might be happening, not in adult life, but in very early life. As we began to examine the data, it became clear that we were talking about a very early period of life indeed; life in the womb and in the first few months after birth.'

The MRC team suggested that what a woman eats when she is pregnant may determine the disease that her offspring will die of well over half a century later, affecting not only her own children but her children's children.

Birth records can indicate health

Old birth records recording details of babies born in Hertfordshire from 1910 to the 1920s provided a fascinating source of information for the MRC team. Meticulously kept details of such children up to the age of five had survived the advent of computerisation to provide vital clues to their health in later life. 'We traced some 5,800 men who were born in six villages in East Hertfordshire,' said Professor Barker, 'and we were able to relate their cause of death to their growth in early life. The result was absolutely clear. Men who'd had lower birth weight, and lower weight at one year of age, had a higher risk of dying from coronary heart disease.'

The next step was to study the present health of a younger generation of Hertfordshire men who were still living. Men who were listed in the birth records were traced and invited to take part in a medical examination. The team were particularly interested in determining the incidence of disorders such as late-onset diabetes, which has been associated with heart disease. However, the volunteer Hertfordshire men were also tested for a range of other disorders. These were then correlated with their birth weights.

'We found,' said Professor Barker, 'that low birth weight, and low weight at one year, predicted not only death from heart disease, but also higher levels of what are called the risk factors from heart disease. That is, higher levels of blood pressure, higher levels of the factors that make the blood tend to clot, higher levels of cholesterol, and higher rates of diabetes.'

Hypertension

A second source of information from birth records was discovered in a maternity hospital in the north-west of England. These records from the nineteen thirties and forties contained exceptionally detailed data about every baby born in the Preston hospital at that time. Measurements had been taken of the baby's length, and the head size had been measured in seven different ways. These measurements enabled the MRC team to reconstruct fairly precisely what the baby had looked like at birth.

Once again the people listed in the birth records were traced and invited to return to the hospital where they were born, to take part in a medical examination. 'We found,' said Professor Barker, 'that these measurements are powerfully predictive of later health in relation to, for example, blood pressure.'

But there was another kind of information in the Preston records which turned out to be particularly interesting: the weight of the placenta had been recorded. At birth, the placenta is usually about one sixth of the weight of the baby. However, Professor Barker's team found that occasionally the placenta weighed more than expected. They found that this also was associated with blood pressure later on in middle age. The men and women in the study group who had the highest blood pressure were those who had been small at birth in relation to the size of the placenta. 'It wasn't that we were looking for very small babies,' explained Professor Barker. 'Many of the babies who subsequently developed hypertension in adult life, had been of average weight. But they were seven to eight pound babies who, from the size of the placenta, should have been nine to ten pounds.'

Fetal development and later health

So what happens during fetal development that could account for this? Throughout life in the womb, the fetus is totally dependent upon the supply of nutrients from its mother. Professor Barker believes that if anything goes wrong and not enough nutrients reach the developing baby, there will be evidence of it. The placenta may enlarge and the eventual weight of the baby at birth could be low, because many organs will not have grown sufficiently and may never be able to catch up.

During life in the womb and immediately after birth, particular organs undergo phases of rapid growth at certain critical and often brief periods, so for each organ there is a window of opportunity when it has to achieve maturation. 'The phenomenon is called programming,' explained Professor Barker, 'which is, in broad terms, the long-lasting effects of stimuli occurring at particular critical early periods of growth.'

This phenomenon is only just beginning to be understood in relation to the emergence of important diseases in adult life, such as coronary heart disease, stroke, diabetes and hypertension.

The way that nutrition during pregnancy influences the health of the offspring could be the key to the north/south divide. It is suspected that sixty or seventy years ago, young women working in the factories and mills of the industrial north may have had a more restricted diet than their counterparts living in the south. 'A consequence of our findings', said Professor Barker, 'is also that attempts to remedy inequalities in nutrition and other influences today, may not yield immediate benefits. There may necessarily be an interval of some years before the north/south divide is removed.'

Building a healthy lifestyle

As part of their medical checkup, the men and women of Hertfordshire and Preston had been weighed and asked about their lifestyle. The MRC team found that the strong relationship between early growth and adult health could not be explained away by any identifiable factor in adult lifestyle.

But those who disagree with the team's findings point to what has happened in America where, in general, people are more interested in health issues than the average European. Premature deaths from heart disease in the USA are decreasing, and this, it is argued, is as a result of the change to a healthy lifestyle adopted by the Americans in the last twenty years or so.

But Professor Barker argues that the reduction in heart disease is as much to do with the better diet of their mothers sixty or seventy years ago. These people are benefiting from the better nutrition they received in the womb and infancy.

According to Professor Barker, the same effect is beginning to be seen in Britain. He insists that the key to the long-term trends lies in the nutrition of young women, whilst recognising that the decline in coronary heart disease could be hastened if people avoided smoking and becoming overweight in adult life. These factors clearly do influence rates of heart disease. 'But of themselves,' he says, 'changes in these adult lifestyle factors do not seem able to explain the long-term trends.'

What about us?

But let's go back to Johnny and his grandfather, Tommy. The hardship endured by Tommy and his family is typical of many people growing up in the early years of this century. Chris, John, Ian and I all come from a working-class background in the north-west, and our family histories are similar. Professor Barker's findings about the long-term effect of hardship on the children and grandchildren of the young working-class women of the north-west don't sound very encouraging for us, do they?

And what implications do the findings have for our children? Are the effects of poor diet during pregnancy limited to heart disease and related disorders, or could there be a link between the health of our parents and grandparents, and the increasing incidence of allergies, asthma and behavioural problems in our own children?

Some people think that health concerns are self indulgent or irrelevant. 'I don't know what illness will eventually see me off,' they say. 'I'm more interested in how I feel right now. Let's just eat, drink and be merry and then pop off early to see what the next life has to offer.'

Up to the age of twenty-eight I ate and drank whatever I liked, but I was anything but merry. My mother and grandmother had both been chronic bronchitics and I would get bronchitis twice a year. In addition I had ulcerated throats several times a year, flu, colds and anything else that was going around. My concentration was poor, my memory awful and my moods unpredictable.

But then I discovered that what I put in my mouth made all the difference in the world. Let me tell you more.

3

BEGINNING TO BUILD HEALTH

Each evening Mother's fingers would deftly twist my long hair round strips of material, then twist the material back around my hair, tying it firmly in a bow. Our little nightly ritual not only gave me pretty ringlets the next day, but provided a wonderful opportunity for us to talk by the fire, as it crackled cheerily in the hearth.

Dad often worked late shifts down at the docks. There was no television in those days, and Mother always found time to listen to our little problems, and to talk to us. Looking back now, perhaps the most precious gift she gave me was her time, as she gently and subtly encouraged me to learn how to express my own feelings, and to try to understand other people.

Mum would also tell me stories about 'the old days', and I loved to hear about my mother's childhood and about what Liverpool was like in those pre-war years. Mum would describe the horse-drawn trams that ran from her home in Old Swan to the Pier Head on the River Mersey.

She would tell me about the neighbours who lived in the cobbled, terraced, two-up, two-down street, where every front door would be left open, and people cared for each other. Grandfather had died during World War One, and life was hard in those days for Grandmother, a widow with two young children. Yet Mum's stories were full of laughter and happy memories.

Even when my hair was finished, I would ask question after question, putting off bedtime as long as I could, 'hanging the latch', as Mum would say. I wanted to know what it was like during World War Two when the docks and munitions factories of Liverpool were mercilessly bombed, night after night, and the shopping streets of the city centre were left in smouldering ruins.

My birthday

But my favourite story of all, as a little girl of six or seven, was the story of the day I was born. Mum and Dad had married at the end of the war and I arrived in May 1946, just a year after the fighting stopped. Mum had set her heart on a little girl, she told me, and when the nurse gave me to her, she immediately took off all my clothes and counted every finger and toe to make sure I was perfect.

But I was a very small, underweight baby. Like most people in those post-war years, Mum and Dad smoked heavily and had no idea of the damage it could do. Smoking, as we now know, is one of the causes of underweight babies. I grew into a skinny child, often ill, and I didn't do particularly well at school.

During my school years I had great difficulty concentrating on the lessons, and my memory was so poor that I couldn't remember what had been said anyway. Swotting was impossible since my brain simply wouldn't store facts, and I scraped through grammar school, hating almost every minute of it. I left school and went into photography.

By then, I seemed to have very little immunity to infection. One lot of antibiotics would follow another as I came down with every 'bug' that happened to be going around at the time. I was anaemic, listless, completely lacking in motivation and I had very little appetite. At eighteen, I began to suffer from the awful bouts of bronchitis that were to confine me to bed for a fortnight, twice a year for the next ten years.

In all that time it never occurred to me that my health problems had anything to do with what I was eating. Not that I'd been eating very much at all! I simply didn't have the appetite to eat enough to put on weight, and I stayed painfully thin for years, weighing under seven and a half stone. 'Just you wait and see,' Mum said when I was a teenager, 'you'll be glad of it when you're older.' But that wasn't much consolation to a gawky, flat-chested teenager with arms and legs like matchsticks.

A solution?

'You've got an appetite like a sparrow,' said our friend and neighbour, the local doctor. 'I'm going to give you something to improve it.' By now I was married and, along with several other young couples, had moved into a newly built estate. As new neighbours, we often took turns to cook a meal and invite each other round for the evening. That night it was the turn of the doctor and his wife. The drug that he prescribed, Periactin, took effect within days and suddenly I was ravenous. I could eat several bars of chocolate in an evening and frequently did, as I strove to accomplish my dream of having curves where ladies ought to have curves. Little did I realise then the damage I was doing to myself.

At eight stone four pounds, I was very pleased with myself indeed. I'd filled out nicely, my bones no longer stuck out and I decided to stop taking the drug. Immediately my appetite disappeared and I soon slipped back to my old weight. By the time I'd had several prescriptions for the drug, countless bars of chocolate and a year or so of see-sawing weight, I was becoming ashamed to show my face at the doctor's surgery. I seemed to need antibiotics every couple of months, since no sooner was I over one infection than I'd caught another.

My memory and concentration were no better and my moods were becoming more and more unpredictable. One day I would feel positive, optimistic, and full of energy, cleaning the house from top to bottom. The next I would feel negative, pessimistic, and lethargic, unable to motivate myself even to tidy up. If only I'd known then what I know now!

Having a family

When I was expecting my first child I would wake up day after day feeling positive, calm and contented. For the sake of the coming baby I'd been eating as well as I knew how in those days, cooking myself proper meals three times a day and making sure that I had plenty of fruit, vegetables, milk and protein.

I still caught my usual colds, flu and ulcerated throats, and spent the annual fortnight in bed before and after Christmas, but I treasured every minute of that pregnancy. As it drew to an end,

I was excited at the prospect of having the child I longed for, but I rather wished that I could stay pregnant for the rest of my life.

Mark was a beautiful and contented though ravenous baby, soon sleeping through the night and wonderfully placid so long as he was fed promptly. By the time I'd breast fed him for six months, however, I was feeling drained. Most days I felt negative, lethargic and pessimistic.

Shortly afterwards we were told that Mum was dying of lung cancer. The next twelve months were probably the most heartbreaking of my life, as the strain of watching Mum waste away took its toll on my emotional and physical health.

I was pregnant again by the time Mum died. The emotional well-being I'd experienced during my first pregnancy was there again, though not so markedly, but this probably helped me to cope with Mum's death.

Adrian was an unhappy, fretful baby, prone to stomach upsets and colic. He was eighteen months old before he slept through the night, but he too was beautiful, and it wasn't long before he learned how to twist me round his little finger, even at five o'clock in the morning!

Looking back now, I can see that Adrian suffered as a result of our lack of knowledge about the role of nutrition both before and during pregnancy. In addition, the anguish I'd felt as I had watched Mum suffer, had added to my health problems.

The family's health

After years of the long hours, missed meals and stress-producing newspaper deadlines that are the lot of most journalists, my husband Ian began to suffer from digestive problems. Twelve months and a good deal of pain and sickness later, he was diagnosed as having a stomach ulcer.

Around that time the first programmes on food and health began to appear on the television, and I started to take an interest in the subject. I went into an old-fashioned herbalist-cum-health shop for the first time in my life, and there I picked up a health magazine. It contained an article on stomach ulcers, which explained the importance of natural wholefoods.

I changed Ian's diet to the suggested high fibre, raw vegetable regime and within a month all the sickness and pain had disappeared, even though his job remained as stressful as ever. Within three months Ian found that he could eat whatever he chose without a return of his symptoms. He enjoyed his new diet so much, though, that he prefers salads to this day, and has never suffered a recurrence of the symptoms of a stomach ulcer.

A few weeks later, when my usual post-Christmas attack of bronchitis came along, I staggered back to the herbalist's shop to ask for advice. 'Garlic tablets,' said the proprietor, 'that'll cure your bronchitis.' I crawled back to bed with my garlic tablets, and a great deal of scepticism.

Two days later, I was out of bed, chest clear and feeling fine. I couldn't believe it. Was it just a coincidence? Perhaps it hadn't been bronchitis at all, but simply a cold. That was the winter of 1974, and I've never had bronchitis since. It took me a couple of years to completely free myself from the ulcerated throats, but once I'd broken the vicious circle of infection, antibiotics and more infection, I haven't suffered from an ulcerated throat since.

I've never looked back since the day I picked up that magazine. It opened my eyes to a whole new world and I began to read avidly everything I could about the subject. Years later I had learned enough to realise why those changes in my diet made such a difference to my memory, concentration and emotions as well as to my immune system. I also learned why garlic had been so effective in the treatment of my bronchitis – but more about that later. I'd been an underweight baby, born to parents who both smoked heavily. I'd suffered from constant infections up to the age of twenty-eight. Yet I was able, through optimum nutrition, to begin to build up my health.

Making a start

I wish that I had learned about nutrition before I became pregnant so that my own children could have had a better start. But at least I was able to begin to build their health when Mark was two and Adrian just a few months old. Mark had had infections up to the age of two. From then onwards, though, both boys developed good resistance to infection and neither of them ever needed to take antibiotics.

By substituting wholemeal products for white flour products, by cutting down drastically on sugar, and by increasing our intake of fruit and vegetables, the health of the whole family improved quite dramatically. Both boys caught all the usual childhood illnesses, measles, German measles, and chickenpox, but were so little affected by them that it was often difficult to get a doctor's appointment in time to have them diagnosed before the symptoms disappeared. While other children were covered in spots, with a high fever and feeling very poorly indeed, my two little rascals drove me crazy because they were virtually spot-free, full of energy, and bored because they weren't allowed to play with their friends.

The change to a wholemeal diet, however, didn't solve every problem immediately. I had to go on to learn about allergies, food sensitivity, candida, hypoglycaemia, and the problem of an inherited subnormal ability to utilise nutrients in the diet. These are conditions which underlie many illnesses today, and are among the subjects I'll be covering in this book.

Breaking hereditary health and emotional problems

It is too easy to dismiss health problems, learning difficulties, or unpredictable moods as being hereditary, and simply accept them as inevitable. My mother and grandmother had both suffered badly from bronchitis, and during the ten years that I suffered from the condition myself, I assumed that it was hereditary and therefore unavoidable. Yet, with a few changes in my diet I had banished it completely.

Smoking, of course, can be another cause of bronchitis but there are many non-smokers – including my grandmother – who still suffer from bronchitis. In my own case, it was only after I was cured of bronchitis that I began to consider the possibility that it wasn't the bronchitis that was inherited, only the *predisposition* to bronchitis. Could it be that the effects of poor nutrition in prenatal life may, to some extent, be ameliorated by optimum nutrition in later life? This certainly seems to have been my experience.

Dare to be different in your diet

In the mid-nineteen seventies I took an awful lot of criticism for suggesting that what you put in your mouth had anything at all to do with your physical, let alone your mental or emotional health. It's easy to forget that not so very long ago there was widespread antagonism to the notion among both the public and the health professions in Britain.

As time went by the role of nutrition in health became more widely accepted, and the work of the early nutritionists began to be vindicated. Consequently I began to realise that just because a great many people disbelieve something, the sheer weight of numbers is no guarantee that they are right. And just because only a few lone voices speak out against the majority, neither does that mean that they can't possibly be right. Vested interests, well-placed funding, and massive advertising campaigns may drown the warnings of doctors and scientists who have limited resources available to them.

In the next chapter I'd like to introduce you to some of those voices of the past whose work has not only stood the test of time, but is of vital importance now in the face of conflicting opinions about diet. These were the men and women who challenged the widely held views and vested interests of their day.

Even today I find that, though the general idea of the importance of nutrition is much more widely accepted, it is just as important to listen carefully to those who are speaking out and warning about some widely held views. We still have to make a choice.

Later in the book, we'll be looking at some of the views and the warnings that are coming from a few present day doctors, scientists and nutrition writers. Some appear to be confirming the observations of those pioneers of nutrition who, early this century, challenged the medical thinking of the day. Let us see what their findings have to tell us. In their brilliant and scientifically documented records of healthy races, I suspect that we may find some clues to the reasons for our present appalling health statistics. We'll also discover some tremendously encouraging information about the effect of optimum nutrition on health and longevity.

4

HEALTHY RACES

At an altitude of 5,000 feet in the beautiful mountains of Switzerland, a sixty-two-year-old grandmother, amazingly fit and in good physical shape, carried an enormous load of rye on her back. After being threshed by hand, and ground by a stone mill, the rye flour would be baked into enough coarse black bread to feed her family for a month.

Far above her, cattle grazed on the rich pastures where the winter's snow had melted in the warm summer sunshine. The idyllic, flower-strewn meadows provided the cattle with a feast of nutritious grasses and they, in turn, produced delicious, creamy high-quality milk for the villagers of the Loetschental Valley.

While sturdy, sun-tanned children played barefoot on the fragrant slopes, young mothers milked the cows and produced the cheese which would feed them through the coming winter. Goat's and cow's milk, cream and cheese, together with the coarse rye bread, formed the greater part of each family's diet, which was supplemented once a week by meat, and delicious broths made from the meat bones and scraps.

Down in the fields, the menfolk harvested the rye crop by hand. Without tractor or even horse and cart to lighten their work, they had to rely on their strong backs, and fine, muscular physiques to enable them to carry their heavy loads up and down the mountainside.

Health, happiness and vitality shone out of the people of this simple community who had no need of doctor, dentist, or policeman. Blessed with beautifully developed bone structure, strong, even teeth, and individual strength of character that was reflected in their communal spirituality, they thrived on their frugal lifestyle.

Weston Price

It was to this community that the American scientist Weston Price came to make some significant studies. With a brilliant career in dentistry behind him, Price had set off from America at the beginning of the nineteen thirties, to travel to the most inaccessible corners of the earth. Accompanied by his wife, he covered 150,000 miles in nine years, looking for the cause of the narrow faces, deformed jaws, crowded, irregular teeth and rampant tooth decay that had confronted him daily in his Cleveland dental practice.

From reports that had been brought back by early explorers, Price knew that primitive people, cut off from civilisation, generally possessed excellently formed sets of teeth, free from decay. He wanted to compare isolated groups of people with those of the same race who had access to the refined and processed foods of the modern world.

Here in the Swiss Alps Price found whole communities with healthy, uncrowded teeth in wide jaws. He also found that they had excellent general health, wonderful personalities and 'the finest physiques in all Europe'.[1] What he saw of them caused him to wonder if there was something in the life-giving vitamins and minerals of their food that built not just strong, healthy bodies, but minds and hearts capable of a higher form of life. This was something that he was to see time and time again and he studied, photographed and documented primitive people of many races.

Contrast

Surrounded by snow-capped mountains, the elegance of Saint Moritz was displayed in the fashionable clothes of its residents, and in the sophisticated hotels, restaurants and shops that lined its stylish streets. All the luxuries of the world were available here, brought in by the railway which linked the town with the rest of Europe. Light and fluffy white bread rolls spread with jam or marmalade could be eaten by all for breakfast. Exotic tinned fruits and vegetables offered endless variety, and locally produced chocolate was made into a popular hot, sweet beverage.

But the children here lacked the beautifully developed features, personality, stamina and glowing health of the mountain children. Tooth decay was widespread in the area, as it was in general in the lowlands of Switzerland. Once a healthy population had lived here, but now tuberculosis ravaged modernised communities.

At the beginning of the nineteen thirties one doctor alone had 3,500 patients under his supervision. When Price asked him how many of them came from the isolated mountain villages he replied that there was not one. Apart from a few who had come from other countries for treatment, his patients, he said, came from the lowland towns of Switzerland.

So was it just the isolation and the mountain air that protected the mountain communities from TB? Time and time again Price would see the devastating effects of this dreaded disease on certain sections of populations while other sections of the same races of people remained free, not only from TB but also from the degenerative diseases which tended to be found among the communities struck down with TB.

He would write later in his book *Nutrition and Physical Degeneration,* that abandoning the primitive diet was the key factor in the devastating effects of diseases such as TB, introduced through contact with civilisation.

Hebridean crofters

Raging Atlantic seas and wild storms continually buffeted and thrashed the islands of the Outer Hebrides, often shrouded in thick fog, and mainly inhabited in the nineteen thirties by crofters and fishing communities. With pasture too poor to support dairy herds, and acid soil that would grow little more than oats, isolated communities, like generations before them, used stone mills to grind their harvest into a coarse oatmeal.

On a breakfast of porridge, with oatcakes for supper, and an abundant supply of seafood, these rugged islanders could survive being cut off by severe weather for many months of the year. The stout walls of their crofts kept out the worst gales of winter, and peat fires burned day and night. Thick, black smoke often filled the room, filtering out through the thatched roof which was renewed each autumn, the old thatch being used as manure for the next crop of oats.

Yet, in spite of such primitive living conditions, and the smoke-filled atmosphere of their crofts, the islanders possessed excellent physiques, and enjoyed remarkable health and resistance to diseases such as TB.

These were gentle, refined, intelligent people, Price noted, with great strength and sweetness of character, and high moral standards. Sundays would be set aside for church services, and in the evening, fishermen would meet together in the streets and on the piers of the little ports, to sing hymns and to pray for the safety of their next fishing trip.

The less isolated communities of the Hebridean islands, however, had been connected to the outside world by a daily steamboat service that delivered tinned goods, confectionery, and white flour. In these areas Price found that there had been a rapid decline in the health of the population. Though previous generations had remained free from TB, the young people quickly succumbed to the disease. In spite of smoke-free homes and more modern living conditions, the number of TB patients increased rapidly.

Here again Price saw the change in personality, motivation and energy levels as well as the lowering of immunity, all of which followed the dietary changes. Deterioration in bone structure, jaws, and teeth, accompanied the degenerative illness, and the incidence increased with the length of time that refined foods had been eaten by communities.

Same pattern

From Alaska to the islands of the Pacific, Peru to Africa, Australia to New Zealand, Price found the same pattern repeated over and over again. From the bitterly cold climate of the Arctic to the hot, sultry weather of the tropics, he sought out races of people, some of whom had remained in isolation while others had gained access to modern foods.

Those who continued to eat their native foods retained their robust health and excellent physiques. Once refined foods became available and native diets were abandoned, however, people's health declined rapidly and resistance to infection was soon lost.

Of particular interest to Price was the effect on the children born to those who had forsaken their traditional diets. Here Price found the narrow faces, crowded teeth and rampant tooth decay which became progressively more marked with each succeeding child. Price observed that this was not due to heredity but was happening in spite of it, and he called it 'disturbed heredity' or 'intercepted heredity'.

He painstakingly documented and photographed the physical changes in dental and bone structure, comparing them with isolated peoples, and the skeletons of past generations of the same races. Foods were sent back to his laboratory in America for chemical analysis and detailed records were built up and stored as a result of his investigations.

Change in character

A change in character also accompanied the use of refined foods, Price noticed. The lethargy and apathy of so many of the modernised sections of communities contrasted markedly with the enthusiasm, humour, stamina and vitality which Price came to associate with the perfect physiques of those who remained isolated.

His observations caused Price to wonder if the civilised communities of Europe and America would ever have the strength of character to give up their convenience foods and to take the time and trouble to rebuild their health with a natural diet.

The staple foods of the primitive people that Price studied varied enormously but, over and over again, Price found that races who lived on vegetables alone lacked the excellent physique of those who had access to seafood or animal produce. Price stressed the vital role of these products in supplying the nutrients essential to the health of every organ of the body, including the brain and nervous system.

Skimmed milk, he warned, was less useful for building health than whole milk. And vitamin-rich butter could restore the health of children who had been unable to utilise minerals to build healthy bones and teeth. Interestingly, some nutritionists, doctors and scientists are now beginning to question the value of replacing whole milk and butter with skimmed milk and margarine, as we shall see in chapter 11.

Health and beauty

The relationship between food and physical and mental health had been established some years earlier by a British army doctor working in India, who had already made a name for himself through his brilliant research into deficiency diseases.

Lieutenant Colonel Robert McCarrison was so stunned by the health and beauty of a certain race of people living in northern India that he stepped back from his usual preoccupation with the cause of illness, and began to wonder instead about the reason for such robust health.

At 8,000 feet above sea level, surrounded by sheer precipices that rose 10,000 to 15,000 feet, fierce winter gales would rage through the valley of the Hunza people, keeping them huddled in their houses until spring beckoned them out to plant their new season's crops. Their summers were hot and arid with little rain to water the produce that was grown in the small terraced fields clinging tenaciously to the mountainside. The remoteness of the area had preserved the traditions of generations of industrious peasant farmers who, by an incredible feat of engineering, had built an immense aqueduct to irrigate their carefully tended soil.

Goats skipped about on the higher crags, while cattle grazed lower down in the valley, providing the milk, yoghurt, butter and cheese that formed an important part of the diet of this hardy mountain race. Since there was a very limited supply of wood for fuel, vegetables were mainly eaten fresh from the fields and raw. Chick peas were sprouted to make them more nutritious and digestible, particularly during the winter and in the months preceding the new season's harvest.

Freshly ground wheat and other cereals were made into nutritious wholemeal chapattis. Meat was eaten occasionally, and this would be cooked carefully with vegetables and very little water, preserving all the flavour and valuable nutrients. Hunza apricots are legendary to this day, and these and other fruit formed a significant part of the diet, not just of the people of the valley but also of their domestic animals.

Healthy people, healthy emotions

But not only did these people live long, active lives; they simply didn't suffer from illness. They were a tall, graceful, athletic, perfectly formed race, and the young army doctor found that they had very little need of his services.[2] However, there was something more, McCarrison noticed, than just good physical health.

Never before had he encountered such cheerful, contented souls. Never had he seen such willingness to help, such motivation to work, or such satisfaction in their labours. This aspect of the Hunza's character fascinated McCarrison as much as did their glowing health.[3]

There were other races too, such as the Pathans and Sikhs who, like the Hunza people, had magnificent physiques and endless vitality. Yet, in the very next valley to the Hunzas, in identical climate and terrain, lived the Ishkomanis, a tribe who contrasted conspicuously with their neighbours. They were stunted in height and physique, prone to illness, lazy, ungainly, apathetic and ill humoured. These people reminded McCarrison of many of the races of southern India who were often small in stature, and dogged by mental and physical ill health. They also reminded him of many of the patients he'd tended back home in England during his medical training.

A controversial theory

McCarrison resolved to prove his then controversial theory that quality of the diet was a vital factor in health. He built up a stock of healthy, disease-free rats by feeding them the diet of the healthiest races of India. Then he divided the rats into seven groups and fed each group a different diet. These were the diets eaten by different races, from the strong, healthy tribes of northern India to the weak, disease-prone races of the south of the continent. All of the rats were kept in identical conditions.

Before long, the once healthy rats whose foods had been changed from those of the vigorous races of the north, to those of the poorer classes of southern India, began to deteriorate. The diseases that made their appearance, McCarrison noted, were the same as those that afflicted the groups of Indians on whose diets the rats had been fed. Diseases of the eye, ear, nose, throat, lungs, and stomach together with skin disease, heart disease and, in fact, diseases of every organ of the body were observed. The rats' endocrine systems degenerated, they didn't reproduce well, and they became prone to incomplete pregnancies, premature births and still births.[4]

But not only did the diets of the unhealthiest races affect the physical health of the rats, it also altered their temperaments. Rats that had once lived peaceably together now became bad tempered and started to squabble and fight. Though once they had been amenable to being handled, now they literally bit the hand that fed them.

At the same time, the groups of rats who had been fed the diets of the healthiest races continued to thrive, reflecting exactly the health of the tribe whose diet they had adopted. The difference in temperament observed among McCarrison's rats paralleled both his own, and Dr Price's observations of the change in human temperament that accompanied the abandonment of natural foods.

What to look for in food

The foods of the healthiest Indians varied significantly, from the Pathan who ate considerable quantities of meat, to the Sikh and the Hunza who used meat sparingly. All, however, contained an abundance of fruit and vegetables and fresh, coarsely ground cereals.

McCarrison wrote later that, from his observations of the people, confirmed by his experiments, he believed that fresh vegetables and whole milk were essential to the building of good health.

As Price was later to discover, there wasn't just one healthy diet – there were many. When faced with some of the conflicting dietary advice often given these days, it is helpful to remember that whole races of people in the past remained healthy on widely differing diets, provided the foods were natural and unprocessed.

The Hunza, like the isolated Swiss, relied mainly upon dairy produce, grain and vegetables. Like the isolated Hebrideans, the foods of the inhabitants of Iceland and of the Faroe islands consisted mainly of meat or fish. The Eskimos of Greenland lived almost entirely on seafood, birds and their eggs.

Tristan da Cunha, an island in the South Atlantic, was once inhabited by a people who ate fish, potatoes, a few vegetables and a great many eggs. The Indians of North America once hunted for the wild game of the prairie and the Chinese grew rice to eat with their seafood, eggs, meat and vegetables.

Always eat your food whole

Over many generations, each of these healthy races learned to make the best use of the foods that were available. The key to their health lay in the quality of their food, which was eaten whole. There was no refining, no stripping away of the most nutritious parts of the product, and there were no chemicals to add to the food.

When meat and fish were eaten, there was no waste. The nutrient-rich organs were recognised for their ability to promote health and were often eaten in preference to the muscle meat which was relatively poor in nutrients. Even the bones and bone marrow were used to make stock for soup.

Degeneration came with the change from natural foods to refined flour and sugar, tinned foods and confectionery. No matter what the manufacturers of sugar may claim about it being a natural product, it is still a refined natural product and, as such, has been stripped of the nutrients necessary for its utilisation by the body. Though it supplies instant energy, it does so at great cost to long-term health.

Bread was once truly the staff of life. But when the germ and bran have been stripped away, it becomes another source of instant energy with limited ability to build health. Convenience foods lose a great deal of the nutrients they contained when they were fresh and raw.

Though it is widely accepted that prolonged stress and destructive attitudes and emotions can cause illness, McCarrison's and Price's work demonstrated that poor nutrition can affect emotional, as well as physical health. This is an important factor that, even nowadays, is often overlooked in the treatment of mental and emotional conditions.

Though infectious agents and poor sanitation can play a part in illness, the research of both men highlighted the importance of nutrition in the building of a strong immune system. This is no less relevant today in the treatment of immune deficiency diseases such as AIDS, as we shall see in chapter 10.

But what about *before* we are ill? What implications could the work of McCarrison, Price and other far-sighted individuals have for us and for our children right now? Isn't our diet here in Britain much better than it was in the early part of this century when many people had to survive on tea, white bread and margarine?

Let's take a look, shall we?

RECOMMENDED READING

Nutrition and Physical Degeneration by Weston Price (Keats, 1989). (In case of difficulty obtaining this book, it is available through Wholefood Books – see 'Useful Addresses' on p 307.)

Nutrition and Health by Robert McCarrison, published by The McCarrison Society 1982 – see 'Useful Addresses' on p 307.

5

SO WHAT'S WRONG
WITH OUR DIET?

Some health professionals say that no one who is eating a 'balanced diet' can be deficient in vitamins and minerals. This is a concept that is, naturally, popular with those who prefer to use convenience food, and also with those who produce and sell such food. In an ideal world a balanced diet would indeed supply every nutrient necessary for the maintenance of good health. Sadly the reality is quite different.

To begin with, one person's idea of a balanced diet may be markedly different from another's. Also, the nutritional value of the food is dependent on factors such as the quality of the soil upon which it has been grown, the amount of pesticides with which it has been sprayed and the way it has been treated during food production. To claim that a 'balanced diet' will automatically promote or maintain health is to dangerously over-simplify the situation.

Equally erroneous is the idea that any old diet will do so long as vitamin and mineral tablets are taken daily as a supplement. The health-promoting factors of natural foods consist of much more than the sum total of their vitamins and minerals. And the whole subject deserves a deeper understanding of the many factors that affect the nutritional status of the body. Let's take a look at what we often have too little of, and what causes such deficiencies.

The vital role of vitamins

Vitamins are usually required by the body only in very small amounts for normal biochemical function but they are essential for good health, as was dramatically demonstrated by diseases such as scurvy, beri-beri and pellagra. The symptoms of pellagra are sometimes called the four Ds – dermatitis, diarrhoea, dementia, and death – and they graphically portray the disastrous effects of a severe deficiency of nicotinamide (vitamin B3). Less severe forms of vitamin B deficiency are implicated in many skin, gastrointestinal and mental/emotional conditions.

Vitamins and minerals often work together as cofactors. For this reason the deficiency symptoms of a particular vitamin or mineral may be caused not by a shortage of the nutrient itself, but by a deficiency of another vitamin or mineral. Magnesium and vitamin B6, for example, must both be present for either to be useful. The same applies to zinc and vitamin B6.

The balance of vitamins is very important indeed, and a deficiency or excess of one can affect another. The B vitamins in particular enhance each other and, if one B vitamin is taken on its own, it can cause a deficiency of other members of the B complex. Yet many vitamin supplements on the market can upset the balance and do more harm than good.

Some practitioners regularly prescribe high doses of vitamin B6, for example, and I've seen people become quite ill when the B6 taken alone causes them to become deficient in vitamin B2.[1] The most common effect of vitamin B2 deficiency is to lower immunity and cause the person to be vulnerable to infection.

Because of the delicate balance between these two vitamins, it can work the other way around, too. Taken on its own, vitamin B2 can produce a vitamin B6 deficiency.[2] Much safer are vitamin B complex supplements containing approximately equal amounts of these two vitamins, together with correctly balanced amounts of the rest of the B vitamins.

Minerals are essential too

It is well known that iron is essential for the formation of the pigment that colours our red blood cells, which carry oxygen to every cell of our bodies. A deficiency of iron causes us to become anaemic and we become pale, tired and listless. Yet many more minerals and trace minerals are known to be essential to health.

Minerals and trace minerals are vital to a collection of inter-linked systems of the body, so complex that some of their roles are not yet fully understood. It is known, however, that they are crucial to bone and tissue formation, and to the production of DNA and RNA, the expression of genetic heredity. They also activate a huge number of vital enzymes and are needed for just about every function of the body.

Zinc, for example, is essential for growth and for sexual development. Boys have a particularly high requirement during puberty, and a dramatic example of zinc deficiency was reported in 1961 on male dwarfs from an Iranian village.[3] A major part of their diet consisted of unleavened bread, which is known to contain phytate, a compound that interferes with the absorption of zinc. In addition to stunted growth, the dwarfs also had defective development of their sexual organs and a lack of mental acuity. In a controlled study, the use of zinc supplementation was able to bring about an increase in height in up to twenty-year-old dwarfs because the growing ends of their bones had not closed. Zinc is also known to be an important nutrient in many aspects of reproduction and is a component of enzymes that regulate mental processes.[4]

Balance

As with vitamins, the balance of minerals in our diet is extremely important. Calcium and magnesium must compete for absorption so an excess or deficiency of one inversely affects the other.[5] We've already seen that vitamin B6 should not be taken alone. So supplements containing just magnesium and vitamin B6 can cause deficiencies of calcium and vitamin B2, which would be most likely to affect immunity and nerves!

To further illustrate the intricate web and delicate balance of nature, minerals are needed as cofactors so that vitamins can be properly utilised. Essential fatty acids are dependent upon certain vitamins and minerals before they can be built upon and used by the body. Nutrients are interrelated and interdependent, and supplementation of isolated nutrients can never compensate for poor nutrition.

Nevertheless it is true that if it is taken together with dietary improvements, careful, balanced supplementation can be very useful at times, particularly during illness. The reasons why this may be necessary will become clearer if we take a little time to look at some of the causes of nutritional deficiencies.

Intensive farming

There are many reasons why our food nowadays is lacking nutrients, and the first place to look for the cause of deficiencies is to the soil. The composition and mineral content of soil depends mainly on the type of rock from which it originally came. Environmental factors over many millions of years, however, can change the nature and quality of soil.

All over the world, soils have been studied for their trace element content and it has been found that shortages of trace minerals such as zinc or selenium are far from uncommon. Areas, particularly, that have been cropped for centuries can become exhausted. Soils that drain easily can lose trace minerals and may be too poor to provide a healthy environment to support the crops grown on it.

Over the last half century or so, developed and developing countries are increasingly relying on the use of inorganic fertilisers to produce high crop yields. Artificial fertilisers do not supply the complete range of minerals and trace minerals, so repeated intensive cropping of farmland removes more and more of the trace elements vital to health.

Over-liming the soil can prevent the crop from taking up certain minerals, and the use of many insecticides, by de-activating choline-containing enzymes, can prevent the uptake of manganese. The crops themselves may obtain enough minerals to appear healthy, yet may be short of other trace elements that are needed by the animals and humans who eat them.

Refining

The greatest loss of essential fatty acids, vitamins and minerals, however, occurs during the refining of food. Wheatgerm and bran are rich sources of fibre, and nutrients. Their removal during the production of white flour leads to substantial nutrient losses. Replacing minerals such as iron and calcium cannot solve the problem since many other nutrients are not restored.

Raw sugar is rich in nutrients but when it is refined to produce white sugar almost all the vitamin and mineral content is lost. Molasses, the black treacle-like substance which is removed, is an excellent source of vitamins and trace elements, and it has been used for many years as a food supplement. Indeed, it is often used to enrich cattle feed!

Grown naturally on good soil, crops contain the nutrients that enable us to digest and utilise them. If these are stripped away by refining, then we must use our own reserves of vitamins and minerals in order to be able to metabolise these now unbalanced foods. Not only do such foods fail to supply the nutrients needed for health, they also rob our bodies of vital nutrient reserves.

Essential fatty acids

Plants supply two of the essential fats, linolenic acid, which is found in the leaves, and linoleic acid, which is found in the seed. An important reason for eating the whole food, rather than the extracted oil is that these polyunsaturates are unstable and easily affected by oxygen. Powerful anti-oxidants such as vitamin E accompany the polyunsaturates in leaves and seeds, preserving the fatty acids and supplying us with important protective nutrients.

The refining of cereals such as wheat (a seed food) removes the germ which contains vitamin E and the essential fats, as well as other vitamins and minerals vital to our health. Heat damages polyunsaturated oils, and many of the vitamins and minerals in plants are lost in the water in which they are boiled. So a diet that doesn't contain a variety of raw fruit and vegetables may be deficient in essential fatty acids, vitamins and minerals.

Whether or not we are obtaining enough nutrients from our food doesn't just depend on whether we choose refined or unrefined, chemically or organically grown food. Our choice of food or, in the case of babies, the type of milk given, can influence our nutritional status. Meat, and in particular organ meats such as liver and kidney, supply linoleic acids. So vegetarians need to be extra careful to ensure that they obtain enough linoleic acid from seeds, peas and beans.

They are much less likely to be deficient in linolenic acids than non-vegetarians, however, since green vegetables are a good source. Breast milk is rich in essential fatty acids while cow's milk is a very poor source, so babies who aren't breast fed may be deficient.

There are other essential fatty acids from the linolenic family, unique to fish, which have received a lot of publicity because of their ability to lower blood levels of certain harmful types of fat. So oily fish is good for the heart and arteries. It may have tasted awful, but grandmother was right to insist that her children took a spoonful of cod liver oil every day! If you don't eat fish or take fish oil you may be deficient in these essential fatty acids.

Over-indulgence

Too much food and drink are also factors that cause deficiencies. Eating more than is necessary can overwhelm the digestive enzymes and create a much greater demand for the nutrients used up in the metabolism of the food. The drinking of large quantities of liquid of any kind causes water-soluble nutrients to be excreted in the urine, a factor that is all too often forgotten by those who maintain that a 'balanced diet' will supply adequate nutrition. Tea, coffee, and alcohol, or diuretics or other medication given to stimulate urine production, increase the loss of all nutrients that dissolve in water. Of the forty or so nutrients required for health, all but five are readily lost in the urine.[6] Our social drinking habits as well as eating and smoking may well be boosting the sales of vitamin and mineral supplements!

Poor health in the rich West

Some people, however, suffer from conditions which make it difficult for them to absorb enough of what they eat. Coeliac disease in which the cereal protein gluten causes trouble, chronic diarrhoea, poor digestion and, I'm afraid, simply getting older, are all factors that can reduce our ability to absorb nutrients. Candida and food sensitivity are also conditions which can impair digestion, and we'll be looking at these later on in the book.

Lack of exercise or prolonged enforced inactivity during illness or old age causes calcium to be lost.[7] Without adequate exercise, no matter how wholesome the diet eaten, nutrients are not circulated properly to the cells that need them continuously.

So we don't replace all the nutrients we take out of the soil. We use chemicals that prevent the plant from taking up some nutrients. We strip yet more nutrients from the food when we refine it. We rob our own reserves of nutrients then wash even more away by drinking too much tea, coffee or alcohol! Our 'balanced diet' may not be as balanced as we thought it was!

To make matters worse, many of us overeat, don't absorb enough, and take too little exercise! But that, I'm afraid, is not the end of this sorry tale. We have yet to consider the 'anti-nutrients', as they have become known. These include coffee, tea, alcohol, cigarette smoke, various drugs, and environmental toxins.

Understanding anti-nutrients

I appreciate that the list of deficiencies brought about by modern living may be confusing and even disheartening, but the names of the separate nutrients are less relevant than the factors which are bringing about their loss. It really is worth taking the trouble to read about and to understand these causes. When the pressures of life or health problems come along, you may be suffering unnecessarily by being unaware of the effects of these antagonists.

Anti-nutrients are antagonistic to, use up, or lock up vital nutrients. The drinking of tea and coffee at meal times reduces the absorption of iron and zinc.[8] White sugar has been stripped of virtually all the vitamins and minerals found in the original plant,[9] so we must draw on our own reserves in order to metabolise it. Excessive saturated fat depletes magnesium,[10] and salt causes the loss of calcium and potassium.[11]

Some food additives lower zinc levels and probably other nutrients. Then there are environmental pollutants such as lead (antagonistic to calcium, molybdenum, zinc), cadmium (lowers zinc and copper) and mercury (antagonistic to zinc).[12] Aluminium, mainly from cooking utensils, lowers calcium and phosphorous levels.[13]

Life's little pleasures

And what about life's little pleasures? Recent research has shown that a glass of wine is good for you. Too much alcohol, however, uses up calcium, magnesium, zinc and the B vitamins B1, B2, B3, B6 and folic acid.[14] Smoking can reduce levels of vitamin C, and the B vitamins.[15]

The contraceptive pill can cause deficiencies of magnesium, zinc, iron, iodine, vitamin C and the B complex vitamins, particularly B6 and folic acid; it can also raise levels of copper[16] which, particularly when combined with smoking, can be toxic.

Got a headache?

So, unless you are a celibate, non-smoking, teetotal food crank, you may need to pay a visit to your doctor for a prescription to cure your self-inflicted illness. But will it? Antibiotics are antagonistic to vitamin K and the B complex,[17] and cortisone reduces potassium and vitamins A, C, D and the B complex.[18] Sulpha drugs deplete the B complex vitamins[19] and diuretics and laxatives cause the loss of potassium.

It's enough to give you a headache isn't it? Before you reach for the aspirin, however, you ought to know that it could make you deficient in vitamins A, B, C, calcium and potassium![20]

Should we be surprised then, that allergies, behavioural problems, learning difficulties and conditions such as ME or chronic fatigue are on the increase? Let's start right at the beginning, before pregnancy, in order to see not only what can be done to improve the health of the next generation, but also to look for explanations for and ways to overcome our present health problems.

6

BEFORE LIFE BEGINS

One day, all the young lady worms in the garden decided to have a contest to see who was the most beautiful of all. Heats were arranged and judged by the older worms, and the contestants were eliminated down to the dozen most beautiful worms.

With their long, elegant, slimy bodies, and their refined, pointed heads, it was very difficult indeed to decide who to choose. Eventually, the judges made their decision and a proud and excited Miss Worm World slithered forward to receive her sash and crown.

At that moment a butterfly fluttered gracefully down to a nearby hollyhock, her wings shimmering blue and gold in the summer sunshine. The worm audience looked at the exquisite beauty of the butterfly, then they looked at each other.

Miss Worm World turned to see what it was that had caught the attention of her audience, and she watched as the butterfly flitted daintily from flower to flower. Then Miss Worm World looked at herself in the mirror. Slowly, sadly, all the worms in the garden went back to their homes.

I used to tell that silly story to my sons when they were little, to try to teach them that our views are subjective. We think we are doing fine so long as we don't have anyone better to compare ourselves to. It is the same with health matters: each generation tends to compare itself to other members of the same generation.

Comparing child development

It is natural for a young mother to compare her child's development to that of her friends' children. Her child may seem to be constantly suffering from coughs, colds or ear infections. But then doesn't just about every other child? Perhaps the child had been a wakeful, restless baby, fretful in the evenings. But then, isn't every new baby?

Teething was difficult of course, those sleepless nights pacing the floor trying to console a red-cheeked, crying toddler. But isn't that to be expected? Then it was the 'terrible twos' – and what a temper he had! But then, don't they all?

His teacher said he had a short attention span and was inclined to be disruptive. But then, boys will be boys, won't they? The dentist said that his narrow jaw was due to the fact that we don't chew such tough foods nowadays as did our ancestors. Well, they all have crowded teeth, don't they? He'll just have to have a brace like all his friends.

And the greasy hair and spots! Ah well, that's teenagers for you! At least he didn't get into trouble with the law like so many other teenagers. And he didn't take drugs either, even when they were being sold like sweets in the lane behind the school. He went through a very moody phase, of course, but what teenager doesn't? He doesn't seem to have much ambition, but given time he'll probably start to work, when he decides what he wants to do. He's lethargic and lazy, but aren't they all?

After all, there are others who are much less fortunate. What about all those people who can't have children? At least they've come up with some clever ways of bypassing some of the problems now, with artificial insemination and in vitro fertilisation and the like.

Or what about those who have children who are born with something wrong with them. Why does God allow these things to happen? Thank goodness for the skill and dedication of our surgeons who are performing successful heart operations and liver transplants on increasingly younger patients.

But wait a minute, are we doing the same as the worms in my little story? Are we failing to be objective about the mental, emotional and physical health of this generation?

Health before conception

At the beginning of the century McCarrison was able to see for himself the phenomenon of whole races of healthy, happy, hard working people, who contrasted vividly with the ill health, discontent and apathy of neighbouring communities.

In the nineteen thirties Price was able to search out races of healthy primitive people and compare their immunity, physique, and temperament with those of the same race who had begun to degenerate both physically and mentally. Their observations enabled both to be objective about health, happiness and heredity.

Both men came to the conclusion that the health of the individual begins before conception takes place, and Price recognised that the health of the father, as well as the health of the mother, has a bearing on the health of the child. Neither McCarrison nor Price presented these conclusions as new, innovative conjecture. They merely confirmed what some primitive races had known and practised for many centuries.

Price found,[1] for example, some African tribes where the young girls were placed on a special diet for six months prior to marriage, to prepare them for motherhood. The Eskimos of Alaska recognised the importance of fish eggs for fertility and reproduction. Certain African women ate a special diet while they were pregnant and, later, breast feeding their infants.

The Hunza, among other races, considered that it was unfair to the next child for the mother to conceive again too soon after a pregnancy. The child would be breast fed for three years, and the mother would prepare for each pregnancy with special foods to build up her nutrient reserves.

McCarrison went further, by demonstrating the effects of faulty nutrition on reproduction. When he fed his healthy rats the diets of the unhealthiest races of people, he found that they began to suffer not only physical and mental health problems, but also reproductive problems. While the healthy rats who were given the best diets produced healthy offspring of a good weight, the rats given the poor diets had difficult pregnancies and labours. As we have seen, there was a high incidence of incomplete pregnancy, still birth and maternal death, and many of those offspring that survived were underweight, weak and sickly.

Underweight babies

A present day scientist, Professor Michael Crawford, is concerned about underweight babies. 'There is a high incidence of disorders such as mental retardation, deafness, blindness, spasticity, cerebral palsy, autism and epilepsy in babies weighing less than five and a half pounds,' says Professor Crawford.

His study of 513 mothers[2] showed that nutrition at the time of conception is of vital importance, since much of the development of the brain takes place during the first weeks of pregnancy. 'This is a vital time for fetal growth,' he says, 'yet it comes long before the mother sees a specialist!'

Professor Crawford's research was centred on the population of the London suburb of Hackney where the incidence of low birth weight is higher than the national average, and where it costs £770 a day to care for each baby in a special care unit. By 1990, the evidence from his studies, together with data from America, had convinced Hackney Health Authority of the need for further research. Professor Crawford was invited to open the Institute of Brain Chemistry and Nutrition in Hackney, 'to be', he says, 'in the front line'.

Babies who are born prematurely are at a higher risk of neuro-developmental damage. The Institute researches into the possibility that dietary intervention can reduce premature and low birth weight babies, and looks at the impact of such intervention on the incidence of neurodevelopmental disorders.

The Institute also uses the knowledge gained from the programme of intervention to try to establish ways and means by which nutrition can be used to prevent such damage. This has enormous significance for all prospective parents, but particularly those who've previously conceived children with neural tube defects, such as spina bifida. This malformation is due to the failure of the fetus's spinal cord to develop properly. It occurs very early in the development of the fetus; about the twenty-second to the twenty-eighth day of pregnancy. Since neural tube defects occur during the first four weeks after conception, when women are unlikely to know that they are pregnant, it is important for women to eat well, not just once they find that they are pregnant, but when they are planning a baby.

Foods containing folic acid, one of the vitamins associated with neural tube defects, are particularly important. Leafy green vegetables, wholemeal bread, liver, kidney, eggs, and whole grain breakfast cereals are excellent sources of nutrients which include folic acid, as are nuts and pulses. These of course are the 'unsophisticated foods of nature' extolled by McCarrison and Price for their ability to build healthy bodies.

Some scientists are now calling for white bread and other basic foods to be fortified with folic acid. Calcium, iron and some vitamins are already required by law to be added to white bread to make up for some of the nutrients that are lost in the refining of the flour. Over sixty per cent of the folic acid in wholewheat flour is lost when it is refined.

Of course every nutrient is important for conception, pregnancy and the health and size of the baby, so supplementation with single nutrients is not advisable. Poor nutrition can result in infertility or miscarriage, and can affect the growth of the fetus, the baby's birth weight, and his immunity. The lower the birth weight, the higher the risk of congenital malformation. Congenital defects of the heart, nervous system, and skeleton, for example, are associated with low birth weight.[3] The ideal birth weight for babies, incidentally, is between seven and a half, and ten pounds (3,500g to 4,500g). The risks associated with low birth weight are higher in babies weighing under five and a half pounds (2,500g).[4] Animal research has shown that birth defects can be easily produced by manipulating diet around the time of conception.[5]

Food shortages and malformations

Research earlier this century showed that the effects of nutritional deprivation could be clearly seen in some occupied countries following the War. Epidemics of congenital malformations or birth defects were reported in the medical journals of continental Europe following World War Two, and these were attributed to food shortages.[6]

During the Nazi occupation of the Netherlands, there were severe shortages of food, and conditions were at their worst from October 1944 to May 1945. With the help of detailed medical records, research workers were able to look back, years later, and chart the effects of the famine on the reproductive capacity of the population.

One epidemic of congenital malformations or birth defects was recorded during the autumn and winter of 1945/6, months after food supplies had been restored. Detailed medical records indicated that poor nutrition just before pregnancy had been much more damaging than during pregnancy.[7]

There was a one hundred per cent increase in perinatal mortality among babies who were conceived during the famine and in the four months after it had ended. The deaths were due in part to low birth weight, and in part to congenital malformations which themselves had increased by one hundred per cent during the same period.

This indicated that it had taken four months for the women to recover their health and build up their nutritional reserves sufficiently to be able to conceive and produce a healthy baby. There were increased miscarriages in early pregnancy and fetal deaths in later pregnancy, among the women who had conceived during the famine and in the four months following it.

Babies born to the women who were already pregnant when the food shortages began were generally normal though they weighed less and suffered from impaired immune systems and lowered resistance to infection.

The study of the effects of the famine demonstrates the importance of nutrition at the time of conception and its role in fertility. Infertility or lowered fertility can be caused by many different nutrient deficiencies – zinc and the B vitamins, for example. If conception does take place, the risk of malformations, growth retardation, sub-optimum mental functioning, and other fetal disorders increases as the supply of nutrients is reduced.

Birth defects

Many women today are suffering from malnutrition, either through poverty or the wrong choice of foods, anorexia or over-zealous attempts to lose weight. Nutritional deficiencies can cause the endocrine system to fail to maintain the menstrual cycle. Or conception may take place, with fetal defects occurring during the first weeks of the pregnancy, leading to miscarriage or congenital birth defects. Less severe deficiencies may result in a baby born without malformation, but with poor immunity, dyslexia or other health problems.

Poor nutrition in men can result in a lowered sperm count with a high proportion of defective sperm. A marginal deficiency of zinc, for example, can affect testicular function and cause infertility, loss of libido and even impotence. Zinc is needed for the movement of sperm, and where there is an insufficient quantity of this trace mineral available, the sperm may not be strong enough to reach the ovum.

Occasionally, however, defective sperm do fertilise the ovum, resulting in fetal abnormality. It is now known, for example, that either parent may be responsible for a Down's syndrome baby. It is also known that zinc plays an important role in the development of the fetal brain.

Back in the nineteen seventies one of the pioneers in this field, Isobell Jennings, MRCVS, of the University of Cambridge, pointed out that fetal abnormality could be caused by damage to the father's chromosomes. 'Phenocopies', she explained, 'are non-hereditary defects which mimic the defects induced by mutant genes.'[8] In other words, nutritional and environmental factors could cause chromosomal damage in either parent, that could be mistaken for hereditary chromosomal damage.

Examples of this, she said, were the cleft palate, webbed fingers and eye defects that had been induced by vitamin A, vitamin B_2 or folic acid deficiency. The sperm, she pointed out, though it contains only one cell, is nevertheless responsible for half of the programme for the fashioning of the fetus and, therefore, is capable of transmitting genetic defects.

Jennings warned that it was important to distinguish between phenocopies and true genetic defects. If congenital malformations are presumed to be caused by a genetic chromosomal defect, when in fact they are caused by nutritional or environmental damage to the chromosome, then the possibility of preventative treatment can be overlooked. 'Much more could be done in the field of preventative medicine', she said, 'to cut down the large number of preventable congenital defects.'

Work on the same lines is now voluminous and there are journals on these topics. Preconception care is no longer just a fringe or alternative medicine interest, and is now the policy of the British government's Department of Health, following House of Commons Committee reports, and volumes of evidence. This is good news for ordinary couples as it influences what is available for them on the National Health Service.

The Maternity Alliance has had a policy of preconceptual care since 1980. The organisation has sold thousands of its leaflets for women and now has one for men (see 'Useful Addresses' on page 307).

Side effects of Western life

Belinda (Nim) Barnes is an indomitable, enthusiastic, and tireless campaigner for preconceptual nutrition, voluntarily putting in long hours for Foresight, the organisation she helped set up. I asked her what motivates her. 'It's the suffering I see,' she replied. 'The utter misery of reproductive failure is an agony that feels like a physical pain. Women ask me, "Why? Why can't I conceive? Why did I have a miscarriage? Why was my baby born handicapped?"'

Though Foresight believe that a wholefood diet is important in successful reproduction, they feel that it is not enough simply to leave it at that. Much of the Foresight team's work is concerned with those factors which complicate the nutritional status. The contraceptive pill, for example, causes a deficiency of folic acid, among other nutrients. Pollution reduces levels of certain vitamins and minerals. Allergy or intolerance to food prevents nutrients from being absorbed and so on. Genito-urinary infections place a strain on the immune system, thus depleting reserves of nutrients such as the mineral zinc. Smoking can slow down development and increase the risk of miscarriage or reduce birth weight.[9] Alcohol or drugs can be harmful, and animal experiments show that low birth weight in offspring can be produced by damage to the germ cell of the mother before mating, by chemicals or radiation.[10]

Nim herself was asking, 'Why?' in the late nineteen sixties, and was searching for a way to help children who were suffering from allergy, hyperactivity, and dyslexia, the physical and emotional conditions and learning difficulties which statistics show have increased markedly in the last thirty years.

Having read an article in the *Journal of Orthomolecular Psychiatry*, Nim invited the American author of the article, paediatrician Dr

Elizabeth Lodge-Rees, to come over to England to talk on the subject. Among the books that Dr Lodge-Rees brought with her was Dr Weston Price's book *Nutrition and Physical Degeneration*, in which he presented the findings of his studies of primitive people. Nim quickly saw the relevance and potential of the work of Weston Price, Robert McCarrison, and of many other classic books on nutrition that she avidly devoured in the months and years that followed.

Health of both parents

She realised the importance of adequate nutrition for both parents before pregnancy and for the mother during pregnancy. With wisdom and insight she recognised the relationship between refined foods, alcohol, smoking, pollution, and infection, and learning difficulties, behavioural problems and mental illness.

This insight prompted her involvement with various organisations concerned with allergic illness, deficiency disease, and environmental problems, at a time when many in the medical profession in general were still extremely suspicious of these areas of health.

However, a small number of doctors and research workers were involved in nutritional and environmental medicine. From among them, Nim and her friends contacted doctors with the knowledge and commitment to pioneer preconceptual care. In 1978 the aptly named organisation, Foresight, was set up.

From those small beginnings, the Foresight team has grown into a small army of doctors who treat prospective parents privately, assessing their nutritional status and recommending a wholefood diet and, if necessary, vitamin and mineral supplementation. Allergies and infections are dealt with, smoking, alcohol and the effects of the contraceptive pill are eliminated, and steps are taken to clear any build-up of toxic metals in the body.

Some, but not all of the treatment is available on the National Health Service, and it is Nim's dearest wish that all of Foresight's preconceptual care will one day become part of the National Health Service.

Concern, however, for those who cannot afford private treatment and don't want to wait for the results of research, was one of the motivating factors which led to the publication in 1990 of the book

Planning for a Healthy Baby,[11] of which Nim is co-author. It details the work of Foresight, covering subjects such as toxic metals, drugs, alcohol, harmful contraceptive methods, chemical hazards, infection and food-related illness. The book makes excellent reading for those who are planning a family and want to know how to ensure the best possible start for their baby.

'Some say that the trouble is caused by poverty,' says Nim, 'but that is only partly relevant. Ignorance about the right choice of food is also an important factor.' She points out that the relevance of nutrition has not been lost on stock breeders who recognise the importance of the correct diet for their male, as well as their female animals, if they are to produce healthy offspring. Ever since food was first refined, the germ of the wheat and molasses from the sugar have been recognised as excellent foods for animals. The miller could make a bigger profit by selling the white flour and the wheat germ separately, than by selling the wholewheat flour as one product.

As we have seen, primitive races ate their foods whole and unrefined, providing plenty of nutrients for the building of healthy babies. But profit and convenience have produced many modern convenience foods that simply do not contain optimum amounts of nutrients. Let's now go on to look at the long-term implications of nutritional deficiencies during pregnancy, in relation to various health problems in later life.

RECOMMENDED READING

Planning For A Healthy Baby by Belinda Barnes and Suzanne Bradley (Edbury Press 1990).
Eating Well for a Healthy Pregnancy by Dr Barbara Pickard (Sheldon Press 1984).
Getting Fit For Pregnancy, leaflet published by the Maternity Alliance (see 'Useful Addresses' on p 307).
Thinking About a Baby, A Man's Guide to Pre-pregnancy Health, leaflet published by the Maternity Alliance (see 'Useful Addresses' on p 307).

7

A PHYSICAL CAUSE OF MENTAL SYMPTOMS

By now the importance of good nutrition for both parents before conception, and for the mother during pregnancy and breast feeding, should be clear. But what if we feel that the diet of either our parents or even our grandparents may have had an adverse effect on our physical or mental/emotional health?

And what about our own children if, like me, you now realise that your diet during pregnancy could have been better? Hyperactivity, learning disabilities and behavioural problems in children are becoming more common. Can anything be done to improve the situation? Let's begin by looking back again to what has been known by some doctors for quite a long time.

The cause of health

A small group of individuals, including Dr Scott Williamson and Dr Innes Pearse, launched the first Pioneer Health Centre in April 1926. They were motivated at first by concern about the extent of infant mortality and sickness in the East End of London, and then by the amount of ill health among the general population. But instead of allowing their interest to centre on the cause of disease, they sought to understand the cause of health.

The Peckham experiment, as it became known, lasted until 1950, though it was interrupted by World War Two. From its small beginnings in a house in the London suburb of Peckham, to the establishment of a well-equipped health centre in the same district,

Dr Pearse, Dr Scott Williamson and their colleagues examined and observed a cross section of families recruited from the area.

The aims of the experiment were to monitor the health of these families by regular medical examinations, and to provide the food and the recreational facilities that would enable them to improve their health. The doctors were able to move freely among the members enjoying the facilities provided by the centre. This enabled them to make observations which supplemented those that they had gathered in the consulting room.

The importance to health of exercise, of adequate sleep, and of emotions and relationships, was seen by the Peckham doctors to be paramount. They were looking primarily at the way to build health, rather than simply at the way to treat illness. We'll be returning to these important aspects of health later in the book, but first I'd like to deal with some of their far-sighted observations on certain physical conditions that also caused mental or emotional problems. These have become more, rather than less relevant with the passing of time.

Shaping future generations through nutrition

The families that were being studied at the centre were not living below the poverty line. So the doctors were surprised to find deficiencies even in people who told them that, 'Father was a great gardener and we grew all our own vegetables and kept hens, and Mother was particularly fond of liver, which we had not less than twice weekly.' In their book *Biologists In Search Of Material*,[1] Drs Pearse and Scott Williamson called this paradox, 'malnutrition in the well-fed'. They recognised that, for some individuals, it was not enough to simply recommend a balanced diet.

The Peckham doctors warned that deficiencies in pregnant women could shape the constitution of the child. These deficiencies, which could be passed on to the child, could have long-term effects if they weren't put right. Growth and development could be limited. So here again we can see a recognition, in the early part of this century, of the role of nutrition in the shaping of future generations.

The Peckham doctors found that they were at times faced with the problem of the individual who had been deficient for a long time, but who didn't respond immediately even when the diet was improved. The long-term deficiencies, they concluded, had caused the body to become so inefficient at utilising food that even an adequate diet wasn't immediately capable of improving the individual's health.

It also became clear to the doctors that a deficiency of one nutrient could prevent the effective utilisation of another. The study of nutrition therefore, they insisted, shouldn't simply be a matter of supplying the right foods, but should also be linked to the individual's ability to utilise available nutrients.

Chronic fatigue

After the mild influenza epidemic of 1936, some of the members of the centre remained unfit for work or school long after the acute infection had passed. Their symptoms included chronic fatigue, muscular weakness, breathlessness, lack of motivation, and apathy in family and public relationships. Low or very variable blood sugar levels were also detected, along with reduced levels of red and white blood cells.

In response to the all-too-popular view that such symptoms were simply psychological, the doctors emphasised in their report that the personalities of the sufferers varied enormously. They warned that it would be premature to attempt to seek some psychological characteristic before the physical nature of the condition had been adequately studied.

None of the symptoms of the patients' condition, the doctors insisted, were subjective facts; 'all are objective, demonstrable features'. Yet these individuals were often signed off as fit for work in what the Peckham doctors described as a 'state of gross physiological insufficiency'.

They also pointed out that the medical history of many of the sufferers had been known for some time before the onset of the condition. These individuals had not been lacking in energy, vitality or motivation before they succumbed to the influenza or some other infection. Chronic fatigue, it was noted, also often followed either minor or major surgery.

The Peckham doctors suspected that nutritional deficiencies had been induced by the infection or surgery. They were hampered, however, by a lack of information about individual nutrients. But they noticed that a diet which, before the onset of illness, had appeared to have been adequate, was often incapable of putting right any of the present deficiencies. Only an intensive study of each person, they insisted, could reveal the full effects of illness on the general health of the individual.

Some people today suffer from chronic fatigue, and it often follows a bout of influenza. This condition may be called yuppie flu, post-viral syndrome or myalgic encephalomyelitis (ME). Yet, even today, sufferers can be told that it's 'all in the mind'. How many of the mental/emotional effects of inadequate nutrition are diagnosed as purely psychiatric disorders and treated with tranquillisers?

Adverse drug reactions

The book, *Power and Dependence*,[2] a detailed enquiry into the safety of medicines, was published in 1992. Charles Medawar, the author, is an expert on drug safety policy. He was Rapporteur of the World Health Organisation's Expert Committee on National Drug Policy (1988), and has acted as expert advisor for plaintiffs' lawyers on many drug injury and medical accident cases. Medawar points out that over 12,000 people in the UK are currently claiming compensation through the courts.

Tranquillisers, prescribed for social as well as strictly medical reasons, account for around one in ten of all drugs prescribed on the National Health Service. From moderate estimates, all of which were derived from industry or government sources, Medawar conservatively calculated that serious adverse drug reactions in the UK total around 50,000 per year, but it could be much more. An estimated 2–3,000 of these cases result in death. Medawar reports that adverse drug reactions are believed to be wholly or largely responsible for three to five per cent of hospital admissions in the UK. This means that about 10,000 people are estimated to be in hospital each day, suffering from the adverse effects of medically prescribed drugs!

About one person in four in Britain has been prescribed a benzodiazepine tranquilliser such as Ativan, Librium and Valium (as well as Halcion, which was withdrawn in October 1991). Medawar points out that around half a million people in Britain alone have become addicted to such drugs. He believes that lack of control over the benzodiazepines and other drugs remains a serious problem in most, if not all, developing countries.

'Increasingly the benzodiazepines are being replaced by new kinds of anti-anxiety drugs and sleeping pills,' writes Medawar. 'The manufacturers of these alternative drugs have claimed that they present little if any risk of dependence. Time will tell.'

'Virtually every anti-anxiety drug and sleeping pill ever prescribed has proved to be a drug of dependence,' he says. 'The history of sedative-hypnotic drugs to date has been marked by belated recognition of drug-induced psychiatric disorders, chronically mistaken as evidence of illness or a character disorder, rather than something to do with the drug.'

Medawar calls for a radical revision of present day views, including widely held beliefs about the role of personality in creating and sustaining dependence. 'Most benzodiazepines are prescribed for anxiety or insomnia, but anxiety and insomnia are also the most common symptoms of drug withdrawal,' he explains. 'If patients become distressed when benzodiazepines are withdrawn, this still indicates to many doctors that they need more treatment.'

Minor effect on health and personality

The report of the work of the Pioneer Health Centre was published in 1938 and then republished in 1947 in the book, *Biologists In Search Of Material*. Since then an increasing number of drugs have been employed in the treatment of illness. Surgery has become more and more sophisticated, and organ transplants now seem almost commonplace. Some suffering is undoubtedly being relieved, and people are generally surviving longer. But we would do well to ask ourselves if the cure of *obvious* disorders has had only a minor effect on the overall health of the population, as the Peckham doctors warned it would.

No matter how sophisticated medicine becomes, it can never substitute for the prevention of disease. As long ago as 1938 the Peckham doctors warned that a physical cause of apparently psychological conditions should always be sought first. Among the symptoms of magnesium deficiency are irritability, confusion, personality changes and insomnia.[3] And depression, mood changes, apathy and sensitivity to stress are all symptoms associated with zinc deficiency.[4] These are just two of the many nutrients that are vital to the health of the brain and nervous system. However, the study of nutrition, as these doctors insisted, shouldn't just be a matter of supplying the right foods, but should also be linked to the individual's ability to utilise available nutrients.

An increase in information on nutritional issues has resulted in public demand for dietary advice, and some health professionals have been responding. Careful research is being done by some scientists who recognise the existence of a complex of disorders underlying many illnesses. But are we seeing enough action at grass roots level in response to the research that has *already* been done? Because, as we have seen, all too often the treatment of *obvious* disorders can have a *detrimental* effect on the patient's health.

Ahead of the medical profession

Dr Kenneth Barlow, now in his eighties, first acquired an interest in nutrition through his contact with Dr Scott Williamson. He started in general practice before the war, in the days when GPs could also serve as hospital registrars. This Dr Barlow did in Coventry. When at sixty-five years of age he was compelled to retire, he turned his attention to nutrition, and eventually became the editor of a nutritional journal.[5]

I went to visit Dr Barlow and asked him how far he felt we have really progressed in the prevention of illness. 'The Peckham doctors were far ahead of the general medical profession of the day,' he replied. 'They started their work in 1926 and here we are, almost seventy years later, still not really preventing disease.'

In his book *Recognising Health*,[6] published in 1988, Dr Barlow wrote, 'It is remarkable that, in the medical view of the "service of health", interest in nutrition has been so slight.' He pointed out that, though the general public are preoccupying themselves more and more with the relationship between nutrition and health, 'in the teaching of the principles of medicine, nutrition was neglected'.

Nutritional reserves

For Dr Barlow, the work of the Peckham doctors pointed to an important factor in preventing illness. 'A diet that appears to be capable of maintaining health is one thing,' he said. 'But a diet capable of enabling an individual to fight infection effectively, or of restoring health after illness, is another matter altogether.' Dr Barlow explained that, to achieve full potential health, the individual must have some nutritional reserves in order to be able to fight infection.

Optimum health, therefore, requires more than barely adequate amounts of nutrients. And this applies to both physical and mental health. It's hard to understand why nutritional causes of mental illness are not more widely sought, since there is a classic historical example of the effect of poor nutrition on mental health that is widely recognised nowadays.

Pellagra

The nutritional deficiency disease, pellagra, often resulted in insanity. Untold numbers of its victims suffered the appalling manifestations of the deficiency, many of them in asylums. The symptoms of pellagra, recorded as long ago as the eighteenth century, usually began with weakness, aching, and fatigue. It then progressed through to debilitating diarrhoea, reddened, cracked and painful skin, insanity and, finally, death. The pellagrin's eyes would become fixed and glassy, and the individual would tremble uncontrollably and stagger about as if drunk, falling down, laughing senselessly, or sobbing piteously.

The appearance of pellagra, once unknown in Europe, followed the introduction of maize which was introduced first to Spain. From there both the crop and the disease spread to Italy, France, Hungary, Romania, Turkey, Greece and Egypt.

At the beginning of the twentieth century wheat and rice were already being refined. The introduction of factory-milled maize then had a devastating effect on the poor of the southern states of America. There pellagra quickly reached near epidemic proportions, filling hospitals and asylums. In response to the dramatic increase in the incidence of the disease, some American scientists began to look for a physical, rather than a psychological cause. An infectious agent was suggested as the probable cause of pellagra.

One man's battle

The story of one man's battle against the medical establishment of the day, is related in Barbara Griggs's thoroughly researched book, *The Food Factor, an Account of the Nutrition Revolution*.[7] It tells how in 1914, Dr Joseph Goldberg, an American scientist, was asked to undertake an investigation into pellagra. He very quickly recognised its true cause. Not only was he able to wipe out the disease among children in orphanages by improving their nutrition, but he was also able to induce it in volunteer convicts by feeding them for six months on an inadequate diet.

His evidence failed to satisfy the adherents of the infection theory, however, and Goldberg was even accused of faking the convict trial. A series of further experiments followed, with first Goldberg himself, then a party of volunteers, and finally his wife, acting as 'guinea pigs' in order to disprove the infection hypothesis. No matter how they tried to infect themselves with a variety of substances from pellagra patients, not one of them ever showed any symptoms of the disease.

The results of the trials were made public in 1916 and finally silenced almost all of his critics. Pellagra was at last accepted by the medical profession as a deficiency disease. Goldberg and his team, desperate to find a food that the poor could afford, went on to discover that the addition of wheat germ to the diets of people suffering from pellagra was able to cure them. Also, supplements of brewer's yeast, another cheap but rich source of nutrients, were found to be able to prevent pellagra.

Fatigue, stress and insomnia

Pellagra is now widely recognised as having been caused by a deficiency of vitamin B3. Maize is naturally low in an amino acid called tryptophan which can be converted into vitamin B3, and the milling of the cereal increased the deficiency by stripping away the vitamin B3 in its outer layers.

What is perhaps much less widely recognised is that a less severe vitamin B3 deficiency can produce a mild form of the symptoms of pellagra. Vitamin B3 assists in the production of energy from food, and is essential for the proper functioning of the brain and nerves. It is also essential to the maintenance of healthy skin, tongue and digestive organs.

The early symptoms of this deficiency are muscular weakness, general fatigue, loss of appetite, indigestion and minor skin complaints. A shortage of vitamin B3 can also cause insomnia, irritability, stress and depression.

Vitamin B3 is by no means the only deficiency capable of producing such symptoms, of course, and it should never be taken in isolation from the other vitamins in the B complex. The wheat germ and brewer's yeast that Dr Goldberg used to cure and prevent pellagra would have supplied not only vitamin B3, but other associated nutrients too. These products are still an inexpensive way of supplementing the diet.

How much suffering could be prevented?

This brings us back to the symptoms displayed by the members of the Pioneer Health Centre. The Peckham doctors recognised that many of their symptoms were due to nutrient deficiencies, and could be treated by supplementation. They also warned that a physical cause of apparently psychological symptoms should be thoroughly investigated first.

How much money could the Health Service save on tranquillisers and anti-depression drugs if that warning was really taken to heart? And how much suffering caused by the addictive nature of many such drugs could also be prevented?

There are far-sighted campaigners, nutritionists, doctors and scientists even today who are still encountering the bias of the medical establishment. However, as I wrote in chapter 3, just because only a few lone voices speak out against the majority, that doesn't mean that they couldn't possibly be right. Of course it doesn't mean, either, that we should accept any and every hypothesis that is put forward.

The Peckham doctors called for action based on *careful research* which, they said, would be 'more likely to be effective than mere reaction to popular outcry'. There's a great deal of difference between careful research and medical bias. And the problem we have now is that people *are* reacting against drugs and surgery, but many are turning to all sorts of questionable practices in their search for health and wholeness.

Nowadays I find that on the one hand, some of the most sensible and well-documented nutritional therapies are still considered to be controversial. And on the other hand, bizarre ideas abound in the alternative scene. But let's return now to Johnny who, as we saw in chapter 2, had been suffering from chronic fatigue, weakness, poor memory, and lack of energy, motivation and concentration.

RECOMMENDED READING

Recognising Health by Dr K Barlow (The McCarrison Society 1988).
The Food Factor by Barbara Griggs (Penguin 1986).
Biologists In Search Of Material by Dr G Scott Williamson and Dr I H Pearse (Scottish Academic Press 1982).
Power and Dependence by C Medawar (Social Audit 1992).
Three booklets available from T-Plan Books, PO Box 20, Liverpool L17 6DS, price £1.50 each including postage and packing: *Escape From Valium/Diazepam* by Larry Neild, *Escape From Ativan/Lorazepam* by Larry Neild, *Escape From Sleeping Pills* by Larry Neild.

8

UNDERLYING PROBLEMS

Johnny, like many teenagers, has a sweet tooth and enjoys junk food, late nights and mornings spent lying in bed. He doesn't spend very much time out in the fresh air, and he gets very little exercise since his pride and joy, a bright red car, came into his life!

Once boys reach their teens, they need considerably more nutrients to supply their rapid growth and development. When the diet doesn't supply enough, digestion, energy levels, motivation, learning and behaviour can suffer, along with the immune system and, in some cases, the skin.

We saw in the previous chapter that it has been known for many years that a diet which appears to be adequate for the maintenance of health may not be nourishing enough to rebuild health after infection or illness.

Similarly, the diet that may have appeared to be adequate for the younger child may not be nourishing enough to sustain periods of rapid growth. No wonder the teenage years can be difficult! Moodiness, listlessness, and laziness aren't always simply a matter of deliberate rebellion. Fathers, especially, please take note!

The deterioration in Johnny's concentration, motivation and learning ability had begun just as he reached his teenage years, coinciding with his development of asthma, and of allergies to animals and house dust. But now he felt tired all the time, was suffering from poor memory, lack of motivation and depression.

What really worried him was that his friend had just been diagnosed as having myalgic encephalomyelitis (ME) and Johnny realised that his own symptoms were very similar to the symptoms his friend was experiencing. ME is known by a variety of names, the most

well known of which are 'post-viral syndrome' and so-called 'yuppie
flu'. The names ME and post-viral syndrome describe the symptoms
experienced by the patient, rather than the cause of the disease.

ME

Dr Belinda Dawes is Assistant Medical Advisor to the ME Association, and Medical Advisor to the ME Action Campaign. Dr
Damien Downing is co-founder of the British Society for Nutritional
Medicine. They are co-authors of the book *Why ME?*, published in
1989.[1]

In the book they point out that 'the multiple malfunctions that
make up ME do not descend upon you out of the blue. They have
been quietly developing, in most cases, for months, years, maybe
even decades.' Though ME is very often triggered by a virus or
similar infection, the infection itself is very often simply the last
straw, leading to a partial collapse of the immune system.

The subject of ME is controversial, though it's difficult to understand why it should be so. Perhaps this is due to the fact that
a diagnosis cannot be made on the basis of a blood test or a
microscopic examination of a piece of tissue obtained by biopsy.
Rather, the diagnosis must be made on the basis of the patient's
history and the cluster of symptoms experienced.

The multiple health problems that make up ME, and which may
have been developing for a very long time, are common, widespread,
underlying conditions that we all need to be aware of, whether they
eventually lead to a diagnosis of ME or not.

Why ME? therefore, is a very useful book since it includes such
subjects as immune dysfunction, food allergies, and candida. It sheds
light not just on ME itself, but on conditions that are of great
relevance to each of us and our children, and it is very helpful to
have so much information in one book.

Johnny's symptoms are typical of such health problems that can
develop over a very long time. He isn't ill enough to be diagnosed
as having ME but, like many people, he is experiencing less than
optimum health. His asthma and already diagnosed allergies provide
the first clue to what is going wrong.

Allergic reactions

Very often, people suffering from allergies like Johnny's frequently also suffer from food allergy or intolerance, caused by a faulty immune system. Drs Dawes and Downing point out that a large proportion of ME sufferers turn out to have had food allergies for nearly all their lives.

I reminded Johnny that I had always felt that he had food sensitivities, even as a small boy. Our parents in the north-west of England, just like Johnny's grandfather, Tommy, had lived through very hard times. Many existed mainly on white bread and margarine, and would go without food themselves rather than see their children go hungry. Their enforced diet, however, may have had far-reaching implications for their children and even grandchildren.

Experiments with cats fed on a deficient diet, have shown that the effects of the diet persisted throughout several generations in spite of the fact that the offspring were returned to an adequate diet. Allergies, it was noted, persisted longest through the generations.[2]

Other experiments with rats and mice who were given diets deficient in the trace mineral zinc, demonstrated that the resulting impairment of immunity lasted for three generations.[3] Yet the only period of deficiency was during the initial gestation period. In other words, the nutritionally adequate diet given to the next three generations failed to correct the impairment of their immune systems.

The zinc test

A lack of zinc is the only nutrient deficiency which is really easy to detect. An inexpensive 'taste test' has been developed by Professor Derek Bryce-Smith of Reading University (see 'Useful Addresses' on p 307 for the supplier). I made up a solution of this taste test and asked Johnny, his brother, and his mum to take a mouthful, to hold it for ten seconds then spit it out and describe what they had tasted.

The person who has adequate levels of zinc will experience a quite unpleasant metallic taste. However, since zinc deficiency reduces the sensation of taste, anyone who is very deficient will taste nothing at all. They all tasted nothing. Johnny was amazed. 'I realised I had a health problem,' he said, 'but it never occurred to me that it might have anything to do with food.'

Since zinc is particularly needed whenever there is rapid growth,[4] and is so important to the correct functioning of the immune system, Johnny now began to realise why, at the beginning of his teenage years, he had started to suffer such clear allergic reactions. We later checked other members of Johnny's family, including his uncle, and going right back to his grandmother. They all had a negative reaction to the test, indicating a zinc deficiency. And they all suffered from allergic conditions, indicating faulty immunity.

Zinc is, of course, highly unlikely to be the only deficiency, but it's easy to detect and can give the first clue to one of the underlying causes of health problems.

The ability to utilise nutrients

In their excellent book, *The Zinc Solution*,[4] Professor Bryce-Smith and Liz Hodgkinson examine the role of zinc in anorexia nervosa, bulimia, reproduction, immunity, schizophrenia and other mental disorders. They point out that a shortage of zinc before birth can be a factor in learning difficulties, increased sensitivity to stress, and susceptibility to infection.

Nutritionists have long recognised that some people appear to have inherited the need for much larger amounts of certain nutrients than the average individual. Professor Bryce-Smith talks about an 'inherited subnormal ability to utilise available zinc'. Even on a good diet, people in this category remain deficient, though as children this may not be so obvious, and may only cause problems in later life. That inherited subnormal ability to absorb minerals, however, can affect children right from the start, causing allergies and behavioural and learning difficulties.

Johnny's brother, Andy, had always had very clear reactions to food colouring. Johnny, his mum and even his mum's mother and brother all suffer from allergies to a variety of substances, including pollen. They all tested negative on the zinc test. All were very deficient.

Is it just that they all eat a diet which doesn't contain enough zinc? Or could it be that there is, running through the family, an inherited subnormal ability to utilise this mineral, and possibly others? I explained the 'domino effect' to Johnny – the fact that deficiencies can be passed on to the child and impair the immune system, causing allergies or food intolerance. This in turn can interfere with the ability to absorb nutrients and aggravate the deficiencies even more.

For Johnny the obvious place to start was by improving his diet and eliminating the foods which most commonly cause allergic reactions. As Johnny's eyes began to glaze over at the thought of having to give up his chocolate and fizzy drinks, I played my trump card. 'Give me just two weeks,' I said, 'and then decide for yourself if your sweets and snacks are really worth having.'

We struck a bargain. He agreed to a really restricted fortnight so that we could find out quickly what effect his diet was having upon him. His mum promised him that he could decide for himself at the end of the fortnight whether to continue with the diet or to give it up. I finished my little lecture, Johnny and his brother made their escape, and Mum and I sat and plotted how to achieve the maximum impact in just two weeks.

You see, I've learned to be a realist when it comes to nutrition. Teenagers and, for that matter, sceptical fathers, need something tangible, something dramatic to convince them. Better to bargain for a couple of weeks of real restrictions than to suggest gradual change. Teenagers have neither the incentive nor the patience for that. In fact it was only desperation that had driven Johnny to agree to any change at all.

What I didn't tell Johnny then was that if, as I suspected, he had food sensitivities, after a fortnight's abstinence, he would react much more severely to the reintroduction of the offending foods. If the improvement in his well-being wasn't enough to convince Johnny of the need to improve his diet, the bad reactions he would experience almost certainly would.

Masked allergies

Johnny's problems all along, I suspected, were due to the fact that he has been suffering from what is known as 'masked' or hidden food allergy or intolerance. Drs Dawes and Downing describe this phenomenon in their book *Why ME?* Masked allergy is when food sensitivities do not cause an immediate and obvious reaction when eaten daily, such as Johnny's brother had experienced with his food colours. Instead they do their damage steadily and insidiously, producing symptoms which are rarely linked to the diet. However, once such foods are eliminated from the diet for about a week, their reaction is 'unmasked'. In other words, when they are then reintroduced, within a short time they cause a much more severe reaction, because the body has by that time lost its tolerance to them.

The most obvious analogy is with alcohol. After drinking steadily for many years the heavy drinker can consume, without apparent effect, quantities of alcohol that would leave the rest of us flat on our backs under the table. Through alcohol abuse, he has lost the ability to react to it in a normal way, and he can go on damaging himself without appearing to do so.

This is what happens in masked food intolerance or allergy. The analogy can be carried even further in that the foods which are doing the damage often cause addiction just as alcohol can become addictive.

When a person is considering the possibility that food sensitivity could be the cause of his problems, suspicion must first fall on those foods he would most hate to have to do without. Often these are the least suspected foods, such as wheat, milk, cheese, eggs, or chocolate. Abstention and reintroduction can confirm the awful truth, and the breadoholic or chocoholic will experience a much more marked reaction to his 'tipple'.

I planned a menu for Johnny which would cut out the foods which most commonly cause reactions. It also eliminated all those high sugar snacks and fizzy drinks that teenagers love so much, concentrating instead on raw vegetables, protein, and whole grain cereals such as rye and brown rice. It was a simple thing for me to plan the menu. The problem would be for the teenager, used to frequent snacks and midnight feasts, to stick to it.

Will Johnny be able to stick to his diet, and what effect will it have on his mental faculties and physical health? While we wait to see what happens, let me tell you a little more about another underlying condition that can be caused by a poorly functioning immune system: candida.

Candida

Just as a faulty immune system can cause allergies, which place even greater strain on the immune system, so a poor immune system can result in candida, which places even more strain on the immune system. To make matters worse candida itself can be the cause of allergic reactions, as we shall see shortly, and the two conditions frequently occur at the same time.

Candida is the most well known of the intestinal yeasts and it can, in certain circumstances, cause problems. There are others, but the treatment for candida is also effective for the other yeasts. Refined sugar has a lot to answer for. Not only has it been stripped of its nutrients so that it has to rob the body's own reserves for its digestion and metabolism, but it is also the perfect food for the candida yeast.

If you've ever made bread or wine, you'll know that, because yeast is a living organism, when sugar is sprinkled on it, it grows very quickly. Similarly, a diet high in refined sugar feeds the parasitic yeast candida which, like bacteria, is common to everyone.

While the sugar is robbing the body's nutrient reserves, it is providing a banquet for the candida yeast.

Symptoms

The symptoms of candida will vary according to genetic individuality, the present condition of the immune system, the extent of candida infestation, and the quality of the diet currently being eaten.

Often the mental symptoms are no more than a general inability to concentrate, or lethargy. But the most distressing symptoms of severe candida overgrowth can be its effects on the emotions. These symptoms may be caused partly as a result of toxins reaching the brain and nervous system, but they may also be the result of the depletion of the nutrients needed by the immune system, which are also needed for the functioning of the brain and nervous system. The symptoms include irritability, personality problems (particularly unnatural or explosive irritability), anxiety, fatigue or exhaustion, depression, hopelessness, feelings of unreality, poor memory, difficulty in concentration, difficulty in reasoning.

Not surprisingly, candida affects the digestive tract. Indigestion, discomfort, abdominal pain, bloating and distension of the abdomen are frequent symptoms and may be accompanied by abdominal noises, heartburn or 'acid stomach'. Either diarrhoea or constipation may be present or may even alternate, and 'spastic colon', cramp-like pain and colic are common.

The presence of candida in the female reproductive organs are a frequent cause of inflammatory conditions of the womb, fallopian tubes and ovaries. Cystitis and vaginitis, menstrual problems, heavy bleeding or cramps, premenstrual tension and loss of interest in sex often result.

Very commonly, the effect of candida on the mucous membranes of the body produces recurrent sore throats, bronchitis, running nose, catarrh. Other symptoms include asthma, hay fever, and sensitivity to fumes and perfumes, chemical smells or tobacco.

Nobody is likely to have all the symptoms. The various symptoms are due only partly to candida's direct activity, but also to nutritional deficiencies caused by the immune system's increased requirements of all nutrients, as it battles to keep candida under control.

Deficiencies are aggravated still further by malabsorption to which candida contributes, and the interference by candida with the intestinal production of certain vitamins, and the utilisation of essential fatty acids (see chapter 10). For these reasons many of the symptoms seen in candida sufferers are symptoms of the deficiency of particular nutrients.

How candida works

What causes this wide range of symptoms? The candida yeast is best known as a 'dimorphic organism'. This means that it has two separate identities or forms, and is able to change from a simple yeast to what is known as its mycelial or fungal form.

The mycelial or fungal form has the ability to produce rhizoids, similar to roots, which enable it to burrow through the walls of the gut. As it does so, it affects the permeability of the gut wall, leaving it rather like a sieve, and allowing particles of undigested food to pass through the intestinal walls.

The intestines are designed to deal with partly digested food and toxins, but let them get into the rest of the body and alarm bells are set off. The immune system recognises them as foreign and responds to them. The type of reaction depends on how far these undigested foods, the candida, and the toxins it produces, are able to get.

Depending upon which tissues they come into contact with, the resulting reactions may include asthma or wheezing, constant catarrh, swelling or skin reactions, aching or palpitations. These are the symptoms commonly recognised as allergic reactions. Candida is a major cause of food sensitivity and allergic reactions, and should always be considered in such cases.

The immune system may spend years fighting off the candida and dealing with undigested food particles and toxins, before it overwhelms the immune system. During that time, the candida yeast is flourishing in the gut, coating the walls of the intestines, letting food particles out before they are digested, and inhibiting the absorption of nutrients further down the line.

Eventually, however, the strain begins to tell on the immune system. Allergies to pets, dust, pollen, or chemical pollutants can develop, and infections may become more frequent. All of this continues to deplete nutritional reserves, affecting both physical and emotional health.

Drugs such as steroids prescribed for conditions such as asthma and rheumatism, weaken the immune system further. One of the most wide-spread uses of steroids, however, is in the contraceptive pill and its prolonged use can have devastating effects on the immune system's ability to control candida.

Over-use of antibiotics

Antibiotics, prescribed in good faith to combat infection can cause further problems. Imagine an army, locked in fierce hand-to-hand fighting with the enemy. At the height of the fighting, the general in charge comes up with a very effective strategy to stop the fighting. He orders the air force to fly over the battle zone and drop nerve gas on the whole area, killing his own soldiers as well as the enemy troops. It certainly puts a stop to the fighting, but our general is soon facing a court martial, accused of insanity!

This absurd story illustrates what I had been doing for many years, and what many people are still doing now. Every time we take antibiotics, we kill off our own army of helpful bacteria as well as the infecting enemy bacteria.

Furthermore, antibiotics kill only bacteria; they have no effect whatsoever on viral or fungal infections, other than to encourage them by killing off the friendly army of bacteria. This leaves plenty of room for the candida yeast to grow and spread.

Antibiotics can also interfere with the intestinal production of certain vitamins, normally synthesised by friendly bacteria. In the absence of one of these vitamins, biotin, the change from candida's relatively harmless simple yeast form to its much more invasive fungal form can take place much faster.

As we shall see in the next chapter, a deficiency of biotin can also interfere with the utilisation of essential fatty acids, with far-reaching consequences.

To make matters worse, the candida sufferer may have been absorbing, for a number of years, antibiotic residues from commercially reared meat such as beef, pork, and chicken. These residues continually destroy friendly bacteria and enable the candida yeast to flourish unhindered.

It was only many years after I had cured my bronchitis and ulcerated throats that I realised why the garlic tablets had been so effective. Garlic is both anti-bacterial and anti-fungal. It can be a very useful weapon in the battle against candida. Though I hadn't known it at the time, my poor immunity had resulted in candida, which was the cause of my bronchitis and ulcerated throats. The reason that the garlic tablets had been so helpful for me was that they are very effective against candida.

As the years went by, I found time and time again that apparently separate conditions so often proved to be inter-related. Poor immunity, infection, food sensitivity, allergy and candida all need to be considered together since, like a circle of dominoes, any one can knock down another.

The extent to which candida becomes a problem depends on the efficiency of the immune system which, in turn, is dependent upon factors such as stress, nutrient deficiency, diet and lifestyle. Often it goes on for years causing minor problems which go unrecognised.

But if the onslaught becomes too great or is too prolonged, it can cause the immune system to break down completely. This can cause a condition very similar to AIDS.

AIDS

It is interesting to note that AIDS patients invariably suffer from severe candida infestation. At first glance it would seem that this is brought about by their immune system's inability to control bacterial and yeast overgrowth.

But could it be the other way round in some cases? Could it be that nutrient deficiencies and other immune-depleting factors in some individuals, over many years, has altered the intestinal flora, and caused allergies, placing an intolerable burden on the immune system? There has been speculation that underlying conditions which damage the immune system may have created a susceptibility to the AIDS virus. Could it be that such factors can make the difference between the individual who comes into contact with the AIDS virus but is able to deal effectively with it, and the individual who goes on to develop full-blown AIDS?

A group of eminent scientists has challenged the direction that AIDS research has taken over the past ten years. One of them, Professor Luc Montagnier of the Institut Pasteur in Paris, is the scientist who first isolated the HIV virus in 1983. Now fifty scientists have formed The Group for the Scientific Reappraisal of the HIV/AIDS Hypothesis. At the Alternative AIDS Conference in Amsterdam in May 1992, they launched a newsletter called *Rethinking AIDS*.

The HIV virus, they claim, is not a significant factor in the onset of full-blown AIDS. It has been suggested that, in high-risk health groups, the use of drugs, coupled with poor diet, could lead to physical degeneration which may then be diagnosed as AIDS. It is possible, say these scientists, to be HIV positive and not develop full-blown AIDS. However, it is also possible to develop AIDS without first developing HIV.

The theories of such scientists are controversial, and have shaken the medical world. But more recently, at the Eighth International AIDS Conference in Amsterdam in July 1992, new findings appear to support them. According to the latest thinking, our bodies have mechanisms both for rejecting the virus if it reaches us in small quantities, or for keeping it dormant inside the cells that it succeeds in infecting.

Complicating factors that can weaken the body's defences, it has been suggested, can allow the virus to become more active. At that point, in a further attempt to control it, the body begins producing HIV antibodies designed to immobilise it, causing the individual to test HIV positive.

The new discoveries, combined with conference disclosures that some AIDS patients seem to have no trace of HIV in their bodies, lends further support to 'dissident' scientists who have questioned the relationship between HIV and AIDS. This is not a reason for panic. Dr Tama Jehuda-Cohen, a clinical immunologist said, 'I think it's wonderful news. It means that getting infected or being exposed is not equivalent to being doomed.'[5]

The role of nutrient deficiencies

This will come as no surprise to those nutrition writers who have long warned of the effects of immune depleting conditions such as nutrient deficiencies, allergies, or candida on the immune system. In his book *Candida Albicans*,[6] Leon Chaitow explains that the immune system, with all its checks and balances, may become disrupted to such an extent that AIDS may occur. The treatment of such underlying conditions, therefore, should play an important part in any immune deficiency condition.

On the subject of nutrient deficiencies and AIDS, the authors of *The Zinc Solution* write:

> On the currently intractable and growing problem of AIDS, we have ventured to make some informed suggestions that go beyond what has so far been definitely proven; in particular, that it is not sufficient simply to seek a vaccine or 'wonder drug' to attack the infective virus. Ways must also be found to strengthen the immune system – which is weakened by zinc deficiency – so that asymptomatic AIDS may be prevented from developing into the very dangerous symptomatic variety.

The book was first published in 1986. Six years later that controversial view on the importance of boosting the immune system, now appears to be supported by other scientists. Though the controversy will no doubt continue, common sense must surely suggest that natural methods of building immunity can only be good for health.

A diet high in refined carbohydrates and the over-use of antibiotics play havoc with intestinal health. Nutrient deficiencies inhibit the efficient functioning of the immune system, and cause allergies and food intolerance, exacerbating the problem still further. Pollution in food and the environment adds to the burden, and stress makes matters even worse. Some or all of these immune damaging factors are very likely to be present when conditions such as ME, AIDS and, for that matter many other illnesses, are diagnosed.

Natural methods of treatment

We may know more about these underlying factors now, but the early nature cure practitioners have been treating them successfully for many years. One of the very first books I bought on the subject of nutrition was *Everybody's Guide to Nature Cure*, first published in 1936.[7] The author, Harry Benjamin, a nature cure practitioner, based much of his work on the detoxification of the whole system with raw food and cleansing regimes.

Though little may have been known then of the specific yeast and bacteria involved, the need to cleanse and detoxify the body was well recognised. The treatments advocated by the nature cure practitioners were able to detoxify the system and to build health and immunity. Admittedly, we now have to take into account factors like pollution, but this increases the need for methods of detoxification and immune strengthening, rather than supersedes it.

To simply think in terms of treating allergy by avoiding certain foods can result in more and more nutrient deficiencies, and in the constant development of new sensitivities. Often a person will experience an immediate improvement in health by removing an important food from the diet. But this may be followed by a long slow decline if the nutrients contained in that food are not replaced by other equally nutritious foods.

Private treatment for the testing and treatment of allergy or food sensitivity can cost more than many people can afford, whereas the long-used methods of cleansing through nutrition usually cost more in will power than in hard cash!

At first it may all seem very complicated, yet a programme of dietary improvements, fresh air, daylight, exercise, stress reduction, and supplementation, if necessary, to boost immunity, can treat all of these conditions. The treatment of candida can improve absorption and utilisation of nutrients, and so boost immunity that allergies and food intolerance often disappear, along with recurrent infections.

A great deal of valuable research has been and is being done in the area of nutrition but let's not forget tried and tested health-building methods, as we benefit from more recent findings. It is the balance of the old with the new, I believe, which brings the most benefits.

Can I have some chocolate?

It was with all this in mind that I had worked out a two-week plan for Johnny to see if dietary improvements could relieve his chronic fatigue, and poor memory, and help him to concentrate better on his all-important exam revision. It didn't take very long to get some results.

After a week of abstinence from all junk foods, refined sugar and flour, and a diet rich in vitamins, mineral and essential fatty acids, Johnny's mum said, 'He seems lifted – that's the only way I can describe the change in him. It's lovely to see him like this.'

The enforced restriction to natural foods had resulted in Johnny being willing to try foods he would once have refused point blank. Moreover, he found that he actually liked them. The initial preparatory shopping had been difficult and Chris had spent much longer than usual searching the shelves for healthy products. But later, shopping became easier.

Johnny made it to the end of the fortnight – just. 'Can I have some chocolate tomorrow?' he asked his mum. But I got there first. I asked him to describe the changes he'd felt on the new diet and he told me that the most dramatic difference had been in his ability to concentrate. One incident in particular brought this forcefully home to him.

He arrived at a lecture on Shakespeare's *Twelfth Night* to find that he hadn't packed his notebook, and wasn't able to take notes. 'Afterwards,' he said, 'I was amazed at how much of the lecture I could remember!' The essay he later wrote on the subject earned him a higher mark than he normally achieved, in spite of his lack of notes.

Generally, he felt more motivated and had a much better appetite, but he'd missed his chocolate most of all. This strengthened my earlier suspicions that Johnny is not only sensitive to chocolate but is also addicted to it.

Chocolate, wheat, milk and cheese are among the most common foods that can cause allergy or sensitivity. Cheese wasn't a problem since Johnny didn't like it so, in addition to chocolate, I'd asked him to avoid wheat and milk for the fortnight. Now I explained that, as he reintroduced these foods into his diet, he could well react to them in a much more obvious way than before. So I suggested that he reintroduce them one at a time, beginning with milk, followed by wheat and finally by chocolate.

Over the next week or so, Johnny again lost his ability to concentrate and went back to feeling as he'd done before the fortnight's restricted diet. Easter Sunday was an appropriate day to reintroduce chocolate and, after three weeks' abstinence, those Easter eggs tasted especially good.

On Easter Monday, however, Johnny had one of the worst headaches he'd ever experienced. This has now left him in no doubt at all that his diet has been a factor in his poor performance at school during recent years.

Johnny's mum now buys flavoured spring water instead of fizzy drinks, and makes sure that really nutritious snacks are always available to replace chocolate biscuits. But what about Johnny's dad, who has always maintained that Johnny's problems were all due to the fact that he'd had too much too easily in life? Was he convinced at last? Sadly no. 'Anyone can get a headache,' he muttered!

An encouraging example

A few months later Johnny telephoned to tell me that he'd passed his exams and had achieved a higher grade than anyone had expected. This means that he will now be able to go on to university. I asked him if he thought that the diet had helped. 'Definitely,' he replied. 'It enabled me to get on top of everything, and to get down to some serious revision.'

By the way, do you remember Johnny's brother Andy, from chapter 2? He suffered behavioural problems whenever he ate foods containing certain synthetic colours. Andy is now a teenager and looks like following his father into journalism. Recently he spent a week on a local paper, gaining work experience.

Shortly afterwards, his parents received a letter from the personnel officer, an unusual procedure, apparently. 'It has been a long time since I have met a fifteen-year-old who has been so pleasant and polite and interested in what he was doing,' she wrote. 'You must be justifiably proud of a son like Andrew. I know I would be.'

Chris and John are very proud of both their sons. They are a credit to the way that they have been brought up. But they are also an encouraging example of the way that allergies and learning difficulties can be overcome by improved diet.

Now both Johnny and Andy must decide for themselves how far they are prepared to go in avoiding the foods that adversely affect them. It can be difficult for teenagers, with so many more exciting things to do in life, to have to watch their diet. But at least they both now know that their health is in their own hands.

Their experiences will stay with them for the rest of their lives, and they will always know that what they choose to eat may affect not only their physical health, but also their mood, motivation, concentration or memory. Shortly we will take a look at another health problem that Johnny's new diet was intended to help. This is hypoglycaemia, or low blood sugar, and it can often be treated by optimum nutrition.

ACTION SUMMARY

There is a lot to be said for considering allergies and candida together, and thinking about the possibility of low blood sugar, which is dealt with in chapter 9. The following recommendations allow for the possibility of candida, low blood sugar, and the foods most likely to cause reactions. (See also appendix 1.)

These foods are wheat, milk, cheese, eggs and chocolate. (Remember to reintroduce them, beginning a week or so later, one at a time, with at least three days between, so that any effects may be recognised.) Chocolate must be avoided anyway, because of the sugar content. If eggs don't cause a reaction, however, they can then be used as part of an anti-candida diet.

Even after they have been reintroduced to check for immediate reactions, cheese and milk are best avoided or at least cut down drastically for a few months, if candida is suspected. Provided there is no reaction to it, natural, unpasteurised yoghurt is an excellent source of friendly bacteria and should be eaten every day.

If after implementing the following suggestions for about six months, there are still problems, then further allergens may have to be sought (see appendix 6). However, once health has been improved, some sensitivities can disappear, particularly when candida is brought under control, in which case there's no point in testing for too many sensitivities too early.

Avoid all sources of refined carbohydrates (sugar and flour), and substitute whole grains and cereal. (In both allergy and candida, bread may be a problem due to sensitivity to either wheat or yeast. Ryvita can be a better option.)

Cut out as far as possible processed, hydrogenated, and reheated fats. To begin with, valuable foods such as milk, eggs and whole wheat must be avoided. So it is important that very nutritious foods should be substituted. Ensure that the diet contains natural sources of essential fatty acids (see chapter 10) and the vitamins and minerals needed for the conversion process.

Good examples are dried beans, nuts (freshly shelled), seeds, whole grains and cereals (rice doesn't often cause problems for those who are food sensitive), green and root vegetables (jacket potatoes can be very useful), and fresh oily fish such as sardines, mackerel, herring, tuna, trout or salmon (there is some loss of EFAs when fish is canned). Meat which has been intensively reared may contain small amounts of antibiotics, so lamb or organically reared meat would be better. Keep some cold and sliced in the fridge, for when you need a snack.

Snacks tend to be the biggest problem, so keep plenty of fresh nuts and seeds in, and have raw vegetable sticks or florets ready prepared in the fridge. Plan ahead, and prepare enough cold rice or three bean salad, for example, to keep the extra in the fridge (see chapter 14, and also appendix 2 for recipes for these, for junket, and for yoghurt cheese).

Garlic, acidophilus powder or tablets (the friendly bacteria found in yoghurt), and olive oil are particularly helpful in candida, as are raw foods (see chapter 15). Molasses, wheat germ, and brewer's yeast are not appropriate in the early stages since they may cause a reaction. Cod liver oil, however, could be used to provide an inexpensive source of essential fatty acids and vitamins A and D.

Read chapter 9 on blood sugar handling problems, and chapter 10 on essential fatty acids.

See appendices 3, 4 and 5 for methods of providing optimum amounts of nutrients. Discuss with your doctor any nutritional changes you plan to make.

See 'Useful Addresses' on p 307 for information about The Hyperactive Children's Support Group and ECHO, and also for 'Nature's Best' (the supplier of the zinc test).

RECOMMENDED READING

Allergy Prevention For Kids by Dr Leo Galland (Bloomsbury 1989).
Candida Albicans by Leon Chaitow, ND, DO (Thorsons 1991).
Why ME? by Dr B Dawes and Dr D Downing (Grafton 1989).

9

SWEET COMPLICATIONS

Gillian and I sat having lunch together, talking about food. We had met up in London to discuss another subject altogether but, as so often happens when someone mentions that they haven't been too well, the topic of conversation had turned to nutrition. Gillian had been feeling chronically tired for months and was having great difficulty with mood swings and concentration. Her doctor had diagnosed hypoglycaemia, also called low blood sugar.

Symptoms of hypoglycaemia include craving for carbohydrates, irritability, and tiredness, weakness or even fainting, and are most commonly felt mid-morning and mid-afternoon or after exercise. Stress can also cause the symptoms of hypoglycaemia, though the condition itself can cause feelings of stress and depression.

Patients may wake up hungry during the night, they often feel sickly, or they may suffer from migraine headaches. Anxiety, panic attacks and racing heartbeat are common symptoms. Mental confusion, emotional instability, and neurotic and even psychotic behaviour can result from a sudden drop in blood sugar.

Hypoglycemia: A Better Approach[1] was first published in 1977 in America. Now into its seventeenth printing, its author Dr Paavo Airola points out that hypoglycaemia, its symptoms, and its underlying causes, vary with almost every individual patient. 'Although we do not know exactly how it develops in every case, we do know how we can successfully control its symptoms and even help to correct the condition permanently and restore health.'

A sugar-laden diet

Basically there are three types of hypoglycaemia. It may be caused by the malfunction of organs such as the pancreas, the liver, the adrenals and other endocrine glands. It may also occur when an insulin-dependent diabetic gives him or herself too much insulin. But the type of hypoglycaemia we are discussing here is known as reactive hypoglycaemia.

In the healthy individual, blood sugar levels are controlled by the hormone insulin, produced by the pancreas. When too little insulin is secreted, or it is unable to be utilised, the blood sugar stays over high and this results in diabetes. In hypoglycaemia, however, the opposite happens and the pancreas produces too much insulin.

The blood sugar level then drops and the cells of the body and the brain are starved of the sugar they need to function properly. Dr Airola believes that much of today's irrational and anti-social behaviour, on an individual as well as a collective basis, can be traced to our denatured, chemicalised, nutritionless, sugar-laden diet. 'White flour and white sugar are more devastating to a person's health on an individual level, and to the physical, mental and social health of the whole human society, than any other single factor,' he writes.

We've already looked at the research of Professor David Barker and his team, Dr Weston Price, Sir Robert McCarrison, and Drs Pearse and Scott Williamson, all demonstrating the damaging effects of refined foods. Here we have another voice of warning.

At its most serious, hypoglycaemia can cause the sufferer to pass out completely, and blood sugar must be restored very quickly before serious consequences occur. Patients are usually recommended to carry sugar lumps around with them at all times. Gillian had been eating frequent high carbohydrate snacks to keep her blood sugar high. However, she found that her symptoms were getting much worse, and she was putting on weight at an alarming rate.

Though sugar can be useful in emergencies when the blood sugar level drops dangerously low, refined sugars and starches are not the long-term answer to the problem of hypoglycaemia, since they are one of the most common contributing factors to the condition.[2] And the continued use of these products to treat hypoglycaemia can create a vicious circle that results in more severe symptoms.

Blood sugar levels

All foods turn into one or other form of sugar in the blood. The crucial factor is the speed at which they release their sugar into the blood stream. Those between-meal chocolate snacks, full of glucose and energy that are advertised on television certainly do give you a lift and boost your energy – for a little while. They release their sugar into the blood stream with a great whoosh, which triggers the pancreas to produce the insulin needed to deal with it, causing the blood sugar level to drop again pretty quickly.

After years of such stimulation, however, the pancreas can become trigger-happy,[3] over-producing insulin and causing a drop in blood sugar as dramatic as the soaring blood sugar level which takes place shortly after eating refined sugar or flour.

All unrefined foods, however, also release sugar into the blood stream, but the fibre and the nutrients they contain safeguard the pancreas in three ways. To begin with, the fibre provides bulk which makes it very difficult to eat enough unrefined food to obtain the same amount of simple sugar as can easily be obtained by, for example, a bar of chocolate or a few sweets. Secondly, these foods take a lot more breaking down by the digestive processes, which means that the sugar is released gradually into the blood stream, preventing that over-stimulation of the pancreas.

The minerals chromium, manganese, zinc, magnesium and potassium are all associated with blood sugar abnormalities.[4] These minerals are found in their largest quantities in the parts of the foods which are stripped away in the process of refining. Molasses, bran and the germ of the cereal are rich sources of these minerals.

Refined carbohydrates are one of the commonest contributing factors in hypoglycaemia,[5] and should be avoided, in order to prevent even more serious health problems. Unfortunately molasses, though it is rich in some of the necessary nutrients, does nevertheless contain sugar, albeit in one of its most healthy forms. This means that it cannot be used to treat the diabetic, and is not advisable in the early stages of the treatment of hypoglycaemia.

I know one lady, however, who suffered from hypoglycaemia and, after using mineral supplements for some months, was eventually able to gradually switch over to molasses, with no adverse effects. She remains well so long as she continues to take two teaspoonfuls of molasses every day.

Badly managed hypoglycaemia can go on for years, putting greater and greater strain on the pancreas. Eventually it may become so damaged that its function is inhibited. I explained to Gillian over lunch that the way to deal with her fluctuating blood sugar levels was to eat small, frequent amounts of protein and complex carbohydrates which 'head off' the drop in blood sugar.

Many excellent vegetable and grain foods are suitable. They break down slowly and release their sugar into the blood stream gently throughout the day, keeping the blood sugar at a steady level and preventing the awful craving that occurs when the level drops.

I suggested a high protein breakfast such as natural yoghurt and wheat germ, followed by a handful of fresh nuts mid-morning (fresh wheat germ and nuts are good sources of essential fatty acids, so important to the health of the pancreas). Lunch might be a large salad with a small portion of some form of protein, and a jacket potato. Mid-afternoon, a few more nuts or a handful of sunflower seeds and, for her evening meal, another small portion of protein with, for example, lightly steamed vegetables and whole grain rice.

Finally, an ideal mid-evening snack might be another helping of natural yoghurt, or some other source of protein. Even fruit can be a problem for the hypoglycaemic, especially in the early stages, and should be restricted until the symptoms have improved. Dried fruit and bananas are particularly high in fruit sugars and are better avoided.

In the long term, too much protein in the form of meat and dairy products is not good for health, and whole grains and vegetables are the most useful foods for keeping blood sugar level. However, for the first few weeks, frequent small amounts of protein can be very helpful in confirming the effectiveness of slowly released sugar into the blood, rather than the use of regular sugary snacks. Fresh nuts and seeds are much better, and together with whole grains, pulses, peas and beans provide an excellent form of protein, complex carbohydrate, essential fatty acids, vitamins and minerals.

The dangers of caffeine

Caffeine in coffee, tea, and chocolate and the nicotine in cigarettes all have the ability to stimulate the liver to release sugar. The over-use of such stimulants can aggravate hypoglycaemia. Small amounts of tea, coffee, and cigarettes can destroy the benefits of weeks of work for the sufferer of severe hypoglycaemia.[6]

Alcohol can cause hypoglycaemia and most alcoholics are severely hypoglycaemic. It is unfortunate that recovering alcoholics are often encouraged to substitute sugary snacks for alcohol when, in fact, the treatment of hypoglycaemia should always be part of the treatment of alcoholism.[7]

In fact the mineral deficiencies associated with hypoglycaemia (lack of chromium, manganese, zinc and magnesium) are exacerbated by the consumption of both alcohol and refined carbohydrates. These very deficiencies can be factors in the cause of the alcohol problem and both the deficiencies and the alcohol itself can inhibit the utilisation of essential fatty acids (see chapter 10).

The late Dr Carl Pfeiffer of The Brain Bio Centre in the States wrote: 'Many women in Western countries are so deficient in chromium that the white blood cell chromium level may decrease by fifty per cent with each pregnancy, resulting first in complete alcohol intolerance, and later in glucose intolerance (adult-type diabetes).'[8]

Brewer's yeast is an excellent inexpensive source of the most easily utilised form of chromium, known as chromium GTF (glucose tolerance factor). However, if there is an overgrowth of candida (see previous chapter) or a sensitivity to yeast, it must be avoided, at least to begin with, and supplements of chromium GTF used instead. It's worth trying brewer's yeast cautiously. If there is any reaction, better to stop and try again later.

I heard from Gillian a few weeks later. As so often happens with hypoglycaemia, the dietary changes had brought swift and dramatic results. It was wonderful to hear Gillian's delight at the improvement in her energy levels, concentration and mood. I suggested that she continued with the dietary methods for a couple of months and then we could have another chat and see if there were any symptoms left which might need to be dealt with.

It has been interesting to watch over the years the changing emphasis within nutritional circles. First it seemed that mega-vitamin therapy was the answer to all our health problems. Then it looked as though just about everything could be cured by dealing with hypoglycaemia, but that then seemed to be usurped by the information about candida. The more books and newspaper articles that appeared, the more confusing the situation appears to become.

Information about food sensitivity, allergy and hypoglycaemia, came at a time when people were getting tired of living with symptoms that couldn't be diagnosed, but were all too often put down to psychological problems. They recognised their own symptoms in the descriptions of each of the above conditions, but wanted to know which condition to put their symptoms down to. Was it hypoglycaemia, allergy, food intolerance, or candida? The difficulty was that many of the symptoms described for each condition appeared to overlap.

Now it is becoming more and more apparent that the conditions themselves can overlap. As we saw in the previous chapter, candida, by interfering with the utilisation of essential fatty acids, and making the lining of the intestines more permeable, can cause allergies and food intolerance. However, food sensitivity can produce a reaction which results in low blood sugar.[9] These conditions cannot easily be separated. A diet of natural foods, however, low in refined carbohydrates and high in raw vegetables, can be helpful to all of these conditions.

Food sensitivity

I spoke to Gillian a few months later and she confirmed that she was feeling much, much better than she had been before she made the changes in her diet. However, she still had some weight to lose and was finding this difficult. We talked about her diet and I explained that this was now the time to look at any remaining symptoms and to consider the possibility of food intolerance.

Were there any particular foods that she found herself wanting to eat every day? Yes, she didn't seem to be able to do without wheat and cheese. These are two foods which frequently cause problems of intolerance and addiction, so I suggested that she cut them out to see what happened.

Not long afterwards Gillian wrote to me: 'I have managed a week without wheat or dairy produce and am feeling a whole lot better, trimmer and toned up! When I first started to tackle the hypoglycaemia I began to get lots more energy, sometimes staying awake till midnight. Now I have even more energy and find myself waking up at six a.m.!'

A few months later I received another letter from Gillian, telling me that she had had to go for seven hours without food on one occasion.'I managed it without a tremor or a dizzy spell,' she wrote. 'How's that for progress?' She went on to explain that she was beginning to appreciate food more, and to feel less anxious about getting hungry. 'All in all, I am enjoying a far better feeling of well-being.'

Hopefully, as Gillian's health is restored she will lose her sensitivity to dairy products and will again be able to include moderate amounts in her diet. If not she will have to be very careful to ensure that she doesn't miss out on any vital nutrients. However, since the foods that are most effective at keeping the blood sugar on an even keel are the highly nutritious vegetables and complex carbohydrates, Gillian is likely, in the future, to continue to feel more and more benefits from her change of diet.

If, however, the person who suffers from hypoglycaemia uses refined carbohydrate snacks to keep their blood sugar from dropping, the constant over-stimulation of the pancreas may result in pancreatic exhaustion. Late-onset diabetes can be the result of years of incorrect management of hypoglycaemia.

Diabetes

Diabetes first made its appearance in the mid-nineteenth century. The late Surgeon-Captain T L Cleave, who had been Director of Medical Research at the Institute of Naval Medicine, called one of his books, published in 1974, *The Saccharine Disease*.[10] He used the phrase 'the rule of twenty years' to explain the observation that diabetes inevitably began to appear in a community approximately twenty years after a natural diet was abandoned and refined carbohydrates, particularly sugar, were introduced. This was the 'incubation period' which imposed unnatural strain on the pancreas through the over-consumption and rapid absorption of carbohydrates, made possible by the refining process.

Cleave rejected the idea that diabetes was primarily caused by hereditary defect. He accepted that the individual make-up of the pancreas and related structures could make it appear to be hereditary, and that this was a factor that could be increased when both parents suffered pancreatic insufficiency. He agreed that the more pronounced the predisposing make-up of the individual was, the earlier in life the disease would begin. But he insisted that this was 'utterly distinct from heredity defect'.

Important nutrients

In chapter 2 we saw that the MRC study concluded that what a woman eats when she is pregnant may determine the disease that her offspring will die of well over half a century later.

Low birth weight and low weight at one year predicted not only death from heart disease but also high levels of what are called the risk factors for heart disease. These are raised blood pressure, high levels of the factors in the blood which make the blood tend to clot, raised levels of cholesterol, and higher rates of diabetes. In fact the team particularly looked for late-onset diabetes, since this condition is very much associated with heart disease.

We saw in the previous chapter that animal experiments have demonstrated that the consequences of a deficient diet during pregnancy affected the next three generations even though they were given an adequate diet. We also saw that some people today appear to have a sub-normal ability to utilise available minerals.

We shall be looking shortly at the effects of a deficiency of the minerals chromium, manganese, zinc, magnesium, and potassium which are associated with sugar-handling problems. Then in chapter 11 we'll be looking at the role of these same minerals in the health of the heart and arteries.

These minerals provide one clue to the reason why diabetes and heart disease are so often found together. These nutrients are dramatically reduced by the refining of flour and sugar, and these were the product that made up a major part of the diets of the working-class parents of the early part of this century.

The good news, however, is that we can often compensate for inherited deficiencies in our make-up by utilising nature's richest sources of nutrients and, where necessary, by taking nutritional supplements.

Chromium is intimately related to the way the body uses sugar, and supplementation can sometimes regulate blood sugar levels in both diabetes and hypoglycaemia. It is found in brewer's yeast, which has been used to lower and even remove the insulin requirements of some patients. Brewer's yeast is cheap. There are no great profits to be made from the sale of this product, so there is no expensive advertising. Yet I have known people achieve results with brewer's yeast where everything else had failed. A minimum of six tablets morning and evening should be taken to provide chromium in its most effective form, known as chromium GTF (glucose tolerance factor). Sadly, some people are sensitive to yeast, so start carefully, and build up gradually. Some vegetables will synthesise GTF, provided the soil they are grown in contains adequate supplies of this mineral. Whole wheat, grown on good soil, is another source, as is liver, beef and molasses.

Manganese is also involved in the functions that evolve around sugar and starch[11] and, like chromium, is almost entirely removed when sugar and grain are refined. Brewer's yeast is a good source of this trace element, too, and wheat germ also contains manganese. In fact, both brewer's yeast and wheat germ are useful sources, both of these minerals and also of zinc. Zinc is necessary for a wide range of processes in living cells, including the health of the pancreas, and it is a component of insulin.[12] This is another mineral that is discarded in the refining of both sugar and grains.

In her book *Let's Get Well*,[13] nutritionist Adelle Davis wrote of the importance of magnesium, vitamin B6 and potassium to diabetes. Without magnesium, another mineral which is lost in the refining process, vitamin B6, cannot be utilised and so a deficiency of this vitamin occurs, which can damage the pancreas. Potassium deficiency in rats has been shown to cause prolonged high blood sugar levels.

Molasses, stripped from the sugar cane, is a rich source of magnesium and potassium, as well as chromium, manganese and zinc. Cane cutters working on sugar plantations who, with their families, ate large quantities of raw, unrefined sugar throughout their lives, were found to be free of diabetes.[14] This is one of the diseases which made its appearance only after such foods were refined!

Wholesome diets for diabetics

In diabetes, insulin production is either missing or inhibited, or else the body cells fail to react to the insulin produced by the pancreas. Unlike the hypoglycaemic individual, the diabetic's blood sugar levels remain too high.

But good nutrition can stimulate insulin production, and adequate essential fatty acids, vitamin C, the B vitamins, vitamin E[15] and the minerals already mentioned, can be provided by small, frequent, highly nutritious meals. These should be high in vegetables and whole grains, which contain complex, rather than refined carbohydrates.

Fresh vegetables, together with seeds, pulses, peas and beans, provide an excellent form of protein and complex carbohydrate. Dried fruit and bananas contain excessive sugar but other fruit can be eaten in moderation. Salt in the diet should be reduced since it can cause the loss of potassium. Vegetarian diets often contain considerably less available zinc than diets containing meat and fish, so this should be borne in mind.

Large quantities of liquid flush valuable nutrients out of the body and excessive thirst is one of the symptoms of diabetes. It is very important that these are replaced by a really wholesome diet and food supplements such as brewer's yeast and wheat germ. These supplements also contain the B complex vitamins. Molasses is a good source of many of the nutrients associated with diabetes but unfortunately, since it does contain natural sugar, this can be a problem for the diabetic, and other food sources or mineral tablets must be used instead.

Excessive thirst is also a symptom of essential fatty acid deficiency. As we shall see in the next chapter, high blood sugar levels can block the conversion of essential fatty acids. This can result in high blood pressure and fatty deposits in the liver and the blood vessels which so often accompany diabetes. Excessive saturated or hydrogenated fat should be avoided, while cold-pressed olive oil is helpful. Eggs and yoghurt are also valuable foods.

Stress increases the requirement of nutrients associated with both hypoglycaemia and diabetes, and can interfere with the utilisation of essential fatty acids. Minerals such as zinc, magnesium and potassium are depleted by prolonged stress or damaging emotions and attitudes.[16] Even the very best of diets can be undermined by a lack of peace of mind. When stress is removed, the requirement of nutrients is reduced and the diet is then much more effective.

ACTION SUMMARY

Avoid all sources of refined carbohydrates, and substitute whole grain bread and cereal. To begin with even fruit juice should be avoided, or else considerably watered down. Fruit itself can be a problem, especially in the early stages, and should be restricted until symptoms have improved. Dried fruit and bananas are particularly high in fruit sugars and are better avoided.

Try eating small nutritious snacks between meals. I suggested to Gillian, for example, that she might have a high protein breakfast such as natural yoghurt and wheat germ, followed by a handful of almonds mid-morning. Linseed, also known as flax seed, is one of the richest sources of essential fatty acids, and can be sprinkled on breakfast cereal. Lunch might be a large salad with a small portion of some form of protein, and a jacket potato. Mid-afternoon, a few more almonds or a handful of sunflower seeds and, for her evening meal, another small portion of protein with, for example, lightly steamed vegetables and whole grain rice. A mid-evening snack might be another helping of natural yoghurt, or some other source of protein. Nuts, seeds and pulses such as beans and lentils provide protein and many other nutrients. Meat or fish is better eaten no more than once a day.

Alcohol, coffee, tea, chocolate and cigarettes should be avoided, and herb tea, Carro or dandelion coffee used instead. Try brewer's yeast, in powder or tablet form, to provide chromium, and wheat germ as an inexpensive source of other nutrients. Molasses cannot be used at all in diabetes, and may be a problem at first in hypoglycaemia. But, after a few months of improved nutrition, it may be able to be tolerated by the hypoglycaemic, and this is a cheap source of the nutrients associated with sugar-handling problems (see appendix 2 for recipes).

Consider the possibility of allergies and/or candida (chapter 8). See chapter 10 on essential fatty acids. Read chapter 11 on atherosclerosis. Chapter 12 deals with weight problems, and chapter 13 offers some general planning suggestions. Chapter 15 deals with the benefits of raw food.

See appendices 3, 4 and 5 for methods of providing nutrients such as essential fatty acids, chromium, magnesium, manganese, potassium and zinc.

Discuss with your doctor any nutritional changes you plan to make. *Fasting is not appropriate in diabetes or in the early stages of hypoglycaemia.*

RECOMMENDED READING

Hypoglycemia: A Better Approach by Dr P Airola (Health Plus 1977). *Nutritional Medicine* by Dr S Davies and Dr A Stewart (Pan 1987).

10

HEALTHY FATS

I bumped into a friend in the high street the other day. 'Now tell me,' she said, 'what do you think about evening primrose oil?' She'd just read a full-page article in the *Daily Mail* on the subject and wanted to know if she should try it.

The list of conditions that evening primrose is claimed to help is so long and varied that it defies belief. How can one product do so much? It's certainly a subject that has caught the public's attention and I can't think of any product I'm asked about more often than the one that my friend had just mentioned.

'Tell me first,' I replied, 'what is it that you hope to cure with evening primrose oil?' She didn't really know. The write-up had been so good that she simply thought that it might be worth trying. She could well be right, but this is a fascinating subject that is worthy of a deeper understanding of the reasons for the effectiveness of the oil from this simple cottage garden plant.

Conditions that have been reported to have responded to the oil include eczema, dry skin, brittle nails, dandruff, frequent infections, hyperactivity, arthritis, premenstrual syndrome, obesity, schizophrenia, alcoholism, high blood fats, diabetes, multiple sclerosis, Raynaud's disease, and cancer.[1]

How can so many varied complaints possibly be helped by one product? In order to understand how evening primrose works we must look at the underlying conditions that can prevent the conversion of essential fatty acids into important regulators in the body called prostaglandins.

Essential fatty acids

The idea that we can be deficient in fat may come as a surprise. Fat, it seems, is a 'baddie', and low-fat products are recommended for health, particularly of the heart and the circulatory system. In fact it is possible to be deficient in a very important type of fat, essential to the construction of every cell of the body.[2]

This is not the fat that causes obesity, but a complex of fat components found inside the cell rather than outside. These fats, which are called essential fatty acids, have a different composition and role to the saturated fat we hear so much about. They are vital to the immune system and to the efficient functioning of the organs of the body, including the nerves, brain, liver, kidneys and heart.

Often known as vitamin F, these vitamin-like lipids must be supplied by our food, essential because we cannot produce them ourselves. Unlike saturated fat such as butter or lard, these are polyunsaturated fats and are liquid. They are not simply a substitute for butter or lard, but are absolutely crucial to health.

The idea that a diet devoid of fats is a healthy diet is a dangerous fallacy. In fact essential fatty acids help to keep us slim, since they are vital for metabolism. The higher the level of essential fatty acids in the body, the lower the body weight![3]

Plants in whatever form supply two of the essential fatty acids, linolenic acid, which is found in the leaves and linoleic acid, which is found in the seed. Linoleic acid cannot substitute for linolenic acid, and vice versa, so both green vegetables and seeds must be eaten. In fact an excess of polyunsaturated oils containing linoleic acid can interfere with the utilisation of linolenic acid,[4] so balance really is important. Over-emphasis on polyunsaturated oils, such as sunflower oil or margarine, at the expense of fresh vegetables or oily sea foods (a good source of linolenic acid) can have the very opposite of the desired effect, particularly where heart disease is concerned.

Dried beans such as kidney, haricot and soya beans, however, are an inexpensive source of both types of essential fatty acids, as are nuts, particularly walnuts. Linseed is an excellent source of both types of essential fatty acids and both the seed itself and the oil are available from health food shops. Linseed oil must be fresh, however, since it turns rancid fairly quickly. (Warning: this is not the inedible oil used for decorating!)

Another important reason for eating the whole food, rather than the extracted oil, is that polyunsaturates are unstable and easily affected by oxygen. Powerful antioxidants such as vitamins A, C and E accompany the polyunsaturates in leaves, seeds, nuts and beans, preserving the fatty acids and supplying us with important protective nutrients. A salad sprinkled with a few fresh sunflower seeds will provide both types of essential fatty acids and the all-important antioxidants at the same time.

Hidden nasties in processed food

When the essential fatty acids in vegetable oils are hydrogenated, as in the production of the so-called health margarines, they turn into trans-fatty acids which are toxic. The same thing happens when polyunsaturated cooking oils are heated repeatedly.

The irony is that the trans-fatty acids in products often used as a substitute for saturated fats actually behave like saturated fats,[5] competing with genuine essential fatty acids for a place in the tissues and organs of the body.

Also, without the protection of their antioxidant companions, polyunsaturated oils very quickly turn rancid when exposed to air. Scientists are now pointing out that mono-unsaturated oils such as rapeseed and olive oil, and the hard fats, such as butter, may be safer since they don't oxidise so easily.

Nevertheless, we do need essential fatty acids, and vegetable oils are a valuable source, provided they haven't been extracted by heat treatment. So look for the phrase 'cold pressed' on the label, and use it in salad dressings. Raw vegetables will provide a good supply of the anti-oxidant vitamins which should accompany the extracted oil. Better still, use cold pressed olive oil as a salad dressing, mixed with the juice of half a lemon.

Trans-fatty acids are the hidden 'nasties' in many processed foods, from cakes, biscuits and ice-cream desserts to savoury convenience foods such as sausage rolls and meat pies. So the more natural foods we substitute for processed foods, the less trans-fatty acids we will have to cope with, and the more essential fatty acids we will obtain.

It is only since the nineteen twenties that sizeable amounts of trans-fatty acids have appeared in our diets,[6] in the form of margarine and other processed fats. This could be a significant factor in the increase of so-called 'Western diseases'.

Writing in his book *Allergy Prevention For Kids*, one nutrition expert, Dr Leo Galland, pointed out that our eating patterns have changed radically over the past one hundred years – so much so that, today, we are in the midst of a famine. 'It is hard to believe,' he wrote, 'because our supermarkets are packed with fresh produce and boxes and cans of everything, but we are literally starving for essential fatty acids.'[7]

As milling methods developed, millers found that by extracting the wheat germ, they could prolong the shelf life of flour. This is because the oils in the wheat germ quickly turn rancid once the wheat grain is broken open and exposed to the atmosphere.

Convenience and increased profits for the miller and the food supplier has meant a drastic decrease in this cheap but vital source of essential fatty acids for the populations of countries using refined foods. Here we have another clue to the remarkable health of McCarrison's Hunzas and Price's isolated races. We can of course add wheat germ to our daily diet, but it must be fresh.

Eat more nuts, seeds and beans

Now let's look at the role of essential fatty acids in the production of prostaglandins, those important regulators in the body, needed by every cell and every organ. Prostaglandins control the activity of certain important enzymes, they are vital to immunity, and essential to the brain and the nervous and digestive systems. Because they have a very short life span they must be continually replaced. Essential fatty acids, minerals and vitamins are important 'ingredients' in the production of prostaglandins.

Without essential fatty acids the process cannot begin, and without certain vitamins and minerals the conversion of essential fatty acids into prostaglandins cannot take place. Bearing in mind that every organ and every cell is dependent upon prostaglandins, the wide variety of symptoms and conditions caused by nutrition deficiency is not really so surprising.

The conversion process of both types of essential fatty acids is a little complicated, but worth looking at in order to understand the underlying cause of some illness. A friend of mine had some difficulty with the subject when I sent him something I'd written about it. In reply, he wrote that he had found it very interesting, but hard to follow in places because of the technical jargon. 'Something about your neighbour, Polly Saturate, eating lino at Acid House Parties for fatties, or something!' was his wry footnote. You'll soon see what he meant!

Both linoleic acid and linolenic acid are essential to health and are necessary for the production of important groups of prostaglandins. We are particularly interested here in two groups of prostaglandins, called series one and series three. Series one prostaglandins are produced from the linoleic family of essential fatty acids (from seeds) and series three prostaglandins are produced from linolenic fatty acids (from oily seafoods and the leaves of plants).[8] See diagram on page 118.

Both types of fatty acids must be converted in stages in order to produce the different groups of prostaglandins. The first stage in the conversion of either group relies upon adequate supplies of the minerals zinc, magnesium, copper and selenium and the vitamins B6, A, C, and E.[9] (It's worth remembering here that B6 itself is dependent upon magnesium.) The B vitamin, biotin, is also important and this is produced by the friendly intestinal bacteria.

The foods that are naturally rich in essential fatty acids, are also rich in the vitamins and minerals necessary for the conversion of essential fatty acids into prostaglandins. Nuts, seeds and beans are good examples, and this is another reason to eat the foods themselves rather than just the extracted oils. A deficiency of any of these vitamins and minerals can have the same effect as a deficiency of essential fatty acids.

However, even if these nutrients are available, this first conversion can be blocked by trans-fatty acids, pollution, radiation, some viruses, stress, diabetes, ageing, too little protein, too many calories, too much alcohol, excessive cholesterol and saturated fat.[10]

An enzyme called delta-6-desaturase is also needed for this first conversion of both types of essential fatty acids. If it is not being produced in sufficient amounts, then the production of prostaglandins is inhibited. There can be an inherited inability to produce adequate amounts of this enzyme.

Alternatively, an inherited subnormal ability to utilise minerals could also be the cause of the blockage in the first stage of the conversion of essential fatty acids into prostaglandins.[11]

The value of evening primrose oil

This is where evening primrose oil can be helpful, because it is able to bypass this first stage of the conversion of linoleic into prostaglandins.[12] The oil contains useful amounts of gammalinolenic acid (GLA), which is the essential fatty acid produced by the first conversion process from linoleic acid. So if, for whatever reason, the first stage cannot take place, evening primrose oil can step in.

Similarly fish oils bypass the first stage of the conversion of linolenic acid[13] since they contain eicosapentaenoic acid and docosahexaenoic acid. These tongue-twisting names have been shortened to EPA and DHA, and are normally produced by the first conversion process of linolenic acid. Like evening primrose oil, fish oils can step in to bypass that first conversion stage. In fact, quite a few preparations are now available which contain both evening primrose oil and fish oils.

Though these supplements can certainly be very useful indeed in a wide variety of conditions, they are really only relevant if, for some reason, essential fatty acids are not undergoing that first stage in their conversion to prostaglandins. Moreover, if the factors which are preventing that first conversion can be dealt with, then so much the better.

If the missing enzyme or the blockage is caused by a deficiency of zinc or magnesium, for example, then other areas of health may be affected by such deficiencies, not just those linked to the production of prostaglandins. Or, if the blockage is caused by excessive trans-fatty acids, cholesterol or saturated fat, those same factors are also likely to be causing health problems.

That is not to say that evening primrose oil and fish oils are never useful. Because of genetic individuality, some people simply may not be able to produce adequate supplies of the enzyme delta-6-desaturase and these people may well benefit from supplementation.

And certainly the use of these supplements can be an indicator of the cause of a health problem. If it works, then it is clear that either a deficiency of essential fatty acids or a blockage in their conversion is the underlying problem.

However, whether these supplements are used or not, it is still well worth making improvements in the diet in general, cutting out undesirable foods and ensuring that all deficiencies are dealt with. Nutrients such as zinc and vitamins B6 and B3 are still necessary for further stages in the conversion process. An improved diet will also provide the antioxidant nutrients which should accompany all extracted oils.

I remember some years ago, a young lady told me that she had been successfully treating her eczema with evening primrose oil but was finding that the cost of the capsules was putting quite a strain on her limited finances. I explained how evening primrose works and suggested that she might try making some changes in her diet and ensuring that it contained adequate supplies of minerals in particular. Not only did these changes maintain the improvement in her skin condition without the expense of the evening primrose oil supplement, but she noticed other health benefits at the same time.

Better skin health for all

We've looked at the role of the series one and the series three prostaglandins. To understand another complicating factor, we need to look at series two prostaglandins. The big difference with series two prostaglandins is that they are not dependent upon the first stage of the conversion process because arachidonic acid, the ready-converted fatty acid of this group, is plentiful in meat and dairy products.[14]

This means that the problems preventing the production of series one and series three prostaglandins don't affect the series two prostaglandins since the average diet generally contains plenty of milk, eggs and meat. The proportion of series two prostaglandins to the series one and three prostaglandins, may then increase, with detrimental effects.

Series two prostaglandins have their uses, but when too many are produced in proportion to the other types of prostaglandins, inflammatory responses can occur.[15] Arachidonic acid is converted into powerful inflammatory agents called lukotrienes, and increased levels are associated with, for example, the skin condition psoriasis. This is probably one of the reasons why low animal fat diets have been successful in the management of prostaglandin-related conditions, particularly when such diets have been supplemented with evening primrose and fish oil.

Hydrogenated oils, however, such as those used in margarines and many convenience foods, should be avoided. The real answer is to increase the proportion of series one and series three prostaglandins, which then suppresses the production of series two prostaglandins. The balance is then restored. Moderate amounts of meat and dairy products may then present no problems.

Evening primrose and fish oil capsules are expensive, and if preventable factors are blocking the conversion of essential fatty acids, these conditions need to be dealt with anyway. This may save the long-term cost of the supplement. Where there is an inherited problem with the enzyme delta-6-desaturase, however, or even in the initial stages of treatment, evening primrose and fish oil may be helpful.

It may be worth checking with your doctor to see if he can prescribe it for you. It may also be necessary to check for allergy and food intolerance and to eliminate problem foods from the diet (see chapter 8).

One final point. Providing the mother has sufficient supplies herself, human breast milk provides appreciable amounts of GLA, the already converted form of the essential fatty acid which is contained in evening primrose oil. Here is yet another reason to breast feed rather than bottle feed, whenever possible. It is also important to eat an adequate diet, not only before and during pregnancy, but also while breast feeding.

ACTION SUMMARY

Ensure that your diet contains natural sources of essential fatty acids, and the vitamins and minerals needed for the conversion process. Good examples are dried beans, nuts, seeds, whole grain bread and cereals, green vegetables, and *fresh* oily fish such as sardines, mackerel, herring, tuna, trout or salmon. (there is some loss of EFAs when fish is canned). Chapter 13 offers some cookery suggestions.

The inclusion of such foods in the diet will often be all that is needed to build health. If problems persist, however, it may be worth adding some inexpensive food supplements such as cod liver oil, molasses, *fresh* wheat germ, or brewer's yeast, to supply additional nutrients (see appendix 4).

Deal with anything else that could be interfering with the conversion process of essential fatty acids to prostaglandins. For example, trans-fatty acids from margarine or convenience food products containing hydrogenated oils, too little protein, too many calories, too much alcohol, excessive cholesterol and saturated fat. Pollution, radiation, some viruses, stress, diabetes, and ageing are less easily dealt with, but the right diet can help.

When considering prevention of, or treatment for, any of the conditions mentioned earlier in this chapter, look at all possible causes of deficiencies. For example, a shortage of any nutrients, but biotin in particular, may be due to malabsorption and the lack of friendly bacteria caused by candida.

If necessary, after having dealt with all these factors, use supplements to deal with any deficiencies that remain even after the diet has been improved (see appendix 5).

Discuss with your doctor any nutritional changes you plan to make.

Warning: Evening primrose oil is not recommended in epilepsy without medical supervision, and purified fish oil such as MaxEPA should not be taken by anyone with blood disorders or bleeding problems, without medical supervision.

RECOMMENDED READING

Evening Primrose Oil by Judy Graham (Thorsons 1984).
Fish Oil, The Life Saver by Dr Caroline Shreeve (Thorsons 1992).
Nutritional Medicine by Dr S Davies and Dr A Stewart (Pan 1987).

Metabolism of fatty acids (simplified)

seeds, organ meat, pulses,
nuts provide:

Linoleic acid

leafy vegetables, linseed,
fish, pulses, nuts provide:

Linolenic acid

both compete for

delta-6-desaturase enzyme ✳

helped by: vitamins: A, C, E, B3, B6, biotin
minerals: copper, selenium, zinc, magnesium

blocked by: toxins (eg. from candida infection)
trans fatty acids (see pp 110-111)
pollution
saturated fats
cholesterol
stress
high blood sugar (diabetes)
excessive alcohol
the process of aging
certain viruses
radiation
protein deficiency
excessive calories

gamma-linolenic acid
(also provided by evening primrose oil)

eicosapentaenoic acid
(also provided by fish oils)

di-homo-gamma-linolenic acid

mainly

a little

series 1 prostaglandins   **arachidonic acid**
*(also provided by
milk, eggs & meat)*

series 3 prostaglandins

series 2 prostaglandins

✳ *candida infection interferes with the delta-6-desaturase enzyme
pathway, the utilisation of minerals, and the synthesis of B vitamins,
including biotin.*

11

THE CHOLESTEROL MYTH

Let's now turn to an underlying condition of heart disease, athero-sclerosis. Then we will continue to look at the role of prostaglandins as well as at other factors crucial to the health of the heart and arteries. Smoking is of course a major factor associated with heart disease, and obesity can also increase the risk. But the role of cholesterol is less clear cut, as we shall see shortly.

Atherosclerosis is the narrowing of the blood vessels caused by deposits of fat and cholesterol, and it can begin quite early in life. Monocytes, which are large white blood cells, burrow into the lining of the arteries then turn themselves into macrophages — scavenger cells that engulf tissue debris, cells or foreign particles. They absorb particles of fat from the blood stream, and can eventually form a fatty streak on the lining of the blood vessel.

Damage to the blood vessel caused by, for example, fatty streaks, smoking, or high blood pressure, prompts certain blood cells to clot and to form a lump on the inside of the artery. These blood cells are called platelets and are vital to the process that stops the flow of blood from a cut or wound, and repairs the damage to the skin.

What they are doing inside the artery, in fact, is repairing the damage to the lining of the blood vessel. In order to do this, the platelets release a prostaglandin called thromboxane, which causes further clotting and narrows the blood vessel as the gap in the lining is drawn together.

More fat, including cholesterol, is then absorbed until an athero-matous plaque develops on the lining of the blood vessel. When this happens in the heart, the condition can lead to angina. Eventually, as the lining of the blood vessel becomes thicker and more fibrous, it may haemorrhage and burst, causing a clump of fatty matter to be released into the blood stream.

An embolism occurs if this fatty lump, called an embolus, obstructs a blood vessel. The condition is similar to a thrombosis where a clot, formed by the coagulation of blood and called a thrombus, obstructs the heart or blood vessel.

In the healthy individual though, one prostaglandin, thromboxane, stimulates blood clotting, while another prostaglandin, called prostacyclin, keeps the situation under control, preventing the blood from forming into a clot by inhibiting platelet stickiness.[1] So, to prevent excessive clotting of the blood and lumps of fat on the arterial walls, adequate amounts of the prostaglandin prostacyclin are essential.

This prostaglandin is converted from linolenic acid. As we saw in the previous chapter, the process is dependent upon certain nutrients, and can be blocked by various factors. We also saw that the first stage of the conversion process relies upon the enzyme delta-6-desaturase, which itself may be inhibited by nutritional deficiencies or even genetically missing. Stress, you remember, was one of the factors that can block the conversion process and, of course, stress has long been known to be capable of raising cholesterol levels.

The good and the bad in cholesterol

What has been discovered more recently, however, is that there are two very different types of cholesterol, low density lipoprotein (LDL), the 'baddy', and high density lipoprotein (HDL), the 'goody'. The way to remember which is which is 'low means high, and high means low'. In other words, an excess of LDL means a high risk of heart disease, while proportionately higher levels of HDL mean a low risk of heart disease.

So the health of the heart and vascular system is not simply about reducing the level of cholesterol, but about reducing the proportion of LDL to HDLs. In fact, low HDL cholesterol levels actually increase the risk of heart attack.[2]

It is important to remember that cholesterol is an absolutely vital constituent of every cell of the body. It is manufactured in the liver, and is transported to the different parts of the body by low density lipoprotein (LDL) circulating in the blood stream. We saw earlier that macrophages in the artery walls absorb particles of fat from the blood stream, eventually forming a fatty streak. The important factor here is that it is only the LDLs that are absorbed by the macrophages. Furthermore, LDL stimulates blood clotting.

HDL, on the other hand, actually mobilises LDL cholesterol from the walls of the blood vessels and scavenges excess tissue cholesterol, returning it to the liver to be disposed of. So not only are adequate amounts of the prostaglandin prostacyclin important for the moderation of blood clotting, but a higher proportion of HDL to LDL is essential for healthy blood vessels.

But now let's take another look at those series one and three prostaglandins from the previous chapter. This time, however, we will look at their role in the health of the heart and vascular system. The series one prostaglandins, linoleic acid (from seed oils and evening primrose) can reduce the proportion of harmful LDL to helpful HDL cholesterol, lower blood pressure, inhibit the clotting of the blood and improve circulation.

However, over-consumption of linoleic acid in proportion to linolenic acid inhibits the conversion of linolenic acid. Both types of fatty acid are converted by the enzyme delta-6-desaturase[3] and they must compete. So if one predominates in the diet, the other misses out on the conversion process.

The E3 series prostaglandins, alpha-linolenic (green leafy vegetables, oily fish) are also important to the heart and vascular system. They too can reduce the proportion of LDL to HDL cholesterol, but they can also prevent the build up of fatty deposits. Furthermore, prostacyclin, one of the series three prostaglandins is a particularly effective inhibitor of blood clotting.

Are meat and dairy products good for us?

So the diet should contain adequate amounts of both types of essential fatty acids by including both oily fish, fresh green leafy vegetables and whole grains and seeds. Linseed and fresh edible linseed oil contain both types of essential fatty acids and are considered by some doctors to be at least as good as fish oil supplements.

There is, however, another series of prostaglandins which are less helpful to the heart and blood vessels. Series two prostaglandins, as we saw at the end of the previous chapter, can cause problems. Although the helpful prostacyclin is produced from series two prostaglandins, it isn't in as effective a form as that produced from series three.[4]

Also, a more potent form of thromboxane is produced from series two prostaglandins which is particularly effective at encouraging blood clotting. In fact, too high proportions of series two prostaglandins can increase the risk of high blood pressure, stroke and heart disease.

As we saw in the previous chapter, the first conversion in the production of series one and two prostaglandins relies upon the enzyme delta-6-desaturase and can be blocked by a variety of factors including deficiencies of zinc and magnesium. Series two prostaglandins are derived from arachidonic acid which, at its most plentiful in meat and dairy products, steps in like evening primrose oil and fish oil, to bypass the first stage of the conversion process.

In other words if, for any reason, the first conversion of essential fatty acids into prostaglandins is inhibited, then the least helpful of the prostaglandins will be able to be produced.

It is easy therefore to see why meat and dairy products have become 'baddies'. Now we skim our milk, cut down on eggs, drastically reduce red meat and eat low-fat products. Clearly too high a proportion of fat in the diet is not good for health. And when that fat is used and reused, or it is the hydrogenated fat contained in many convenience foods, it can block the conversion process of essential fatty acids into prostaglandins.

But have we got the whole cholesterol issue in perspective? Have we got the dietary balance quite right? Or is there an underlying condition that deserves more attention?

A second look at cholesterol

Let's take a look back at the story of cholesterol which began in 1951, when autopsies on young American men killed in the Korean War showed degeneration in the arteries of practically all of the casualties examined. In fact seventy-seven per cent of the casualties showed gross evidence of coronary heart disease.

The stringy, streaky, yellow deposits of fat and fibre, though not yet serious enough to have posed an immediate threat to the young men had they survived the war, nevertheless came as a shock to the pathologists. They had expected to find healthy smooth arteries and heart muscles in these young, vigorous men.

A team of physicians from Boston University Medical School undertook to examine the entire population of the town of Framingham, Massachusetts, a programme which began in 1948 and continues to this day.[5] The team wanted to recruit most of the adult residents and study them for the rest of their lives.

Two out of three healthy men and women between the ages of thirty and sixty-two were recruited to be examined and tested and to complete detailed questionnaires every two years. The project has revealed a substantial amount of what is now known about the epidemiology of coronary heart disease.

From the Framingham study it emerged that men were much more likely to suffer a heart attack than women. It also emerged that people with coronary heart disease often have higher levels of cholesterol. Young and middle-aged men with high blood cholesterol levels, in particular, were three or four times more likely to die suddenly or have a heart attack or chest pains, than those with low levels of cholesterol.

However, the findings also showed extensive heart disease among subjects with low or average cholesterol levels. The relationship between cholesterol and heart disease it seemed, was not as simple as it first appeared. High cholesterol levels in women under the age of forty did not appear to increase the risk of heart disease. However, high cholesterol levels did appear to increase the risk factor in women between the age of forty and fifty.

After the age of fifty, for both men and women the link between high blood cholesterol levels and coronary heart disease became weaker. In fact, among the elderly, the group in whom most deaths from coronary heart disease occur, high cholesterol levels did not appear to be a risk factor.

A rather surprising fact that emerged from the Framingham study was that in 912 subjects, there was no relationship between the amount of cholesterol, saturated fats or overall calories in their diets, and the cholesterol levels in their blood. Yet, in young and middle-aged men, the risk of coronary heart disease did appear to rise steadily as levels of cholesterol in the blood increased.

It was not lost on the Framingham team that people were already being advised to lower cholesterol levels in their diets and that plans were being made for much more elaborate cholesterol reducing campaigns. They pointed out that the levels of blood cholesterol varied considerably within the Framingham study group.

These variations could not be related to or explained by the levels of cholesterol or saturated fat in their diets. The team warned that it would be desirable to know what it was that accounted for such variations in blood cholesterol levels before any attempt was made to manipulate the blood cholesterol levels of the general population.

No benefits

The finding of the Framingham team that there appeared to be little relationship between cholesterol and saturated fat in the diet, and blood cholesterol levels, was mainly ignored in the search for a specific dietary approach that might reduce the incidence of coronary heart disease.

Yet feeding quantities of cholesterol-rich egg yolks to volunteers demonstrated that it took huge amounts of dietary cholesterol to affect the levels of cholesterol in the blood. By the mid-nineteen sixties many researchers had dismissed the importance of dietary cholesterol.

However, in 1971 an American task force set an agenda that would guide medical thinking for many years. The Framingham study had identified the risk factors of heart disease as smoking, obesity and high blood pressure, which had by and large, fitted in with other epidemiological evidence. In the expectation that a fall in blood cholesterol levels through dietary measures alone would be too small, the task force instigated the Multiple Risk Factor Intervention Trial, or MR.FIT. This was one of the largest medical experiments ever conducted, taking ten years, and involving twenty-eight medical centres across the United States.

Using the risk factor equations developed for the Framingham study, the researchers selected 12,866 men who were believed to be at highest risk from factors which, the team believed, could be understood and controlled. Aged between thirty-five and fifty-seven, the men's typical diet included more than twice the amount of cholesterol considered desirable. Two-thirds of the subjects smoked cigarettes, two out of three had developed high blood pressure early in life, and sixty per cent were obese.

The men were randomly divided into two similar groups. One group was referred to the usual care of their own doctors. The other group was encouraged to modify their diet and lifestyle. This group cut their dietary cholesterol intake by forty-two per cent, their saturated fat consumption by twenty-eight per cent and their total calories by twenty-one per cent.

At the end of four years nearly three-quarters of the smokers had given up their cigarettes. More than nine years after the experiment had begun, the investigators began to compute the results. No significant difference in the overall number of deaths could be found between the two groups.

The biggest surprise came for the group who had been left to their own devices. The number of deaths from coronary heart disease was forty per cent lower than expected. Even though this group reported only minimal changes in their diet, their blood cholesterol levels declined nearly as much as the special intervention group's, leaving only two per cent difference in the groups. Only twenty-nine per cent of this group gave up smoking, yet the typical blood pressure of the group was only four per cent higher.

The failure of the Multiple Risk Factor Intervention Trial triggered a wide range of comment and criticism in the medical community, but attracted little attention in the general press. The health advice given to millions of Americans over decades had been tested in a large and elaborate clinical trial, and had produced no measurable benefits!

Cancer

Meanwhile, however, the continuing Framingham study was beginning to reveal some disturbing statistics. Subjects who subsequently
developed cancer were found to have had unexpectedly low levels of
blood cholesterol as much as sixteen to eighteen years before their
cancer diagnosis. These findings prompted the National Cancer
Institute, in 1987, to measure the same relationship between
low cholesterol levels and subsequent cancer diagnosis among
over 12,000 men and women who participated in the National
Health Nutrition and Examination Survey.

The men with the lowest cholesterol levels were found to be more
than twice as likely to be diagnosed with cancer as those with
the highest cholesterol levels. That made low cholesterol almost
as powerful a predictor of cancer as high cholesterol was of heart
disease.

In the women taking part in these studies, the link between low
blood cholesterol levels and subsequent cancer diagnosis was shown
to be similar but weaker. The statistical association between low
cholesterol and cancer found in these and other studies neither proves
nor disproves that low blood cholesterol actually causes cancer, but
only that it was statistically predictive of cancer.

However, in a twenty-five page article entitled 'The Cholesterol
Myth' published in the September 1989 issue of the *Atlantic Monthly*,
it is suggested that it is not difficult to find a theory to explain the
link between low cholesterol levels and cancer. The article quotes
the British heart researcher Michael F Oliver, who asks, 'How
much cholesterol can be depleted from cell membranes over many
years without alteration of their function?'[6] In other words, does
the membranes' functioning become sufficiently compromised to
admit carcinogens - the cells that cause cancer?

High fat diets

Dr Uffe Ravnskov, a Swedish GP, believes that claims that a high
fat diet leads to heart disease have been distorted by researchers.
He analysed twenty-two trials involving 114,000 people, which had
been conducted over almost thirty years.

In the July 1992 issue of the *British Medical Journal*, he alleged that the benefits of lowering cholesterol, either through diet or drugs, 'have been exaggerated by a tendency in trial reports, reviews and other papers to cite supportive results only'.[7] Of sixteen reports published after 1970, all but one used the results of supportive or inconclusive trials to back up their findings, while ignoring those that contradicted their conclusions.

He concluded that lowering blood cholesterol does not reduce mortality and is unlikely to prevent heart disease. However, he also pointed out that the association between dietary fat, blood cholesterol levels, and coronary heart disease is beyond doubt. So why have efforts to lower blood cholesterol been so inconsistent?

In her book *Let's Get Well*, first published in 1966,[8] nutritionist Adelle Davis wrote about the effect of low fat diets on blood cholesterol levels. She pointed out that when low fat diets were given to patients with atherosclerosis, the patients' appetites usually became greatly increased.

They consequently consumed excessive calories, mostly from starches and sugars, which were quickly changed into saturated body fat, causing the blood fat and cholesterol to soar. The size of the fat and cholesterol particles became much larger, the amount of cholesterol changed to bile acids was greatly reduced, and coronary patients adhering to such a diet became markedly worse.

The opposite effect explained

She went on to warn that diets low in cholesterol have also achieved exactly the opposite from what was hoped. Such diets throw the liver into a frenzy of cholesterol-producing activity, causing blood cholesterol levels to increase. 'Conversely,' she wrote, 'liver biopsies showed that, when volunteers were fed three or four grams of cholesterol daily, far more than would ever be obtained from foods, the production of cholesterol by the liver was "almost completely suppressed".'

She was outspoken in her condemnation of attempts to lower blood cholesterol levels. 'Experimental heart disease has been produced with diets completely devoid of cholesterol.' She then made a very important observation. 'Low cholesterol diets have restricted so many excellent foods that the very nutrients needed to utilise fat and cholesterol have been decreased or omitted.' *The very nutrients needed to utilise fat and cholesterol!* Here we have a clue to an underlying condition that deserves to be more widely recognised.

She went on to point out that certain ethnic groups obtained sixty to sixty-five per cent of their calories from butterfat and yet they had no atherosclerosis, no heart disease, and their blood cholesterol levels were amazingly low.

'In the days when atherosclerosis was unheard of,' she reminded us, 'butter and cream were eaten by all. Butterfat, in moderation, appears to be a problem only when the nutrients needed to utilise it are undersupplied.'

Of the avoidance of dairy produce she wrote, 'Eggs have been condemned, their high lecithin and methionine content ignored. Even mayonnaise has been forbidden, yet it averages fifty-two to sixty-seven per cent essential fatty acids and ten to fourteen per cent lecithin.' Methionine is an important amino acid used in the building of body protein and in the production of lecithin, which is the substance we are particularly interested in here.

Lecithin, produced by the healthy body, has a similar action to washing-up liquid's effect on grease. It emulsifies fat and breaks it down into microscopic particles which are able to be held in suspension in the blood stream. They can then pass easily through the arterial walls to be utilised by the tissues.

Adelle Davis explained that in the healthy individual, when a meal is eaten which is high in fat or excessive calories, the production of lecithin increases tremendously, and the fat in the blood is immediately changed from large particles into smaller and smaller ones.

In patients with atherosclerosis, however, the blood lecithin stays disproportionately low, regardless of the amount of fat entering the blood, and the fat particles remain too large to pass readily through the arterial walls. 'All atherosclerosis,' she wrote, 'is characterised by an increase of blood cholesterol and a decrease in lecithin.'

Magnesium – an alternative approach to heart disease

So why does the atherosclerosis patient produce too little lecithin? Adelle had the answer. 'Lecithin', she wrote, 'consists of several substances . . . which require essential fatty acids, and the B vitamins choline and inositol for their structure, and numerous other nutrients to synthesise them.' Because lecithin is essential to every cell in the body, however, the demand for these raw materials is tremendous, and a shortage of any one limits the production of lecithin.

The amount needed of one of these nutrients, in particular magnesium, is tremendously increased when the blood cholesterol is high. Magnesium 'is readily lost in the urine', writes Adelle, 'and because of the high intake of saturated fats in the modern diet, the magnesium daily requirement is apparently much greater than was previously realised. For these reasons, inadequate magnesium may well prove to be a major cause of our national atherosclerosis.'

It looks as though her words might now be proved to have been prophetic. According to a survey published in the December 1991 issue of the *British Medical Journal*, deaths from heart attacks might be halved if victims were routinely given magnesium on admission to hospital, saving tens of thousands of lives worldwide.

Seven trials around the world have shown that treating heart attack patients with an intravenous magnesium drip soon after admission, generally within twelve hours of severe chest pains starting, reduced deaths by between a third and two-thirds.

In the review of the trials, it was reported that even if the treatment reduced mortality by only a quarter, it could save tens of thousands of lives a year.[9] The review, conducted by teams from the National Heart, Lung and Blood Institute in the United States and the Clinical Trials Service Unit at Oxford, suggested that intravenous magnesium is likely to be suitable for almost all patients. Serious side effects are rare and the drug costs only a few pence.

It is known that deaths from heart disease are more common in areas with a low concentration of magnesium in the soil, and blood levels of magnesium tend to be low in people who suffer from the condition. Magnesium deficiencies can also arise from malabsorption, stress, deficiencies of related nutrients, diseases such as diabetes, and alcohol abuse.

Magnesium, as we have already seen, was one of the nutrients vital to the first stage of the conversion of essential fatty acids into prostaglandins. We have also seen that prostaglandins are important regulators in the body and are needed by every cell and every organ.

And we have seen that prostaglandins control the activity of certain important enzymes. They are vital to immunity, and essential to the brain and nervous and digestive systems. Now we can see that they are vital to the heart and vascular system.

Magnesium and essential fatty acids are needed for the synthesis of lecithin,[10] so important to the correct utilisation of fats. Along with calcium,[11] it is needed for the healthy contraction and relaxation of muscles[12] and of course the heart is a muscular pump. It is also a nutrient that is used up in large amounts when we are under stress[13] or being 'eaten up' by destructive emotions or attitudes. Time and time again we come back to the importance of minerals.

Alternatives to refined foods

We have already seen in earlier chapters that refined sugar and flour don't contain sufficient nutrients to enable fats to be utilised, and so the body must rob its own stores of such nutrients. The cholesterol story, as many nutritionists have pointed out, is not just about fats but is also about refined carbohydrates. Let's look at what Adelle Davis wrote about sugar:

> A high intake of refined sugar (including alcohol), if not quickly burned, is immediately converted into saturated fat. Animals fed sugar instead of starch develop high blood cholesterol, and the essential fatty acids in their blood and tissues decrease far more than when starch is fed. The blood cholesterol of healthy volunteers fell when they ate unrefined starches, but substituting sugar caused their blood fats and cholesterol to increase markedly.[14]

Instead of refined carbohydrates, natural starches should be eaten (potatoes, dried beans and peas, whole grain breads and cereals) and white sugar and flour should be restricted. Raw sugar and whole grain cereals are rich in the nutrients needed for their metabolism, particularly magnesium and chromium, but these nutrients are almost entirely removed in the refining process.

Not only are these nutrients stripped away during refining but, as we have already seen, in order to metabolise these foods, we must rob our own stores of nutrients. Included in the list of nutrients stripped from refined foods are also manganese, zinc, and potassium which, together with magnesium and chromium, are all associated with diabetes.

So chromium deficiency has been associated with both heart disease and diabetes.[15] Low levels of chromium can raise blood cholesterol and also fatty tissues, or plaques, in the arteries. Both blood cholesterol and blood sugar levels rise and glucose tolerance is impaired when animals are made chromium deficient.[16] Chromium supplementation not only lowers blood cholesterol[17] but increases the proportion of protective high density lipoproteins (see chapter 10).

Manganese is involved in the metabolism of both fat and sugar.[18] Studies have shown that zinc also protects against heart damage after a heart attack, since this trace element is protective against fatty deposits in the blood vessels.[19] Toxic metals such as lead and cadmium are linked to arterial and heart disease, and adequate zinc also protects against these pollutants.

Magnesium plays an important role in the muscular action of the heart and potassium also affects heart rhythm.[20] Low potassium levels are also associated with high blood pressure.[21] Too much salt is known to reduce levels of potassium, but it is also interesting to note that magnesium helps to hold potassium in the cells of the body,[22] so a magnesium deficiency can deplete potassium.

We have now looked at the role of chromium, manganese, zinc, magnesium and potassium in diabetes and heart disease. A diet of unrefined foods, rich in these and other protective nutrients such as the anti-oxidant vitamins A, C and E, fibre and essential fatty acids can help to protect not only against diabetes and heart disease, but also against many other conditions, including cancer.

ACTION SUMMARY

Excess weight, smoking and too much alcohol are major factors in atherosclerosis.

Ensure that the diet contains natural sources of essential fatty acids, and the vitamins and minerals needed for the conversion process into prostaglandins (see chapter 10). Good examples are dried beans, nuts, seeds, whole grain bread and cereals, fruit, green vegetables, and fresh oily fish such as sardines, mackerel, herring, tuna, trout or salmon (there is some loss of EFAs when fish is canned). Chapter 13 offers some cookery suggestions.

Cut out as far as possible processed, hydrogenated and reheated fats, and use small amounts of cold-pressed oil. There is controversy about the value of skimmed milk and the avoidance of butter and eggs, certainly in the prevention of atherosclerosis. Full cream milk is recommended for small children, and eggs and moderate amounts of butter are valuable foods. However, when cholesterol levels are very high they may need to be avoided, but the main emphasis should be on restoring the body's ability to metabolise fats efficiently.

The change to a diet of natural, unrefined foods will often be all that is needed for the prevention of vascular disease. Garlic and onions, in particular, are good for the health of the arteries. If there are persistent health problems, however, it may be worth adding some inexpensive food supplements such as cod liver oil, molasses, fresh wheat germ, or brewer's yeast to supply additional nutrients (see appendix 4).

Read chapter 9 in case of any sugar handling problems. Chapter 12 deals with weight problems, and chapter 13 offers some general planning suggestions. Consider any possible underlying causes of nutrient deficiencies (see chapter 8).

See appendices 3, 4 and 5 for methods of providing nutrients such as chromium, magnesium, manganese, potassium and zinc, which have been mentioned in this chapter.

Discuss with your doctor any nutritional changes you plan to make. He may also be able to prescribe fish oil supplements in cases of raised cholesterol levels.

RECOMMENDED READING

Nutritional Medicine by Dr Stephen Davies and Dr Alan Stewart (Pan 1987).
Fish Oil, The Life Saver by Dr Caroline Shreeve (Thorsons 1992).
The Eskimo Diet by Dr Reg Saynor and Dr Frank Ryan (Edbury Press 1990).

12

WEIGHT PROBLEMS

'Have you been losing weight?' I asked Pat, a journalist friend I hadn't seen for some time. We'd arranged to meet for lunch and Pat arrived looking very fit and slimmer than I'd remembered her. 'Yes,' she replied, 'and you'll be interested to know that I don't get uptight about dieting any more. Once I stopped counting calories and simply started to eat healthily I began to lose weight.' That was just the quote I needed for my chapter on health problems! I asked Pat to tell me more.

We had first talked about nutrition some years earlier and, consequently, Pat took another look at what her low-calorie, low-fat slimmer's products actually contained. 'Some of them were nutritional rubbish,' she told me. 'So I cut out all the junk I'd been having, stopped eating for a quick boost, and prepared proper meals for myself.' So why do people like Pat so often find that slimming products and diets fail to work for them?

Too little fat can cause you to be overweight! There is a special kind of fat called adipose tissue, more commonly known as brown fat, which is found in the back of the neck, between the shoulder blades, along the backbone, and around the kidneys. This fat normally burns up excess calories to provide heat.

People who put on weight too easily often have less active brown fat than those who find it easy to stay slim. Their metabolically underactive brown fat allows excess calories to be laid down as fat in the tissues, leaving them less able to stay warm in cold weather.

Vitamins, minerals and essential fatty acids are believed to be important to the effectiveness of brown fat, and prostaglandins, converted from essential fatty acids, are thought to stimulate the brown fat tissue, accelerating its fat-burning activity. Also stimulated by prostaglandins are enzymes responsible for the storage and transfer of energy.

Only when energy can be efficiently produced, for use both as heat and as energy, can weight be lost. The more essential fatty acids in the body, therefore, the lower the weight! Small quantities of cold-pressed, unrefined vegetable oils can actually help to prevent hunger and make dieting and weight maintenance easier.

However, as we saw in chapter 10, the production of prostaglandins relies not just on essential fatty acids for raw material, but also on vitamins and minerals, and can be blocked by a variety of factors. In order to function efficiently, enzymes also rely on various nutrients, such as zinc.

In fact one of the most common causes of overweight is that the modern diet simply doesn't supply enough nutrients to enable fat to be turned into heat and energy. We are back to the problem that refined foods have been stripped of the nutrients needed for their metabolism. The reason that some diets don't succeed is because they fail to take this into account.

One of the factors that can block the conversion of essential fatty acids into prostaglandins is the consumption of hydrogenated oils. This processed fat is the ingredient in some so-called health margarines often advertised as low in saturated fat. They are also used in many savoury and sweet convenience foods. Hydrogenated oils, like reheated and reused oils, are toxic and they act like saturated fat.

Also, by interfering with the conversion of genuine essential fatty acids they contribute to a shortage of prostaglandins, so important to the efficiency of the calorie-burning, energy-producing enzymes and that all important brown fat! Very small amounts of butter can actually do less damage than liberal amounts of some low-fat spreads.

Unrefined, cold-pressed oils such as olive oil and seed oils, however, along with green leafy vegetables and fish oils, supply essential fatty acids and lecithin, vital to fat utilisation, energy production and the burning of calories. Fat cannot be utilised properly unless lecithin is being efficiently produced by the body or else is supplied in the diet.

As we saw in chapter 11, lecithin acts a little like washing-up liquid in greasy water. It emulsifies fat, breaking it up into microscopic particles which can easily be transported and disposed of. It is effective not only in the blood vessels but also in the tissues, and can help to reduce the high levels of blood fats and cholesterol which usually accompany excessive weight and often result in increased blood pressure, coronary disease and varicose veins.

Dieting can make you fat

There is a lot more to losing weight than just counting calories, and a great deal of truth in the saying, 'dieting can make you fat!'

Often the slim person eats far more than the overweight individual. Needless to say those races who lived on unrefined foods didn't have a problem with extra pounds, since it was very difficult to eat too many calories because of the bulky fibre in such wholefoods. In addition, properly grown, unrefined foods also contain the nutrients necessary for their metabolism.

Refined products, on the other hand, once the fibre is stripped away, can supply excessive quantities of calories in a form that can be eaten without effort. The constant robbing by such foods of the nutrients needed for their metabolism can result in metabolic inefficiency and, as every slimmer knows, an efficient metabolism is the best weapon in the war on weight. But perhaps the greatest problems that refined foods can cause for the would-be slimmer are addiction and craving.

Slimming diets that allow small quantities of foods containing, for instance, white flour, can fail because no matter how small the quantities or how few the calories, they can still set off craving, and fail to deal with the addiction which so often accompanies food intolerance (see chapter 9).

Successful dieting must take into account the possibility of nutrient deficiencies, hypoglycaemia, food intolerance and addiction, which can all cause craving. Faulty nutrition over many years may have resulted in liver damage, so that the production of vital enzymes is reduced.

A deficiency of any of the B complex vitamins inhibits energy production[1] so that foods are inefficiently utilised. Inadequate protein in the diet reduces energy producing enzymes, and fewer calories are burned. Protein itself relies upon other nutrients in order to be utilised, and a deficiency of any one means that protein is turned to fat.

A shortage of essential fatty acids can damage the adrenal glands, allowing the blood sugar to fall and making dieting extremely difficult. Frequent small portions of food, such as nuts, seeds or wheat germ containing essential fatty acids, complex carbohydrate and protein, can prevent the tiredness, craving and irritability which are symptoms of low blood sugar.

Don't miss meals

In order to lose weight people will often miss out on meals, eating just one large meal in the evening. In fact this has the very opposite effect to the one desired. Instead of most of the food being converted to energy as when small frequent amounts are eaten, a large meal can overwhelm the digestive enzymes[2] so that much of the food is laid down as fat rather than used as energy. The resulting drop in blood sugar during the day can destroy the best of intentions and break the will power.

Small frequent amounts of very nutritious food throughout the day can actually help in the battle of the bulge, while inadequate slimming diets can damage both physical and mental health. The over-enthusiastic slimmer may still be paying the price of poor nutrition many years later.

Tea, coffee, cola drinks and cigarettes not only deplete the body of vital nutrients but they also stimulate the liver to release stored sugar. This is how they give you a 'lift'. However, as we have seen, their constant use can make the pancreas trigger-happy as it reacts to the surge of sugar by releasing insulin to deal with it. This is another cause of hypoglycaemia and an often unsuspected reason for the craving for carbohydrates.

It is much easier to maintain a healthy diet without tea, coffee and cigarettes, and often impossible to do so when these stimulants are used regularly. Alcohol is made with sugar and it too can affect blood sugar levels and prevent successful dieting. Spring water with a slice of lemon can be sipped as often as desired.

A deficiency of iodine can damage the thyroid gland, making it underactive, which slows down the production of energy and leads to weight gain and other health problems.[3] Sea kelp powder or tablets and sea foods contain iodine. Fish is also a very good source of essential fatty acids and, since red meat contains saturated fat, fish should replace it wherever possible.

Avoid products high in saturated fat and use instead natural foods rich in essential fatty acids, rather than the processed foods often described as low-fat products. Very little fat is needed for health and for weight reductions, but those very small, frequent amounts of the right oils are vital.

Many attempts to lose or gain weight lose sight of these important factors and often result in lowered health and vitality which simply exacerbates the original problems. So give a little less thought to counting calories and think more about nutrients. The priority must be to restore health and to stimulate energy-producing enzymes.

Real health should not only mean fewer pounds on the scales, but also shining hair, bright eyes, clear skin and boundless energy! Put an end to see-sawing weight and repeated dieting and make healthy food a way of life that provides the energy and incentive to make exercise a pleasure rather than a chore.

Plenty of vegetables, some whole grains, moderate amounts of protein and dairy produce, and small, frequent amounts of nuts, seeds or wheat germ and the use of food supplements such as sea kelp, lecithin, brewer's yeast and molasses will provide the nutrients needed for efficient metabolism.

The mineral magnesium is involved in metabolism, and a deficiency hinders energy production,[4] and also prevents vitamin B6 from being properly utilised. B6 itself aids excess fluid and weight loss. So as well as ensuring an adequate intake of all of the B complex vitamins, make sure that the diet contains plenty of magnesium, balanced with calcium.

Molasses, though it contains some natural sugar, also contains a wide range of nutrients and is one of the cheapest food supplements available. It can be used in moderation (two teaspoons a day) to replace other sweeteners and is well worth the calories it contains. The regular use of artificial sweeteners is not recommended for health and are best avoided as far as possible.

The calories to really avoid are the empty calories that don't provide any nutrients. Make every mouthful count and don't waste a single mouthful on refined sugar or white flour – even if it is advertised as a low calorie slimming product!

Steady weight loss

Forget about crash dieting and aim for a steady weight loss of no more than two or three pounds a week, then maintain your desired weight with a highly nutritious diet. The best diet is one that can be maintained for life, give or take the occasional treat. I've never had to learn to count calories. If I want to lose a few pounds I just make sure that I eat the most nutritious diet I know. The pounds soon disappear.

A carton of natural yoghurt and a piece of fruit makes a good breakfast as does a small portion of home-made muesli. Prepare vegetable sticks or a salad instead of sandwiches for lunch and eat them with a piece of chicken, a hard-boiled egg, or a small portion of cottage cheese. Just five or six nuts or a small handful of sunflower or pumpkin seeds eaten between meals will prevent craving.

Make the evening meal a salad containing plenty of leafy green vegetables, some root vegetables and a portion of protein. For dessert eat either a piece of fruit, a small helping of freshly made fruit salad with a little natural yoghurt, or a home-made junket dessert sweetened with a small amount of honey. If you need a mid-evening snack to stave off those middle of the night hunger pangs, eat either the yoghurt and wheat germ or the muesli, whichever wasn't eaten for breakfast.

If you really have difficulty sticking to such a diet then you may have a problem such as low blood sugar, food intolerance or yeast or bacterial overgrowth (see chapters 8 and 9). If you realise that you are suffering from any of these conditions, don't give up on your dieting altogether, but concentrate on building health.

You may well find that by treating such conditions, you are then able to stick to a weight-reducing diet. However, much better to have to eat a little more than you'd like of really health-building foods than to destroy your health even further by alternately starving and bingeing.

Read chapter 10 on the role of essential fatty acids in the production of prostaglandins and consider the use of an evening primrose and fish oil supplement if you think you really need it. If the cost is too burdensome, try cod liver oil.

Although fasting by itself is not the best way to maintain weight loss, it does have advantages, along with raw-food regimes, in the treatment of some conditions, such as yeast and bacterial overgrowth, and toxic conditions, that make successful dieting difficult (see chapter 15).

Finally, no diet, however good, can be really effective without regular exercise. Walking, cycling, swimming, running or even skipping with a rope are all excellent ways of burning up excess calories, replacing the lost fat with firm muscle and strengthening the heart and blood vessels. Build up gradually, a little and often, and see the difference just half an hour a day can make.

Underweight

Inability to gain weight may be due to a lack of appetite, faulty digestion, a reduced ability to convert food into muscle, or an overactive metabolism or thyroid gland. Vitamin E and iodine deficiencies are associated with overactive thyroid.[5]

Wheat germ is an inexpensive source of vitamin E, and sea kelp powder or tablets and sea foods contain iodine. Lack of appetite can be caused by deficiencies of a variety of nutrients including iron, magnesium[6] and some of the B complex vitamins.[7]

However, the first possible deficiency which should be considered is a deficiency of the trace element zinc. Not only does zinc deficiency affect the appetite and digestion, but it also affects the sense of taste and of smell.[8]

We saw in the previous chapter that this deficiency is, in fact, the easiest of all to detect. A taste test, developed by Professor Derek Bryce-Smith of Reading University, can be used at home. The degree of taste experienced indicates the extent of the deficiency (see 'Useful Addresses' at the back of the book for the supplier).

Time and again I have seen children, teenagers and adults dramatically improve a poor appetite and renew their interest in food after taking zinc supplements. This is one of those cases where supplementation may be necessary to break the vicious circle. With little or no appetite it is virtually impossible to eat enough to supply the amount of nutrients needed to restore the appetite.

Children who are 'faddy' eaters may well be zinc deficient and this is a very common deficiency. Those same children may have allergies, may be depressed or easily upset, have behavioural problems, hyperactivity, or learning difficulties, all of which can be symptoms of zinc deficiency.[9]

Teenagers are often short of zinc and other nutrients, particularly when they are growing or developing rapidly.[10] The level of zinc that may have been barely acceptable through childhood can be grossly inadequate to meet the demands of puberty. Zinc is needed in order for vitamin A to be released from the liver and, when the mineral is in short supply, vitamin A deficiency can manifest itself as spots or acne.[11]

A change to vegetarianism in the teenage years may reduce levels of zinc still further since meat and fish are much better sources of zinc than vegetables. Girls may exacerbate a zinc deficiency through nutritionally deficient slimming diets and the loss of appetite may go unrecognised or even be welcomed.

Optimum nutrition

Stress of any kind depletes the body of zinc,[12] magnesium,[13] the B vitamins[14] and other nutrients, so exams or a broken romance may be the cause of a reduced appetite. However, since these nutrients are so important to the health of the brain and nervous system, emotional or behavioural problems may occur. The danger here is that a condition such as anorexia is put down to a psychological condition while the physical cause goes unrecognised and untreated.

Professor Bryce-Smith, co-author of the book *The Zinc Solution*, believes that one of the factors which could make an individual susceptible to anorexia nervosa is an inherited subnormal ability to utilise available zinc. In such cases the possibility should always be considered that both the lack of appetite and the emotional problems are occurring simultaneously as a result of a deficiency of nutrients such as zinc, iron, magnesium, and the B complex vitamins, so important to the appetite, the digestion and the brain.

A very common cause of zinc deficiency for women is the contraceptive pill, and this can cause problems with the appetite as well as the emotions. Alcohol and cigarettes are factors which can deplete many nutrients including zinc,[15] and so depress the appetite.

The stomach, the small intestine, and the pancreas ought to produce enough digestive enzymes but, if they are inhibited by nutritional deficiencies, the digestion of food is hampered and abdominal discomfort and malabsorption are added to poor appetite. No wonder it is difficult to gain weight!

Poorly digested food stays too long in the stomach, putrefactive bacteria multiply, and histamine is produced, which causes allergies.[16] Bacterial and yeast overgrowth inhibit the production of certain vitamins by friendly intestinal bacteria, and an enzyme is produced which destroys vitamin B.[17] Thus deficiencies are exacerbated and absorption reduced still further.

Bloating or wind, indigestion or nausea take away the pleasure and incentive to eat. Supplementation may be the only way to break the vicious circle, and restore the appetite and digestion enough to obtain adequate nutrients from the diet.

For those who are underweight, the diet should consist mainly of highly nutritious, easily digested food like raw and very lightly steamed vegetables, and yoghurt and junket which are predigested by the addition of bacteria and rennet. Potatoes can often be more easily digested than bread. All too often the high carbohydrate foods which are eaten in the attempt to gain weight are the very foods which have caused the underlying problems.

Refined foods which have been stripped of the nutrients needed for their utilisation may well have robbed the body of nutrients like zinc, magnesium and iron, necessary for appetite and digestion. Much better to concentrate first on restoring health through optimum nutrition, and dealing with any underlying conditions. Once appetite, digestion and absorption are restored, weight should soon be gained.

Bulimia and anorexia nervosa

There has been a lot of publicity recently about the eating disorder bulimia nervosa, with well-known personalities disclosing that they are suffering, or have suffered, from this condition. Anorexia can turn into bulimia, and vice versa. Bulimia victims may eat very little for long periods of time, but then gorge food and use laxatives or induce vomiting in order to prevent indigestion and weight gain.

Professor Bryce-Smith believes that bulimia nervosa may represent a desperate attempt by the body to gain more zinc. 'By gorging,' he points out, 'at least some zinc may find its way into the starved body cells.'[18]

Personality changes often precede or accompany the condition, and it may well be that the neurosis is induced by the mental effects of zinc deficiency.[19] This may interact with other features of an individual's personality to produce the varied manifestations such as anorexia, bulimia or other depressive or compulsive states.

Certain personality types and backgrounds may put some individuals more at risk than others, but of course it is worth remembering that the stress of destructive attitudes leads to increased losses of nutrients such as zinc.[20]

Commenting on findings which suggest that drug abuse is often associated with both anorexia and bulimia, Professor Bryce-Smith offers a possible explanation. He believes that a predisposition to addictive and compulsive states of behaviour could take the form of either drug abuse or food abuse, or both. He points out that there is a well-established link between zinc deficiency and alcohol abuse.

It could be that drug abuse, in some people, may also be connected to a deficiency of zinc. In fact, some of the mental disorders associated with alcohol-induced liver damage have been reported to respond very well to zinc supplementation. Professor Bryce-Smith cites case histories of sufferers of both anorexia and bulimia who have responded quite dramatically to zinc supplementation.

The onset of bulimia or anorexia may also coincide with the use of the contraceptive pill. 'The pill', points out Professor Bryce-Smith, 'raises levels of copper in the blood stream, and this element is also antagonistic to zinc.'

Take zinc in your diet

The individual who has inherited a subnormal ability to utilise available zinc and who, consequently, already has low levels of this nutrient, would be much more susceptible to any of these factors. Low zinc status could also affect their mental and emotional stability, aggravating or even causing the type of personality that puts them more at risk than others to compulsive conditions.

Sadly the treatment for such disorders often tends to emphasise the mental aspects of the problem, rather than physical factors such as the nutrient status of the body. The foods that are eaten, either during bingeing or during hospitalisation, are all too often the calorie laden, refined foods, stripped of many of their nutrients, that may well have played a major role in the original onset of the illness.

Since these foods continue to rob the body of already scarce supplies, it is hardly surprising that such treatment achieves little success. When a zinc deficiency condition is correctly diagnosed, however, supplementation can result in swift and lasting improvement.

As we saw earlier, not only does zinc deficiency affect the appetite, and the emotions, but it also affects the sense of taste and of smell. The taste test developed by Professor Bryce-Smith is so inexpensive and simple to use that it should be the first check that is made on either the anorexia or the bulimia sufferer (see page 308). Not only is the solution a test for deficiency, but it is also a zinc supplement in itself.

Parents can, therefore, slip the solution into a drink for the young teenage victim who imagines that she is overweight and refuses to eat. If zinc deficiency is the problem, the sufferer will be unable to taste the supplement, and will benefit from it. However, if there is no deficiency of zinc, the addition of the supplement to the drink will immediately be recognised. Professor Bryce-Smith does not suggest that zinc deficiency is the only reason for such conditions, only that it is a common and easily diagnosed cause that should always be considered.

The fact that the quality of the diet is so rarely recognised as a cause of bulimia was graphically demonstrated for me recently. A columnist on a national newspaper wrote an excellent article on the social factors that can lead to bulimia nervosa.[21] Revealing that she herself once suffered from bulimia nervosa for eighteen months, the writer put into perspective the difficulties faced by the partners of such victims.

'Looking back on my own insanity,' she wrote, 'without the self-pity that overwhelmed me at the time, I cannot honestly blame anyone but myself. I overcame bulimia by learning to accept my own limitations, and the limitations of those around me.'

It was revealing, however, to read a smaller article at the bottom of her column. She says that she has never understood the pleasure some people get from slaving for hours over a hot stove, when they can achieve much the same in two minutes with a microwave. She finished off the article by writing, 'A visiting child of a muesli-mother said to me the other day as I served up micro-burger and chips, "I love coming to your house. You're such a wonderful cook." Children may not know anything about gourmet food, but they know what they like.'

That may be true, I would like to reply, but do they know what's good for them? So-called muesli-mothers may be an object of fun in the national press, from time to time, but by providing their children with nutritious foods, they are very likely to prevent the deficiencies that can affect the appetite and emotions, and trigger disorders such as bulimia.

Optimum nutrition during childhood provides for the increased demands of the teenage years, when youngsters are most vulnerable.

ACTION SUMMARY

Consider the possibility of allergies and/or candida (see chapter 8).

Read chapter 9 on blood sugar handling problems, chapter 10 on essential fatty acids, and chapter 15 on the benefits of raw food. There are some planning suggestions in chapter 13.

Avoid refined carbohydrates, and substitute whole grain bread and cereal. Cut out as far as possible processed, hydrogenated and reheated fats. Ensure that the diet contains natural sources of essential fatty acids, vitamins and minerals. Good examples are dried beans, nuts, seeds and seed oil, whole grain bread and cereals, fruit, green vegetables, and fresh oily fish such as sardines, mackerel, herring, tuna, trout or salmon.

Try eating small nutritious snacks between meals. Have a high protein breakfast such as natural yoghurt and wheat germ, followed by a handful of almonds mid-morning. Lunch might be a large salad with a small portion of some form of protein, and a jacket potato. Mid-afternoon, a few more almonds or a handful of sunflower seeds and, for the evening meal, another small portion of protein with, for example, lightly steamed vegetables and whole grain rice. A mid-evening snack might be another helping of natural yoghurt, or some other source of protein. Nuts, seeds and pulses such as beans and lentils provide protein and many other nutrients. Meat or fish is better eaten no more than once a day, if possible.

Coffee, tea, soft drinks, chocolate and cigarettes should be reduced or avoided, and herb tea, Caro or dandelion coffee, mineral water and fruit juice used instead. Smoking and alcohol are better avoided.

It may be worth adding some inexpensive food supplements such as sea kelp (in powder or tablet form), cod liver oil, molasses, fresh wheat germ, or brewer's yeast, to supply additional nutrients. See appendices 3, 4 and 5 for methods of providing optimum amounts of nutrients.

If you are suffering from any illness, discuss with your doctor any nutritional changes you plan to make.

RECOMMENDED READING

Let's Get Well by Adelle Davis (Unwin Paperbacks).
Nutritional Medicine by Dr Stephen Davies and Dr Alan Stewart (Pan).
Raw Energy by Leslie and Susannah Kenton (Arrow Books).

13

WHERE DO I START?

I pulled the bedcovers back over each sleeping child. Tousled hair, face flushed in sleep, the adventures of a small boy's day relived in pleasant dreams of bluebell woods and bikes and dens. Of climbing trees and hide-and-seek, of football, cricket, chasing friends and all the simple joys of childhood years. How precious to me now are the memories of the times we shared!

After kissing their peaceful faces, I left them tucked safely up in bed, aware of how lovely were these years, when their happiness was in my hands. Before long they would grow up I knew, and I must let them go. Other people, other circumstances would influence their lives and I would no longer be able to bandage a grazed knee, listen to a tale of woe, or kiss away a tear.

Down in the kitchen, I began to prepare the dough for the next day's bread. As I kneaded and pummelled, floured and turned, I had time to reflect and to count the blessings my children had brought me. The whole family were much healthier now, responding well to the diet we'd been eating for the past few years.

Placing the dough in a big earthenware bowl, I covered it with a cloth and left it to rise overnight in the airing cupboard. It would only need to be quickly shaped into rolls and loaves in the morning, and the smell of baking bread would fill the house, bringing two hungry little boys scampering down the stairs for breakfast.

In those days, I couldn't buy wholemeal bread and so I'd had to learn how to bake it. I soon discovered, however, that it wasn't the time-consuming task I'd envisaged and, with a little planning, I could fit it into my busy day. In fact planning, I very quickly learned, really was the key to the successful changeover to a healthy family diet.

A helping of guile

To planning I added a dash of ingenuity and a good helping of guile, and soon I had the perfect recipe for healthy meals that appealed to children. They would help with the baking, fashioning weird and wonderful shapes from the dough. I could harness their enthusiasm, since if they'd helped to prepare the meal they would invariably eat it.

Daddy, of course, had to get used to the fruit of their labours, arriving home from the office to be presented with an array of well-handled offerings. He'd be watched carefully as he sampled each item to make sure that he really did enjoy every mouthful. I'd quietly slip healthy ingredients, like chopped nuts, raisins and organic oats into home-made biscuits to replace shop-bought snacks loaded with white flour and sugar.

On cold winter days the boys would arrive home from school to a hearty soup, packed with the vegetables they would have refused had they been served separately. But I'd have slipped a handful of alphabeti spaghetti into the soup and they would soon be too busy searching for the letters of their names to think about what they were eating.

Raw vegetables could be arranged into all kinds of plate pictures. I'd make a face and then we'd all have to decide whether we were going to eat the carrot nose first, or the cucumber eyes, the hair made from shredded lettuce or the tomato mouth. Tell a child that he must eat something because it is good for him and you might as well throw the meal straight into the bin. But make mealtimes fun and involve children in the preparation, and you are halfway there.

The occasional treat

I've never tried to force the boys to eat. However, I made sure that there were no unhealthy alternatives in the house. When children know that there are chocolate biscuits or sweets in the cupboard they can make life very difficult until they are allowed to have them.

But if the biscuit barrel contains only healthy snacks, the fruit bowl is full, and the fridge always has a supply of prepared vegetable sticks at the ready, they soon get used to the idea. Chocolate and sweets then become a real treat, eaten occasionally, rather than an everyday occurrence that is taken for granted.

The biggest disservice we can do our children is to allow them to constantly fill themselves with sugary snacks. Nutritious meals are far more appetising to a child with a healthy appetite than to a child whose palate has already been jaded by empty calories.

Deficiencies of nutrients such as zinc and the B vitamins can cause loss of appetite. When the appetite is restored through foods rich in these nutrients, mealtimes become a pleasure instead of a chore. A faddy child who pushes his or her food around the plate at mealtimes, but eats sugary snacks all day, may be suffering from an unrecognised loss of appetite. Parents don't always realise that a poor appetite doesn't prevent children, or adults for that matter, from eating readily absorbed sugar and refined carbohydrates.

I'd love one of your salads, Mum!

The teenage years are probably the most difficult in some ways. It can be hard to find the empty chocolate wrappings and sweet papers under the bed, evidence of a midnight feast, and yet say nothing. What youngster can resist the lure of the school tuck shop, or the sticky contents of a friend's bag of sweets? Those first trips into town with friends can be an orgy of burger bars and coffee shops, but who wants to stand out from the crowd at that age?

This is a time for discretion, a time to allow them to make their own mistakes and to suffer for them. But the child who learned early the importance of good nutrition soon realises that teenage spots are the result of too many binges. And the memory of boundless energy will haunt listless teenagers who know very well that their health is in their own hands.

Once it seemed that we would have our children forever. But the little boy I once bent down to scoop into my arms now towers above me and must himself bend down to give me a hug. Childhood chattering has given way to long, late-night discussions. And those backpacking adventures we shared, trekking over mountains to isolated youth hostels, he must now share with friends.

Not so very long ago the car would be packed, the trailer tent hitched up, and a picnic ready as two little boys dashed home from school on a Friday afternoon, excited at the prospect of a camping weekend. Now the rucksack is packed with light-weight tents, portable stove, and cooking utensils as my independent young man sets off on his own adventures. But I know that my efforts have not been in vain when he arrives home and says, 'I'd love one of your salads, Mum.'

The memories are precious, and always will be, but there are advantages too, now that we have our freedom again. It can seem strange to look into a tidy bedroom, no longer strewn with bits of Lego, and to see an empty bed where once a tousled head lay surrounded by furry toys.

But we no longer take for granted, as we once did before the boys were born, the long walks and leisurely peaceful meals, the time to write or to read a good book. We can eat just what we want to eat, when we choose to eat, and I realise how easy it is to have a healthy diet when there are just the two of you again. It's wonderful to have the energy, health and enthusiasm to start a new chapter in life and to still see it all as an adventure.

A word about students

All that peace and quiet disappears at the end of term, of course, when the house is invaded by students, stopping off on their way home, or to various destinations around the world.

Mark was *en route* to America to work at a summer camp. We arrived at his lodgings to pick him up just as an old, battered minibus disgorged its load of long-legged dishevelled students, arriving back from a camping trip. He loped up to our car saying, 'Five minutes, I haven't packed yet, and this is my friend Paola — she's coming with us.' An hour later we were on our way!

Paola, who has beautiful long blonde hair and blue eyes, comes from Trieste in northern Italy, near the border with Slovenia. Her mother's family came originally from Austria, while her father's family hailed from Bavaria, hence her un-Mediterranean colouring.

We learned during that journey home that Paola's Italian cooking had been very popular with her fellow students. Her idea of a perfect evening was to prepare a dinner party for her friends.

'Students are always complaining that they have no money,' she said, 'but then they go out and drink five pints of beer in the pub and wonder why there's very little left for food!' It made more sense to her to make an evening's entertainment out of a meal and Mark, with his enormous appetite, had very quickly become one of her most appreciative dinner guests! 'Students should get together,' Paola suggested, 'and take turns to cook meals so that everyone only has to cook once every few days.'

She talked with great concern about the health of some of her friends who lived on coffee, toast and breakfast cereals, slept until late morning yet were constantly tired and lethargic. 'Their complexions are so grey and spotty,' she exclaimed, 'yet they don't seem to realise the harm they are doing to themselves through their diet.'

Paola was full of life and vitality and it was lovely to listen to her enthusiastically describing the inexpensive Italian meals she loved to prepare, while Mark chipped in with supporting comments about his favourite dishes.

The benefits of Italian cooking

The next morning Paola dashed off to catch the train, leaving behind her luggage. She was going to a south coast university for an interview for a postgraduate course. Arriving back that evening to pick up her suitcase, she had intended to set off again to visit some friends. I had other ideas.

'How would you like to stay for tea?' I asked. 'And how about showing me how you prepare some of the dishes that were most popular with your student friends?' She was delighted, and on the way home from the station, we stopped off at the local supermarket. Though we bought enough ingredients to prepare three types of salad meals and two pasta dishes, the cost was surprisingly low.

'The most important thing is to use a really good olive oil,' explained Paola. 'Don't try to save money by buying cheap versions. It must be the first cold-pressing of the olives.' She pointed out that there are better ways to cut down on the cost. 'Tuna, for example, is a must for students, so long as it's dolphin-friendly. It's cheap, they like it, and it's an oily fish so it's very good for you.'

Pasta, a staple food of Italy, is also inexpensive and provides enough to satisfy even Mark's appetite! We bought the wholemeal variety of course. We couldn't find a wholemeal ready-made pizza base but Paola says that some supermarkets do stock them.

Too much salad?

Here in England, when we talk about Italian food, we tend to think about pizzas and pasta, forgetting that in Italy, salads and fresh fruit make up a very large part of the diet every day. 'The trouble with salads', objected Mark, 'is that as a student, you don't have time to go shopping so often, and salad ingredients don't last long.' He also found that by the time he'd bought all the different ingredients for a salad, he ended up with too much for one person.

'Ah but', said Paola, 'that's much more the Spanish way of preparing salads. In Italy we usually make salads out of no more than two or three types of vegetables.' She pointed out that you don't have to use lettuce, which doesn't last very long. Tomatoes or peppers, for example, will keep for a week. Root vegetables like onions, carrots or beetroot also keep well and can be eaten raw.

'Well another thing,' insisted Mark, 'students won't take the trouble to prepare a side salad when they've got to cook a meal as well.' Paola has the solution with her 'all-in-one salads' in which the protein, such as butter beans, chick peas, red kidney beans or flaked tuna fish, is tossed with the salad ingredients in the olive oil dressing.

'What could be more simple,' she exclaimed, 'than to slice some tomato and raw onion, then open a tin of tuna or butter beans, and add a little oil, lemon juice or vinegar and black pepper?' In fact she pointed out that these dishes taste even better when they have been kept in the fridge overnight. So the leftovers from today's main course can be used as tomorrow's side salad.

Scared of cooking?

With meals like this the student can eat healthily yet never cook. 'People are scared of cooking,' said Paola. 'They think that it's very difficult, but it doesn't have to be!' I asked her if she'd done much cooking at home in Italy and she told me that she'd never needed to, since her mother had done it all. 'But, of course, I watched my mother and grandmother cooking, so when I had to look after myself, I knew what to do.'

Listening to Paola, I was struck by her attitude to food. She doesn't see it as a chore or an inconvenience. To her it's one of the pleasures of life, and she loves to shop for food as much as she enjoys cooking.

'For Mediterranean cooking,' she explained, 'once you have learned to balance the flavours of herbs, onions, garlic, salt and pepper, you can prepare a basic sauce and a basic salad dressing, then use these recipes for a whole variety of meals.'

I pointed out that for young people learning to cook, the problem is that they don't usually have the various herbs and spices in the kitchen cupboard and it can be too much trouble to go shopping for them. 'Then all you have to do', she replied, 'is to make sure that you always keep in black pepper, tinned tomatoes, a jar of pesto sauce, Parmesan cheese, onions, garlic and dried oregano. If you can buy fresh oregano, so much the better, but dried is fine.'

We spent a couple of chatty hours together in my kitchen, discussing the best way to use wholemeal bread and pasta. Wholemeal baguette, we decided, could take more garlic than white bread, and was better crisped for longer in a hot oven without being wrapped in tin foil.

The spaghetti was better tossed in, and completely covered by, its tomato dressing or pesto sauce, rather than used as a base for a topping. Shell shapes were better with a tomato-based sauce, while pasta twists worked well with pesto sauce. All the wholemeal shapes needed cooking a little longer, however – ten minutes, as opposed to only five for white pasta.

By the time my husband Ian arrived home, everything was ready. 'The proof of the pudding is in the eating,' as they say! Mark thought it was heaven – all his favourite meals at one go! Huge slices of juicy water-melon were followed by three variations of pasta dishes and three varieties of salad. Fresh strawberries and cream then rounded off our lovely evening together, and all agreed that you don't have to spend a fortune or forgo the pleasures of life to eat healthily!

Planning is the key to health

After all these years, Ian and I couldn't bear to swap our delicious nutty whole grain organic rice for the tasteless, pappy white version. Heavy, chewy, dark bread makes white loaves seem like polystyrene to us now. Fresh vegetables, lightly steamed, or prepared raw in an endless variety of salad combinations, put flavourless frozen vegetables to shame.

Ready-meals could never replace fresh fish, lightly sprinkled with herbs then grilled, chick peas slowly cooked in aromatic spices, or lamb chops marinated with fragrant rosemary.

Does it sound as if I spend my life in the kitchen? Far from it. I've simply learned to plan our menu to fit in with our lifestyles. Planning is still the key to a healthy diet that provides the energy to live life to the full, rather than tying you to the kitchen stove.

Where once it had all seemed so confusing, searching for unfamiliar healthy ingredients, now they are just part of the normal weekly shop. Though at first it seemed a lot more trouble to have to think about new menus and recipes, now I hardly give it a thought. Even the planning has become a simple routine.

I was fortunate of course, to have been taught to cook as a child. But as Paola says, it really isn't difficult, and you don't need to be a cordon bleu cook.

Whole grain rice doesn't stick together the way that white rice does, and it's difficult to go wrong with a baked potato. Why spend hours producing a gâteau or a rich dessert, when you can have a fresh fruit salad or a delicious junket dessert ready in minutes?

Wholemeal fruit cakes are so quick and simple. You just throw all the ingredients in a bowl, mix them together, then pop them in the oven. I wouldn't swap them for the sickly sugary, shop bought variety!

What about the cost?

And what about the cost? I spend less in real terms now than I've ever spent on food. Whole grain rice may cost a little extra than the white variety, but it is so filling that it goes much further. The same applies to wholemeal bread and pasta.

Some of the healthiest fish, such as fresh sardines, rich in essential fatty acids, are really cheap, and the smell of them grilling always reminds me of Mediterranean holidays.

Pulses are excellent value. Pay the little extra for the organic variety if you can, then experiment with herbs and spices to create the delicious dishes which used to feed large families.

These meals may take a long time to cook but, if you can invest in a slow cooker or crockpot, you can prepare them very quickly, well in advance, then leave them safely to cook. And how welcoming is the delicious aroma that greets you on a cold winter evening when you arrive home after a brisk hike.

It takes no longer to cook ingredients like rice and pulses in larger quantities than needed, and then you can freeze the extra. They keep well and, if separated partway through the freezing process, can easily be reheated straight from frozen. This is where planning comes in.

A double quantity of rice for Monday's chilli will provide enough for a tasty risotto on Thursday. Cook extra chick peas for Saturday's chick pea casserole and, on Wednesday, the rest can come out of the freezer to be made into falafels, those delicious traditional spicy rissoles from the Middle East.

Keep cooked lentils or beans of any kind in the freezer and you can have vegetable burgers ready for the children in no time at all. Or prepare a double quantity of the vege-burgers themselves and freeze half. These too can be taken straight out of the freezer and grilled or fried straight from frozen. Even without a freezer such freshly cooked foods will keep safely in the fridge for two or three days.

These are really cheap, filling, nutritious meals that will feed a large family for far less money than convenience foods. They are the type of foods that were eaten by the isolated races visited by Weston Price and Robert McCarrison. Expensive cuts of meat aren't necessary and in fact, eaten too often, are not good for health. Liver and kidney are cheap and much more nutritious. This is where the real savings can be made.

Perhaps some of the cheapest and most nutritious foods of all are sprouted pulses and lentils. A handful of beans or green lentils, soaked overnight, then rinsed morning and evening for a few days, will produce a quite amazing amount of sprouts. I hate to destroy the nutrients by cooking them, preferring to add them to chopped raw vegetables to make a mixed salad, dressed with a little olive oil and lemon juice.

For those who are vegetarians or, like us, prefer to eat a good proportion of vegetarian meals, it's worth remembering that pulses need to be combined in the same meal with cereals in order to provide a complete protein. Most traditional dishes have evolved to provide adequate protein, and dishes such as curry or chilli are invariably served with rice.

Cereals are easy and cheap

Try other cereals too. You'll be surprised how easy and cheap they are. Millet cooks quickly to produce three to four times its own weight of light fluffy grains, not unlike mashed potato. It is very high in protein, and easy to digest. Use it in milk puddings or as part of a savoury meal. Buckwheat is rich in vitamin E, the B complex vitamins and also a substance called rutin which strengthens the walls of arteries, and helps to reduce blood pressure.

Use oats in flapjacks which are very simple to make, or try fresh oatcakes with a weekend breakfast. Oats are one of the most nutritious grains, since the protein they contain is in a very easy to assimilate form. They are also rich in the mineral silicon, essential for the development of the muscles, brain and nerve structure.

I use organically grown oats in porridge, and jumbo oats as a muesli base. I make the muesli up once a week or so, adding raisins or sultanas, hazelnuts and sunflower seeds, and a little toasted oat cereal to add crunchiness.

No matter how little time is available in the morning, it's easy to add milk, yoghurt or fruit juice to a serving of muesli to make a really nutritious breakfast. And it will satisfy the appetite far longer than the sugar-coated refined cereals that line the supermarket shelves.

Better still, chop up an apple between two people and add it to the muesli just before serving.

Traditionally, the muesli base was soaked overnight to release nutrients and aid digestion. Grated apple would be added to it as it was served with milk or natural yoghurt. Children love this type of muesli, topped with a little honey.

Natural yoghurt makes a very good breakfast, on its own or added to chopped fruit. It is a very easily digested complete protein, and provides valuable friendly intestinal bacteria. The best way of eating wheat germ is to add two or three teaspoons to natural yoghurt. Usually, I alternate yoghurt and wheat germ one morning, with muesli the next. In fact breakfast can be the easiest meal at which to begin to make improvements.

Young at heart – food for the elderly

About twelve years ago, after listening to me extolling the virtues of healthy foods, a couple we'd known so long we called them aunty and uncle decided to find out if there was anything in what I was saying. The first thing they did was to sprinkle sunflower seeds on their normal breakfast cereal.

I remembered that within a few weeks they were singing the praises of this simple, inexpensive addition to their diet. It's quite a long time since I last spoke to them so, since I was about to write about food for the elderly, I thought I'd telephone them to see how they were.

'Never felt better,' said Bill, who answered the telephone. Yes, he still ate sunflower seeds every day and could clearly remember the difference they had made to him all those years ago. 'I noticed that I had more energy and felt livelier,' he recalled. 'I didn't feel my age so much either.' Bill and Elsie are in their late seventies now, and they enjoy amazing health and vitality. 'I feel absolutely smashing too,' said Elsie. 'No complaints at all!'

A couple of years ago Elsie had been to see her doctor for a check-up. 'You are incredibly healthy,' she was told. 'If you go on like this there's no reason why you shouldn't live to be a hundred!' However, the doctor offered to give them a flu jab.

'Why would we want a flu jab?' exclaimed Elsie, declining the offer. 'We never even get colds, let alone flu.'

She put this down to the fact that they'd both been taking garlic perles for years after I'd recommended them. 'Do you know,' Elsie told me, 'I'll be seventy-nine next birthday and I don't feel anything like that age! I met a friend in town this morning and she couldn't get over how well I looked.'

Elsie and Bill certainly sounded like a wonderful advertisement for sunflower seeds, but was that all they'd changed in their diet, I asked? 'Oh no,' replied Elsie, 'we eat fish and chicken twice a week, wholemeal bread, and lots of vegetables, salads and fruit.' Elsie cooks her vegetables for only a very short time and they both drink the cooking water to make sure they don't lose any nutrients. 'I always use fresh vegetables,' said Elsie, 'not being very keen on all this tinned stuff!'

'Didn't you find it difficult making changes in your diet at such a late stage in life?' I asked her. She pointed out that nobody ever thought about white bread years ago but, in recent years, she'd changed to wholemeal. 'It's like everything else in life,' she said. 'You've just got to try these things. People give up too easily.'

Now white bread is too starchy for her and she much prefers the wholemeal variety. A couple of years ago, however, she did find that her joints were getting a little stiff. 'So I started taking cod liver oil,' she said, 'and I've been feeling a hundred per cent ever since!'

Hard times – on a budget

Elsie and Bill live in the north-west of England and, like many others of their generation, they went through hard times in the thirties. When Bill was laid off work, because of bad weather, Elsie always tried to make sure that he and the children were fed. 'I've known myself sit and eat a baby's rusk,' she recalled, 'because there was nothing else in the house.'

They'd had four children in five years, and there were many hard winters then. 'Looking back now, I don't know how we managed,' said Elsie. 'I can remember one of the children asking their father for a penny. How it broke his heart to have to tell them that he didn't have one.'

And yet, I pointed out, in spite of all those hard times, they still experienced dramatic improvements when they changed their diet around about the time that they retired. I have noticed time and time again that when older people make even a few changes, they can get results so much more quickly than the young. 'Ah, but when we were children,' replied Elsie, 'there may not have been much food around, but it was all grown naturally.'

She commented that her youngest grandchildren seem to suffer from far more infections than had her own children who were born during World War Two. It does seem that older people are inclined to suffer more from simple deficiencies, rather than the allergies and other inherited problems that seem to afflict so many of the young nowadays.

Tied to the office – but healthy

But what about the in-betweens, the career people in the increasingly competitive workplace? How can they avoid the vending machine tea and coffee, the soggy white sandwiches from the tea trolley, and the canteen meals that have been kept warm for hours?

One friend of mine told me that he had replaced endless cups of coffee and tea in the office with bottled water and, after only a month, found that he was feeling much better. I went to see him in his London office recently. He produced two wine glasses and we sipped mineral water while we talked.

'It saves all the arguments about whose turn it is to make the coffee, or to pay for the tea,' he told me, 'and it also helps me while I'm working.' He explained that it was almost as if he needed to do something with his hands at times and that, where some people might reach for a cigarette, he now pours himself another glass of mineral water.

I'd already noticed the bowl of fruit on the top of the filing cabinet, a simple way of avoiding sugar-laden snacks, but I really was impressed when lunch arrived. A paper tablecloth quickly transformed the filing cabinet, which was soon graced by a large silver tray of wholemeal sandwiches with a variety of fillings.

There was more fruit to follow, fresh orange juice, and some wholemeal seed cake, but I was rather surprised to see two very un-wholemeal chocolate and fudge cakes! As I reached for the kiwi fruit, I was told that the girls in the office had been wondering whether or not I'd be tempted!

If you want to avoid wheat, however, take some raw vegetable sticks or florets, and a carton of savoury dip into the office. Or how about rye crispbread with cheese and an apple? Of course, if you're one of those organised early bird types, you could make up a salad and take it into the office in an airtight plastic container. But if you're not a morning person you might grab some shelled nuts and sunflower seeds, a tomato and a carton of yoghurt.

My husband counters the long hours staring at a computer screen and the stuffy atmosphere and artificial lights of the newspaper office by walking to the station every day. He keeps a light-weight waterproof and a brolly in his briefcase, and strides out faithfully, come rain or come shine.

At weekends he 'recharges his batteries', playing golf or hiking, and says that, without that fresh air and exercise, his mind simply wouldn't be sharp enough the following week. I have my own way of 'winding down' and getting fresh air and exercise, but I'll tell you about that in the next chapter.

ACTION SUMMARY

See appendices 1 and 2 for a starter menu and some recipes, including Paola's Italian dishes.

RECOMMENDED READING

The Foresight Wholefood Cookbook by Norman and Ruth Jervis (Aurum Press 1986).
The Food Pharmacy Cookbook by Jean Carper (Simon and Schuster 1991).
Living Without Sugar by Elbie Lebrecht (Grafton Books 1989).

14

TIME TO GO BACK, FOR THE SAKE OF OUR FUTURE

My friend the robin came back this year. With his head cocked to one side and his bright eyes searching for tasty morsels, he hopped about behind me in the pale January sunshine, as I dug the trenches for the next summer's runner beans.

Winter had been dull and miserable rather than severe, and I'd been wistfully recalling the bright summer mornings and long warm evenings I'd spent contentedly, discovering the satisfaction of watching my own vegetables grow.

Once Christmas was over, I couldn't wait to get out in the fresh air and experience again the therapeutic effects of daylight and exercise, and the thrill of planning and preparing for a new harvest of organic vegetables.

Never be afraid to learn lessons

I'd learned some good lessons from my first year as a novice allotment holder. The rows of lettuce had looked very artistic indeed, alternating as they did one crisp green iceberg and one crinkly pink Lollo Rosso. Everyone commented on how pretty they looked as they grew from tiny seedlings into large healthy specimens.

Then came the day that they were ready for eating. All of them! At one go! We had lettuce coming out of our ears! It hadn't occurred to me to stagger the planting times!

Then there was the afternoon I planted out all the cabbage, sprout and broccoli plants I'd carefully grown from seed. I went home for tea feeling very satisfied with myself at the sight of my little plants standing proudly in neat rows.

Next day I went back to see how they were getting on. The sympathetic looks from the holders of nearby allotments should have prepared me for the sight of row after row of little stick-like skeletons, forlornly hanging their heads in shame at their nakedness!

One of the nicest things about having an allotment, however, is that there is always a kindly, experienced neighbour on hand to give advice. With the hasty purchase from the allotment store of a large net to deprive the voracious wood pigeons of their next meal, my little skeletons soon recovered, and eight months later I was still picking delicious sprouts from three-foot-high plants.

Nothing ventured, nothing gained

Shop-bought organic vegetables were putting too much strain on my weekly housekeeping budgets, but for the sake of our health, I wasn't prepared to give up on them completely. Why not grow my own? I might not make a success of it, but nothing ventured, nothing gained. And with an annual rental of eight pounds for each allotment, I didn't have a lot to lose either.

A visit to the town council offices and an exploration of the local allotment site yielded a plot, overrun with waist-high weeds. I roped in my husband to do the heavy jobs like clearing the ground, barrowing down the manure and digging up the ancient, worn-out blackcurrant bushes. Through that first autumn and winter, between us we transformed our tangled land into neat rectangles of freshly dug earth.

I devoured Lawrence Hill's classic book, *Organic Gardening*,[1] and spent long, cosy winter evenings by the fireside, plotting and planning what to sow and where to sow it. The book became dog eared and well worn, underlined and scrawled with notes as I learned about compost making and crop rotation.

Lady Eve Balfour's book *The Living Soil*[2] reinforced my conviction that I was right to 'go organic', and inspired and encouraged me. If only I'd known the pleasure and satisfaction it would bring, I'd have acquired an allotment years ago.

Grow your own

With a flurry of wings, my friendly robin startled me out of my reverie. Satisfied by his unexpected banquet, he flew off as the sun sank lower in a rose pink winter sky, lengthening the shadows that crept stealthily across my now completed bean trench. I turned around to see Tom walking towards me with his usual friendly smile. Not Tommy from Liverpool this time, but Tom the energetic eighty-three-year-old stalwart of the local horticultural association.

He'd been sorting out and restocking the allotment store ready for the new season, and had popped down to see how I was getting on before he locked up shop and made his way home. 'That soil looks a bit acid to me,' he said, spotting the algae that was turning the surface green. 'You want to get that limed as quick as you can.' I wondered how long it would take me to learn all I needed to know, but of course Tom had had a bit of a head start on me.

Born in the Fenlands of East Anglia, he left school at the age of fourteen and went into service at a local manor house. A strong-willed boy, who didn't take well to unfair treatment by his superior, young Tom raised his fists one day, ready to defend himself when the head gardener came at him with a pitchfork. That was the end of his job at the manor house and Tom found work instead at a large market garden near Norwich, which supplied vegetables to the greengrocers of London in the nineteen twenties.

'How did they grow the vegetables in those days?' I asked Tom, and he told me about the contract with a local stable to take all the manure they could produce. This was rotted down and mixed with sterilised soil to produce the potting compost for the trays of seedlings.

No chemicals in those days, and no pesticides. They didn't need to think in terms of organically grown produce, for there was no other way of growing. 'Aye, but they had flavour, did those vegetables,' said Tom.

Old-fashioned horse muck

When Tom was eighty, with a lifetime of experience behind him and a lovingly tended garden bursting with fruit and flowers, vegetables and shrubs, his house came under a compulsory purchase order to make way for a new bypass.

His main concern as he looked for a new home was that it should have a big garden, and he found one. While his new neighbours shook their heads and muttered dire warnings about the inability of Tom's predecessors to grow anything but weeds, Tom began to dig.

A couple of years later, the rich green lawns, colourful massed flower borders, fruit-laden bushes and award-winning vegetables were featured on BBC TV's *Gardener's World* programme. 'How did you manage to bring about such a transformation?' asked the interviewer. 'With old-fashioned horse muck of course,' replied Tom.

And what a wonderful advertisement he is for the benefits of home-grown vegetables. Always cheerful, Tom insists on carrying heavy bags of seaweed meal or seed compost to the car for me. Not only does he tend a large garden, serve in and stock the allotment shop, he also keeps himself busy fitting carpets and doing other voluntary odd jobs for people in need. His energy, motivation and general health would put many a person half his age to shame.

As the sun began to set behind the tangle of a wild blackberry hedge, turning the sky a deep brilliant mauve, the iridescent quality of the fading light of that crisp, January late-afternoon reminded us it was time to make our way home. 'Aye,' said Tom, as we turned to go, 'I've seen it both ways now. I've seen vegetables grown with muck and I've seen 'em grown with chemicals. I reckon it's time to go back to the old ways.'

The minerals we need

Just nostalgia, or could Tom be right? I mentioned in chapter 11 that it is known that deaths from heart disease are more common in areas with a low concentration of magnesium in the soil. Some people believe that if the soil is deficient in nutrients, either crops will not grow, or else plants will be smaller but will contain a balance of nutrients.

This simply isn't true. Yes, it is true that, if the soil is too deficient in minerals such as magnesium, iron or manganese, plants will not grow, but a less severely deficient soil will result in crops with less than optimum levels of these minerals.

However, there are trace minerals that are vital to the health of humans, but which are not necessary to the vigour of plants. When chromium, selenium, zinc or iodine, for example, are absent from the soil, the plant does not appear to suffer. Animals and humans, however, can develop severe deficiencies as a result of eating these apparently healthy crops.

The Hunzas recognised the importance of minerals. From specially constructed channels in a massive aqueduct built to bring water from the glacier, they collected silt to spread on their fields. This silt has been compared to the silt which used to be deposited on the banks of the Nile by the annual flood of the river, before the Aswan dam was built.

Robert McCarrison extolled the virtues of 'the unsophisticated foods of nature', with their ability to provide all the nutrients necessary for good health. But he made one very important proviso. He said, 'provided they are grown on soil which is not impoverished'. In these few words lies the clue to the health of the Hunzas, and also the key to many of our present health problems.

Is the soil good enough?

There is a crucial difference, all too often forgotten now, between the food of the healthy people that McCarrison and Price studied, and most of the food available today. This difference was in the health of the individual plants and animals themselves.

A healthy plant can contribute far more to the health of the animal who eats it, than can an unhealthy plant. In the same way, only a healthy animal can confer real health upon those who use its milk or eggs, and eat the meat.

The plant is dependent on the quality of the soil, the animal is dependent on the quality of the plant, and we are dependent upon the quality of the milk and meat of the animals that contribute to our food, as well as upon the quality of the plants we eat.

Inevitably this cycle of health must begin with the soil. The minerals and trace elements, so vital to this cycle of health, cannot be manufactured in our bodies. They must be obtained either from the crops or from the animal products that make up our diet.

Only crops grown on healthy soil can provide the whole spectrum of minerals and trace elements that, as we have seen in previous chapters, play such important roles in the building and maintenance of health. Optimum health simply cannot be achieved without adequate supplies of these nutrients.

Healthy soil, healthy body

In previous chapters we have seen that certain intestinal conditions can cause or exacerbate nutrient deficiencies. An overgrowth of unfriendly intestinal bacteria or yeast, for example, can inhibit absorption and suppress the production of certain vitamins.

I see a parallel here between intestinal health, and the health of the soil. Lowly friendly bacteria, and humble, beneficial fungi, play their part in the transfer of vital nutrients from the soil to the plant.

Their existence goes largely unrecognised by many today, as this soil life is starved of its own food, and destroyed by chemical fertilisers and pesticides. But though we may not recognise the role of this friendly army, we are most certainly suffering from the effects of its destruction.

Time and again a lack of minerals proves to be the primary cause of ill health, often setting off a chain of consequences which can result in infection, degenerative disease, and mental illness. These minerals, however, must not simply be in the soil. They must also be easily available to the crops.

The success of the Hunzas as agriculturalists lay in their ability to create a soil environment which stimulated the crops to take up these vital elements. Crops grown on such fertile soil would then provide not only an abundance of minerals, but also of vitamins, high-quality protein, and essential fatty acids. Not only did the Hunzas recognise the benefits of the mineral-rich glacial silt, they also recognised the importance of compost.

Essential soil food

With the wisdom of those who live close to nature, rather than the knowledge of those who look through a microscope, they had evolved a system of producing a food for the soil which teemed with life and vitality. Though they may have known little of fungi and bacteria, they recognised that this soil food was capable of producing healthy crops, which in turn promoted their own health and the health of their animals.

The addition to the soil both of glacial minerals and of this rich compost, laid the foundations for the longevity, health and vigour of this beautifully formed race.

The 'recipe' for the soil food had been handed down from generation to generation. Sewage was stored for six months in conditions that rendered it sanitary, then it was combined with vegetable waste, composted, and turned frequently to introduce air into the mixture.

This ensured the return of all the valuable minerals to the soil, unlike modern sewage systems which pollute rivers and oceans and flush precious trace elements into the sea. Moreover, this hygienic treatment of waste materials prevented the problems of sanitation that had long undermined the health of the inhabitants of the slums of towns and cities throughout the world.

To the waste materials would be added fallen leaves, the mineral rich ashes from their wood fires and just the right amount of moisture. The success of this 'recipe' depended on the Hunzas' ability to provide, in this blend of waste materials, the right conditions for the bacteria and fungi to do their job. Animal waste products and plenty of oxygen were the vital 'ingredients' that produced a rich, black, crumbly substance, capable of enhancing the environment of the soil.

The stimulation of the symbiotic micro-flora ensured the maximum uptake of nutrients by the crops. This was true compost, quite unlike the dry, lifeless rubbish heaps of many a compost bin today, or the sterilised contents of the plastic-bagged products sold in garden centres.

Creating a conducive environment

With the benefit of modern science we can now look into the life of the soil and see a fascinating picture of how, given a soil environment conducive to their own health, soil micro-flora, both bacterial and fungal, play a vital role in the nutrition of plants. They do this in two ways: first, by digesting certain substances in the soil and excreting them in a form which is easily taken up by the roots of the plant; second, by invading the roots of many plants with their own mycelium, a type of root which provides a passageway for nutrients to pass directly from the soil into the root of the plant.

The failure to discriminate between harmful and helpful bacteria and fungi has resulted in a lack of understanding of the harm that is done by indiscriminate attempts to kill off pathogens in the soil, the plant, the animal, or in our own bodies.

Like the 'crazy general' in chapter 8, the over-use of antibiotics in animals and humans kills off the friendly, as well as the unfriendly bacteria, and allows harmful intestinal flora to multiply. This increase in unfriendly flora in the gut can cause an inability to absorb nutrients.

Similarly, chemical fertilisers and pesticides are antagonistic to the useful micro-flora of the soil. It is interesting to note that, just as an increase in unfriendly intestinal flora inhibits the absorption of nutrients from the gut, so an increase in unfriendly soil flora inhibits the uptake of nutrients by the roots of the plant.

The key to the health of the soil, the plant, the animal and the human is to encourage in each an environment that is more conducive to the helpful than to the harmful micro-flora.

It is this ability to change and improve the environment of the soil, which makes properly produced compost far superior to any other form of fertiliser. Not only is it a food for the soil, it is also a biological stimulant to the friendly army of soil flora.

The cycle of health

This is where the cycle of health begins. Crops grown on such healthy soil do more than simply provide food for the humans and animals who eat them. If they are eaten whole, they create an intestinal environment that stimulates, and is conducive to, the body's army of friendly micro-flora, so vital to efficient immunity and the ability to resist infection and degenerative disease.

Resistance to disease isn't the prerogative of humans alone. Like the Hunza people and McCarrison's rats, properly fed humans and animals have a natural resistance to infection. In the same way properly fed plants have an ability to resist disease.

We tend to have the same problem today in our attitude to plant health as we have in our attitude to animal and human health. In our attempts to fight the battle against infection and disease with drugs or chemicals, we not only forget to encourage natural resistance but we actually destroy it.

The work of the agriculturalist Albert Howard paralleled the findings of McCarrison and Price in relation to disease resistance. Howard had been appointed Imperial Chemical Botanist of an experimental station at Pusa in India in 1905, where his task was to carry out research into agricultural problems.[3]

Though he had come to India armed with a degree in agriculture, he was willing to learn from the Indian peasants the art of growing healthy crops that were virtually free from disease. After setting up his own experimental station at Indore in 1925, he began to study the effects of these disease-resistant crops on the health of his farm animals.

In an experiment comparable to McCarrison's rat experiments, Howard succeeded in preventing disease in animals fed on compost-grown fodder. When these animals came into contact with cattle infected with diseases such as foot and mouth, their own resistance enabled them to remain free from infection.

The indicator of wrong feeding

Howard claimed that crops grown on land treated with compost had a resistance to disease, which could be passed on to the animals who were fed on such crops. The results of his experiments suggested that 'the birthright of every crop and of every animal is health, and that the correct method of dealing with disease is not to destroy the parasite but to make use of it for keeping agricultural practice up to the mark'.[4]

Howard pointed out that the correct method of dealing with plant disease is not simply to destroy the parasite but to recognise it as an indicator of what is going wrong. He saw a connection between

ecology and health, recognising the link between plant, animal and
human resistance to infectious and degenerative disease.

His wisdom in asserting that the observation of disease should
be seen as an indicator of wrong feeding, applies equally to human
health. Symptoms should be seen as an indicator of underlying health
problems and these, rather than just the symptoms themselves, should
be treated.

Organic agriculture at its best

The crops that Howard grew and the cattle he reared we now of
course know as organically produced vegetables, meat and milk.
Even in the midst of mountainous food surpluses and EC quotas
on milk production, some still claim that we need agrochemicals in
order to produce enough food. Debate still rages about whether or
not it really does taste better or has the ability to improve health.

Any assessment of the taste or productivity of organic produce,
however, must be based upon crops grown with properly made
compost, if the results are to be a true indicator of the benefits
of an organic system of agriculture. Organic agriculture should
involve much more than simply the absence of chemical fertilisers or herbicides. The fertility of the soil must be improved and
maintained.

Another agriculturalist, Eve Balfour, one of the founders of the
Soil Association, spent most of her life researching the cycle of
nutrition, from the soil to the plant, to the animal and to the
human. Her book *The Living Soil* was first published in 1943 and
resulted in the 'Haughley experiment', the first investigation into
the agricultural and nutritional benefits of organic, versus chemical,
agriculture to be done on a farm-scale.

When the book was later republished it also contained the results
of twenty-five years of comparison between three areas of land –
one farmed totally organically, one farmed with agrochemicals,
and one farmed with a mixture of both.

The benefits of optimum soil

Writing on the subject, she points out that for real taste and quality in the produce, the compost must be made from vegetable and animal waste. Moreover, without animal waste in the compost, there was no increase in disease resistance in the crops, a factor which can all too often be forgotten in the debate about the benefits of organic agriculture.

Eve Balfour's observations also pointed to the relationship between food and emotional health. Organically fed cattle were found to be in better condition and were far more placid and contented than any of the others. This led to speculation that the calves, born to cattle who had been organically fed, were able to metabolise their food in a different way – the reverse, in fact, of the inherited subnormal ability to utilise available nutrients, which is becoming increasingly prevalent today. The ability of the individual to metabolise nutrients gives a clue, not only to immunity, but also to emotional health, linking the observation of Price, McCarrison, Howard and Eve Balfour.

Eve Balfour also found that the second generation of organically fed cows needed less food than the cows feeding on chemically grown pasture, and yet they produced more milk. 'This more-milk-for-less-food experience', she wrote, 'has been one of the experiment's more interesting farm findings to date.'

Analytical work later showed the superiority of organic pasture, and the fact that the cows on the mixed section needed to eat twice as much in order to obtain the same level of nutrition. Incidentally, the extra yield of chemically grown crops has been shown to be mainly water.

As to the taste of the produce, Eve Balfour tells the story of a field on the mixed section of the farm that had been previously treated with a chemical fertiliser. However, the strip in the middle of the field had been deliberately omitted. When cows were turned out into the field they immediately found the untreated strip and grazed it bare before feeding elsewhere.

In her book, Eve Balfour quotes the words of a peasant which perhaps sum up the situation best of all. 'If people ate more of what's grown in muck, there'd not be half the illness about. People say that what's grown with artificial manure does you as much good as what's grown with muck. But I know that's wrong. What's grown with chemicals may look all right but it ain't got the stay in it.'

A vicious circle

As the fertility of the soil is reduced, and crops increasingly suffer from disease, we become trapped in a vicious circle of pesticides and agrochemicals which pollute our rivers and damage our own health and the health of wildlife. With inferior fodder, animals have lowered resistance and have to be dosed with drugs, which can end up in the food chain.

When agricultural practices aim for quantity rather than quality there is a corresponding decline in the health of those who drink the milk and eat the meat and crops produced by such a system. They, too, have to rely upon drugs to take over the job that their own immune systems should do, and so the vicious circle is complete. A circle of degeneration instead of a circle of health.

The Hunzas, McCarrison, Howard and Eve Balfour all recognised the value of properly made compost. The isolated people of the Hebridean islands used the smoke-filled thatch from their cottages to fertilise the acid soil and grow their oats. The Swiss of the Loetschental Valley grazed their cows on the high summer pasture, before making cheese from the milk.

Primitive people who hunted or fished for their food lived in an unpolluted environment where the balance of nature was undisturbed, and the circle of health had not been interrupted.

How big a price are we paying, in physical and mental health, for a system of agriculture that creates profit for the agrochemical industries, yet seems to be putting farmers out of business and taking farmland out of production? What are the effects on people of soil depletion and pollution?

Can we break the vicious circle of degeneration, and create a cycle of health, either individually or nationally? Is the research done by McCarrison, Howard, Price and Eve Balfour still relevant today in this hi-tech, fast-moving world in which we now live? Is it too late, or can something still be done to improve the health of the population? Let's look first at an example, earlier this century, of improved national health.

Government food policy

By the time that World War Two broke out, the British government had learned lessons from the recruitment figures of World War One. Then only thirty-six per cent of the men who had volunteered for service had been found to be fully fit.[5] Ten per cent were turned down completely, and the rest were judged to be in poor condition.

The appalling diet, particularly of the northern industrial towns, had been a major factor in the state of the health of the nation. In addition to poverty, ignorance and the wrong choice of food had contributed to a lowered resistance among the population. The 1918 Spanish flu epidemic has been estimated to have affected 500 million people worldwide, killing 20 million.

The years between the wars brought little improvement in the health of the nation but, at the outbreak of World War Two, a national food policy was put into operation by the government.

Rationing meant that some people were forced to eat less, and white bread became a thing of the past as bakers were instructed to produce the 'National Loaf', high in the all-important bran and wheat germ.

Dig for victory

At the beginning of the book, I wrote about Johnny's grandfather, Tommy, and his childhood in Liverpool. Tommy's father had learned to grow his own vegetables in order to provide enough food for his family. With the outbreak of war, however, and government encouragement to the nation to 'dig for victory', Tommy's neighbours in Norris Green immediately turned to his father for gardening advice.

He'd already learned the art of making compost from horse manure and vegetable waste to feed his crops and produce an abundant harvest of potatoes, onions, cabbage, cauliflower, lettuce, leeks and tomatoes.

Although meat was rationed, offal was plentiful and rabbit could be bought to make into a pie or a stew. With neck of lamb to make the traditional Liverpool dish, scouse, plenty of eggs, and an occasional chicken or duck from their own stock, the family not only had enough to eat but they ate better quality food than ever before.

Lawns in gardens up and down the land were dug up so that vegetables could be grown in their place. Tommy remembers that spare land at the side of railways was leased by local councils, together with recreation areas, municipal golf courses and bowling greens, to provide allotments for families who had no garden. He remembers the free seed that was distributed to the poor, and the vegetable competitions that were organised between the allotment holders in Liverpool.

While the affluent had to forgo their rich foods during the war, many of the poor, like Tommy and his family, ate better than they'd ever eaten before, and the health of both began to improve. Everyone was encouraged to eat a salad every day, extra milk and eggs were made available for expectant mothers, and orange juice and cod liver oil were given to babies and small children.

Enforced restriction to naturally grown foods, as Dr Weston Price had earlier found among isolated people, proved to be a blessing in disguise. The infant mortality rate dropped as did deaths from degenerative illnesses such as diabetes and heart disease.[6]

This was achieved not by healthy option convenience foods, or by expensive food supplements, but by a dramatic reduction in refined foods and a diet high in naturally grown vegetables. I often wonder how big a part the change in the nation's diet played in the legendary spirit of the British people throughout the long years of wartime bombing and hardship.

Is it worth bothering now?

Can food still make a difference now, though, in the polluted environment we've created since the war? A doctor friend of mine once asked me, 'With so much pollution around nowadays, is it worth bothering about what we eat?' The successful work of two charities dramatically demonstrates the benefits to health of improved food and environment.

When the nuclear reactor exploded in Chernobyl on April 26th, 1986, it released ninety times more radiation than the Hiroshima bomb, leaving hundreds of thousands sick and dying. The effect of that drifting radioactive cloud on the immune systems of the local population was so devastating that its effect has been likened to that of AIDS.

Children who are suffering dreadful health problems as a result of the massive radioactive fallout are being brought to Britain to spend a month drinking uncontaminated milk, eating uncontaminated food, and breathing cleaner air. The Chernobyl Children Life Line, based in Surrey, is linked with the Minsk-based April 26th Foundation. They co-operate to give a reprieve to children who are not too ill to travel to England.

'You would not believe the difference that one month of this makes,' said Victor Mizzi of the Chernobyl Children Life Line. Interviewed for a *Mail on Sunday* feature,[7] he described the change that he sees in these children even in such a short time. 'They arrive so pale and tired, and they leave with rosy cheeks and lots of energy.' When these children return home, they take with them desperately needed food and supplements for their brothers and sisters.

Yes, it is worth bothering about what we eat, as such dramatic results demonstrate. Sadly, for these tragic children, their stay in England may only mean a reprieve of two to three years from their health problems. But if improvements like this can be seen so quickly, when the immune system has been severely compromised by massive doses of radiation, there is a lesson here for all of us.

Genetic deterioration and agrochemicals

It must make sense to eat as much naturally grown, unprocessed food as possible to counter the immune depleting effects of a cumulative daily cocktail of insecticides, herbicides and chemicals that are sprayed on to crops both before and after harvesting.

The *Mail on Sunday* feature on the children of Chernobyl mentioned that many people in Byelorussia are so worried about the long-term effects of the radioactive fallout that they will only marry people from the same areas. They do not want to be blamed for deformed or sick children, so they marry someone else who is sick and could share the blame.

They know only too well the devastating genetic damage that can be done by radiation. Changes in chromosome structure can cause mutations in the genes, which alter the characteristics of succeeding generations, causing defects and malformations.

Yet many chemicals used in pesticides, herbicides and insecticides have been shown to produce exactly the same effects as radiation. Accumulations of insecticides have been discovered in the eggs of birds, and the sex organs and germ cells of animals from areas that have been sprayed by such chemicals.

Laboratory studies of such radiation-imitating chemicals have demonstrated their ability to damage chromosomes, interfere with normal cell division, or cause mutation. These genetic injuries may cause disease in the exposed individual or they may make their effects felt in future generations.

In her classic book *Silent Spring*,[8] Rachel Carson wrote in the early sixties, 'For mankind as a whole, a possession infinitely more valuable than individual life is our genetic heritage, our link with past and future. Shaped through long eons of evolution, our genes not only make us what we are, but hold in their minute beings the future – be it one of promise or threat. Yet genetic deterioration through man-made agents is the menace of our time, the last and greatest danger to civilization.'

All these years later, a decision has been taken to pay farmers more money to produce fewer crops! What will it take before they are paid to improve the fertility of their soil and produce organically grown crops?

Children are more vulnerable

At the beginning of the book, we saw something of the long-term effects of a diet of refined foods on the children and grandchildren of young women who lived in the early part of this century. Yet many women like Elsie, in the previous chapter, born nearly eighty years ago, recognise that their children were healthier during the war than their grandchildren are now.

Chemical pollution and toxic metals can affect the foetus as well as the growing child and the adult. Young children are more easily affected by lead, for example, which inhibits the production of enzymes and can damage the brain.[9]

Insecticides work by paralysing the insect's nervous system, but these chemicals can also accumulate in the fatty tissue of animals and humans, and interfere with important bodily functions such as oxidation and energy production. Accidental or cumulative overdoses can damage the liver and the nervous system, and cause paralysis.

Observation of such accidental overdoses has shown that children are more vulnerable than adults, with women more susceptible than men. (Incidentally, those who led active outdoor lives showed less severe reactions than those who led sedentary indoor lives.)[10]

Just as some people with faulty immunity develop allergies to dust or animals, for example, so those with lowered immunity are least able to cope with pollution. Pollution itself causes more damage to the immune system and creates a vicious circle.

Toxic metals and chemicals deplete nutrients. Lead, for example, robs zinc from the body.[11] Since zinc is needed for just about every metabolic process, its depletion can cause a wide variety of physical and emotional problems, as we have seen.

We owe it to our children

People will often point to the fact that we now have more old people living longer to justify their opinion that there is nothing wrong with our diet. A good deal of this is due more to our doctors' ability to keep the unhealthy alive than to our ability to create real health.

However, an important fact which is often overlooked is that our elderly people were conceived, born, and went through childhood before most of the chemicals now in use were invented. The fact that *they* are living longer should not make us complacent about the health prospects for the younger generation.

The deficient diets of the young women of the industrial cities of the north who existed mainly on tea, white bread, and margarine resulted in underweight babies. As we saw at the beginning of the book, the Medical Research Council study found that low birth weight was powerfully predictive of the later health, not only of the children, but also the grandchildren.

Must we wait for some future study to confirm the warnings about pollution already being given by organisations like Foresight, the association for preconceptual care, and The Hyperactive Children's Support Group? Their success in the nutritional treatment of infertile adults, parents with a history of miscarriage or abnormal births, and children with behavioural problems, should convince us that it's not too late, either individually or nationally, to make marked improvements in both physical and emotional health.

Both organisations recommend organically grown foods. We owe it to our children and to future generations to deal with pollution and create optimum health now in order to prevent genetic deterioration, 'the last and greatest danger to civilization'.

Keeping everything in perspective

Of course it's easy for me to talk about growing my own vegetables, writing as I do from home, where I can plan my day round the weather. I don't have to commute to an office, shop or factory, spend long, stressful hours clearing a backlog of work, make executive decisions, or deal with awkward customers. I don't get home exhausted from work with my mind still full of the problems of today and the plans for tomorrow. I don't need to collapse at the weekend to recover and renew my energy for the week ahead.

John has an allotment near mine and he is one of those friendly neighbours I can always turn to for advice. There I was last year, in my wellies and old clothes, sweating under the hot midday sun. I was doing battle with the army of weeds that did their level best, during the first summer, to reclaim their territory. Looking up, I saw John strolling down the path to collect some vegetables for the evening meal. In his pale grey suit, crisp white shirt and beautifully polished shoes, he looked business-like and distinguished.

For years he'd driven forty miles each day to and from his office, before a move to a local firm enabled him to wander down and survey his neat, weed-free allotment during a sunny lunchtime. I asked him what he would say to the businessman who had neither the time nor the inclination to grow his own vegetables.

'Digging on my allotment', he replied, 'actually saves me time, by enabling me to get everything in perspective. I've made many a decision, and worked out many a strategy as the physical exercise cleared my mind and helped me to unwind. Time spent reflecting on life can reduce the number of regrets caused by making wrong decisions.'

Finding space to grow

For those whose problems are due not to a shortage of time but of money, remember Tommy's father who escaped from the poverty trap by growing his own vegetables. 'But I wouldn't know where to start,' you may protest. Neither did Tommy's father. He'd lived all his life in the slums of Liverpool and, as Tommy pointed out to me, 'didn't know a weed from a flower – but it didn't take him long to learn'.

Your garden's too small? So is mine, like a pocket handkerchief. That's why I got an allotment. No allotments available in your area? There is a statutory obligation for local authorities to provide allotments for the use of ratepayers (Small Holdings and Allotments Act, 1908, Section 23, and the Allotments Act, 1950, Section 9). Lawrence Hills, writing in his book, *Organic Gardening*, urged would-be organic gardeners to get together to demand their rights.

You are so busy working to make ends meet, that you really haven't got the time to grow your own vegetables or to buy organic ones? Well you could send a letter to your MP suggesting that your taxes could be used more constructively by paying farmers to make the change to organic agriculture, rather than paying them to produce less.

In the meantime, organic pulses like lentils, beans and chick peas, and cereals such as oats and rice, don't cost that much more than non-organic ones. You can even produce your own ridiculously cheap, highly nutritious, fresh vegetables by sprouting the organic pulses. These can easily be grown on your kitchen window sill in just a few days.

RECOMMENDED READING

Organic Gardening by Lawrence D Hills (Penguin Handbooks 1977).
The Living Earth and The Haughley Experiment by E B Balfour (Universe Books 1976).
Silent Spring by Rachel Carson (Pelican Books 1962).

15

THE BEST THINGS IN LIFE
ARE FREE!

Our bodies have quite amazing powers of recuperation and cleansing, if only we will give them the right materials, and use them as they were designed to be used. Even if you've been eating additive-laden foods, drinking less-than-pure tap water, and breathing polluted air for years, you can make a difference that you really can feel, and that shows in your eyes, your skin, your nails and your hair.

If the benefits of optimum health mean that I live a very long and active life, that will be very nice indeed. But I'd have a lot of difficulty motivating myself to work at my health simply for some hoped-for extra retirement years. No, what motivates me today is that I want to feel good tomorrow. I want to have the motivation and energy to enjoy each day, and I want to know right now that I am already reaping the benefits of optimum health.

I didn't start off life with a strong constitution, and I was never blessed with beautiful features or the perfect body, but it's the only one I've got. Endless cups of tea, laced with three teaspoons of white sugar, and large quantities of chocolate biscuits, took their toll during my childhood, teens, and twenties. As a result, I learned about nutrient deficiencies, hypoglycaemia, allergies, and candida as I dealt with them in my own life.

Too busy feeling better!

When people thought my ideas rather cranky and denied that nutrition could make so much difference, I never ever wondered if they might be right. I was too busy feeling better than I'd ever felt in my life before! No more colds, flu, or ulcerated throats! Much more energy and stamina! And, most precious of all to me were the improvements in memory, motivation, concentration and ability to deal with stress. Yet I've never totally given up tea, chocolate biscuits or even cream cakes.

How times have changed since the early seventies. Where once my ideas seemed strange, compared to some who advocate various weird diets, now I'm a moderate! But I've looked into just about every nutritional fad that has come along. From mega-vitamin therapy to extremely restricted exclusion diets for allergies, I found that there's invariably some truth in all of these ideas, but that it's usually necessary to view them in a broader context. Time and time again, I came back to the simple, natural methods of building health that I'd learned right at the beginning. And the most valuable recent findings, such as the role of essential fatty acids, simply confirm the observations of the early nutritionists who insisted on the importance of natural, unrefined foods.

That is not to say there is never a need for nutritional supplements, but they are no substitute for the time-tested, basic principles of health. Not only has the need to detoxify the body been long known, it has now become more crucial than ever before in our additive-laden, pesticide-ridden, polluted modern society. No health therapy I've ever tried has compared to the benefits of a short programme of fasting and raw food designed to cleanse and detoxify the body.

Get serious about your health

People can spend a lot of money trying different products and therapies in their search for fitness, yet miss the health-promoting benefits of moderate exercise, or the immune-enhancing effects of the full spectrum of light in ordinary daylight. They may spend an expensive week at a health farm taking exercise, and eating raw vegetables. Growing my own vegetables saves me a lot of time and money. I get exercise, fresh air, daylight and a great deal of satisfaction, while I'm growing the organic vegetables I use to detoxify my system!

So, if you are really serious about your health, and you want results that you will see and feel each day, this is the chapter for you. If you suffer from allergies, yeast infection or hypoglycaemia, or if middle age is stiffening the joints and making you sag where you shouldn't, then read on. Do you feel more tired than you ought to? Would you like to have more energy? Do you want to look after your arteries and reduce your cholesterol level? Do you need to lose or gain weight? Perhaps you could simply do with improving the condition of your hair, skin or nails.

Cooking destroys many of the nutrients in food, and a diet of mainly cooked foods can lower vitality and lead to a sluggish metabolism. Practitioners of 'Nature Cure' have successfully treated diseases of every part of the body with a diet high in raw food. From digestive disorders to cancer, depression to heart disease, the list of illnesses which have been treated by these natural methods seems endless.

Begin a body cleansing routine

Basic to their treatment, is the need to cleanse the system and stimulate the friendly intestinal flora. The writing of the early practitioners of Nature Cure refer to the importance of this over and over again. We have seen that unfriendly intestinal bacteria and yeast infection can underlie many health problems, from allergies to chronic fatigue. The work of those early nutritionists has been well and truly vindicated. Their methods have been proved repeatedly by people who have experienced the benefits of raw food for themselves.

If I am going to put a bit of effort into keeping fit, I want to see the results pretty quickly. I want to feel so well that I know I'm not wasting my time. When you cleanse the system, you know about it. There is a feeling in your stomach which tells you it's working, just as your stomach can tell you when you've eaten too much rich food. You also know it's working when you lose the desire for stodgy food and stimulants. And you know that it's worth making the effort when you wake up in the morning, leap out of bed and find that you have the energy to work all day yet still feel good in the evening.

Poor health can be a vicious circle as lack of energy and motivation destroy the incentive to exercise. This lowers vitality even further so that it becomes too much effort to prepare nourishing meals.

Raw food can break the cycle of ill health since it takes very little preparation and is easily digested.

How to eliminate toxins

Now for the cheapest of all methods of improving health. In fact it can actually save you money. I first discovered this method in the mid-seventies and I've been using it regularly ever since. A very old method, dating back to ancient times, it is mentioned frequently in the Bible. It sharpens the mind, cleanses the system, and has been used by practitioners of Nature Cure for many years to treat a wide range of health problems. I like to use it two or three times a year and I feel terrific after it. In fact, whenever I want to get a lot done, or I need to write, I find this method very helpful indeed. It enables me to sleep fewer hours more soundly, to wake up thoroughly refreshed, and to get my housework done in half the time.

It's not recommended for people with heart or kidney problems, for diabetics, pregnant women or children, but for anyone else it can be used for short periods of time, say one to three days. I am talking of course about fasting. When you give your body a rest from having to digest heavy meals, it can get on with all the other jobs it needs to do, including the elimination of toxins accumulated from pollution in the air, food and drinking water.

Eating too much protein or carbohydrate produces metabolic byproducts which also need to be eliminated.[1] You'll know this cleansing is taking place by the furring of your tongue and the rather nasty taste in your mouth during the fast. The more your body needs a fast, however, the more toxins it needs to get rid of, the worse you'll feel initially. The better your diet and the more regularly you fast, the less you'll be aware that you are fasting. I can walk or cycle for miles when I'm fasting, particularly once I'm over the first day.

What's that I hear you say? You don't think you could fast? You get a sickly headache when you miss a meal? And you like your food too much? Well so do I. I really love my food and I too can get sickly if I miss a meal. But that's not true fasting.

The key to successful fasting lies in the preparation. It is very important indeed to cut out tea, coffee, soft drinks, and all stimulants for two or three days before beginning to fast. This is when you find out just what your favourite beverage has been doing to you. If you are used to drinking a fair amount of tea or coffee, you are very likely to get a rather nasty headache for a day or so. Get that out of the way first before you make any other changes in your diet.

Ease in through gentle preparation

For the person who has never fasted before I would recommend a programme of preparation over several weeks, using a good proportion of raw food in the diet, cutting out tea and coffee and culminating in a couple of days of raw food only, before embarking on a one day fast. When you first begin to fast, choose a non-working day so that you can take it easy. That may seem like a lot of trouble for one day, but the programme of preparation will bring its own rewards even before the fast is begun. The high raw-food diet will begin the cleansing process gently and avoid the more noticeable cleansing effects of rushing straight into a fast.

Perhaps most important of all is the way you *break* a fast. Eat only a small piece of fruit for breakfast the next day (not banana), and perhaps another one mid-morning. For lunch have a small plate of raw vegetables or salad. Eat another piece of fruit mid-afternoon and for the evening meal another salad. That way you ease your body gently back into eating and continue the cleansing process for another day.

Throughout the preparation, the fast, and the day after the fast, drink spring water with a slice of lemon or little pure fruit juice added to it. Herb tea made with spring water is excellent, and vegetable juice is better than fruit juice for those who suffer from hypoglycaemia or yeast infection.

Fasting is more effective when used regularly. Some people prefer to have a longer fast two or three times a year, while others prefer to fast one day a week, spending the one or two days before the fast on raw food and the day or two after it also on raw food. This can be a very effective way of sticking to a health building regime. Having gone to the trouble of cleansing the system and feeling much the better for it, you are far less inclined to ruin it all for a couple of minutes pleasure eating a bar of chocolate!

Benefits of fasting

Fasting alone is not the best way of slimming, but as part of a generally healthy regime it is a very effective way not only of losing weight, but of maintaining that loss. The fasting and the raw food cleanses the system and stimulates the metabolism. This enables the nutrients in the food to be better utilised, and turned to energy rather than laid down as fat. As with many dietary therapies, fasting and raw food can benefit the person who is underweight, too. Through the same cleansing and stimulating effects, that person can absorb food more efficiently and improve his or her appetite.

Other people prefer to fast two days a fortnight or, say, three days a month, since the first day of a fast is always the hardest. This has the advantage of continuing the cleansing and stimulating process for longer, but the disadvantage is that it can be easier to slip back into old dietary habits between fasts. Fasting is particularly effective after Christmas or a holiday, when dietary excesses are making you feel particularly sluggish. It's worth doing even if you only do it now and again. Once you've tasted the benefits, however, it becomes harder and harder to settle for less than your optimum health.

The benefits of fasting and raw food regimes are not limited to mood and energy levels either. You can see the effects in the eyes, the skin and even the hair when it is used regularly. It has been used effectively to relieve muscle and joint stiffness and pain in conditions such as rheumatism and arthritis. It can help lower blood pressure, stabilise the blood sugar in hypoglycaemia, and reduce cholesterol levels. By restoring the balance of intestinal flora, it is very effective indeed in the treatment of candida. This in turn can be effective in the treatment of chronic fatigue, allergic conditions and food intolerance. Premenstrual tension and menopausal problems can be alleviated by such a regime, and depression and nerve disorders often respond very quickly.

Much longer fasts are used very effectively by Nature Cure practitioners to deal with a wide range of conditions, but a fast of longer than three days should be supervised by an experienced practitioner. By about the sixth or seventh day of a fast the body has really got down to some deep spring cleaning and as toxins are really being thrown off, a temporary feeling of weakness or other symptoms may occur. The inexperienced patient will be reassured by the monitoring and the encouragement of the practitioner. But the cost of private treatment may be prohibitive and a consistent health promoting regime of short fasts and a diet high in raw food can be a better and more effective option.

No desire for stodge

I've used fasting since the children were small, even cooking meals for the rest of the family at the same time. However, I must admit that on the first day that I go without food, they are much more likely to be served a salad than a meal that smells too inviting. I can push my will power only so far! By the second day I don't feel hungry anyway, so it doesn't matter what I cook. Once I stop fasting and begin to eat again, food tastes so much better than before.

There is no desire at all for stodgy meals or sweet foods, and I get a great deal of satisfaction from preparing really varied and interesting salads. In fact I know it's time for another fast when I start to feel like eating heavier meals. This is where the one day a week fast is so effective. The less tea and coffee you drink incidentally, the easier you will find it to stick to a healthy diet. So often it is the dropping blood sugar and the craving caused by stimulants, that defeats the very best of intentions.

I used to suffer from being underweight. In recent years, however, I have found out what it's like to find yourself a few pounds overweight after a particularly indulgent Christmas or holiday. That quickly sends me back to the same regime and those pounds disappear by the second or third day. That may seem strange, but nutritional methods, by cleansing and stimulating, simply return the system to normal and, along with it, the weight.

The value of outdoor exercise

No matter how effective the cleansing or nutritious the diet, it will be of little use without regular exercise to increase the circulation, firm the muscles and keep the joints flexible. Exercise ensures that the nutrients you eat get to where they are needed in the body. This needn't be too vigorous, and a brisk walk each day is more beneficial than a heart-pounding game of squash once a fortnight. Swimming and cycling are excellent and one of the most inexpensive pieces of health building equipment you can buy is an old-fashioned skipping rope. People don't always recognise the importance to health of fresh air and daylight. They may come back from a holiday feeling fit and relaxed and put it all down to lack of stress, forgetting that they've just spent day after day out of the house, factory or office.

Daylight contains the full spectrum of light, as opposed to normal electric lighting, which contains only part of it.[2] When daylight strikes the retina at the back of the eyeball, the signal is carried to the pineal gland which produces the hormone melatonin. It is this hormone that influences our sleep patterns. Daylight tells the pineal gland to stop manufacturing melatonin, and lack of daylight increases the production of this hormone.

This is the hormone which brings about hibernation in some animals as the days become shorter. Melatonin suppresses the production, by the pituitary gland, of hormones that stimulate the rest of the endocrine system of the body. The activity of other ectocrine glands, therefore, is also influenced.

The thymus, the adrenals and the thyroid gland all play an important part in immunity, and the ability of sunlight to stimulate the immune system and restore health is now being recognised again. Of course we are only rediscovering what Florence Nightingale knew and practised. She laid down very strict rules not only relating to the freshness and quality of food, but also for the patients' removal from the hospital ward out into the sunshine for several hours each day.

Victorian hospitals were often built with verandas so that patients could spend as much time as possible benefiting from the health-promoting, immune-stimulating effects of daylight and sunshine. Nowadays the immune-stimulating effects of daylight are recommended in the treatment of allergies, candida, ME or chronic fatigue, and skin conditions such as acne or psoriasis.

Are you SAD?

The stimulation of the pituitary gland in turn influences the thyroid gland so that metabolism is also stimulated. Healthy metabolism increases the efficiency with which we use nutrients, by turning them to energy instead of fat. However, when we huddle indoors during the winter, we don't get sufficient natural light to effectively suppress the production of melatonin. Consequently the metabolic rate of the whole body slows down, we use our food less efficiently, are unable to burn up calories so easily, and may put on weight. Increasing levels of melatonin can cause craving for food and this is seen in the animal who eats to build a store of fat in order to survive the hibernation period.

There may be over sensitivity to cold, a generally run-down feeling, depression and susceptibility to infection. The ability to handle stress is often diminished, along with energy levels, and since melatonin is not properly suppressed, constant tiredness is a common symptom. We have seen that individual requirements of nutrients vary from person to person. It's the same with individual requirements of daylight. We will all be affected to some extent by light deprivation, but for those whose requirement is very high, the effects of our long winters can be devastating. These people suffer from seasonal affective disorder (SAD), which causes them to suffer from depression, tiredness and lack of energy and motivation, and to crave carbohydrates. The condition can be treated with a special lamp which emits the full spectrum of light, mimicking the effects of sunshine.

Unfortunately, glass cuts out part of the full spectrum of light, so even if you work near a window you won't be getting the full benefits of daylight. Those who work in windowless offices and factories under artificial lighting, however, are suffering an increasing number of health problems as their immunity is lowered through lack of fresh air and daylight; the name 'sick building syndrome' has now been coined. More and more firms are recognising the importance of light, and full spectrum light fittings are increasingly being installed in offices and factories. They ought to be fitted in hospitals, since this type of light can promote health and stimulate the immune system. Lack of full spectrum light has been implicated in hyperactivity, which is often caused by allergic reactions, so full spectrum lighting should also be fitted in schools to stimulate children's immunity.

The sunshine vitamin

Vitamin D is manufactured in the skin after exposure to sunshine, and this vitamin is an activator, essential to the absorption and utilisation of minerals. It has long been known that during the lengthy winters of our northern hemisphere, vitamin D deficiency increases. This inevitably means that mineral absorption and utilisation also increases. While studying the isolated people of the Loetschental Valley in Switzerland, Dr Weston Price analysed the vitamin content of the milk from the cows grazing on the rapidly growing grass in the early summer sunshine. He found that the butter made from this milk was several times higher in fat-soluble activators such as vitamins A and D, than in butter from cows fed on poor pasture, or on dried grasses and cereals.[3]

Price later used this vitamin-rich butter to improve the absorption and utilisation of minerals such as calcium and magnesium, so vital to the efficient functioning of all muscles including the heart. It is interesting to note that it has been observed that the further away from the equator, the higher the rate of heart disease.[4] Animals are just as dependent on nourishing food, and a good environment for their health as we are for ours, and unhealthy animals don't produce such healthy milk and butter as do healthy animals. Should we not be concentrating on improving the health of our dairy herds and consequently the quality of their produce instead of skimming the cream from milk and substituting butter for margarine? Though margarine has synthetic vitamin D added to it, as we saw earlier, the hydrogenation of vegetable oils produces trans-fatty acids which are toxic.

Vitamin D and calcium have long been known to be vital to the building of strong bones and it is very sad to see the increase in rickets in the poorer communities of cities like New York. As we get older, vitamin D deficiency can cause osteoporosis. When vitamin D is in short supply and minerals aren't available, the teeth suffer too, and decay sets in. We are all being warned that too much sunshine can cause skin cancer in fair-skinned people who burn easily. What we don't always realise is that dark-skinned people actually need much more sunshine for health.

Those early nutritionists and Nature Cure practitioners who were branded as cranks for their insistence on the importance of fresh, properly grown whole foods, also extolled the benefits of sunshine to health. They may not have had the benefits of our modern knowledge of exactly what effect the full spectrum of light in daylight has upon the endocrine system of the body, but experience revealed to them the importance of sunshine to health. Keen gardeners and others who work outside often have very few infections. So, wherever possible, take your exercise in the fresh air away from traffic fumes.

RECOMMENDED READING

Raw Energy by Leslie and Susannah Kenton (Arrow 1986).
10 Day Clean-up Plan by Leslie Kenton (Vermillion 1992).
Day Light Robbery by Dr Damien Downing (Arrow 1988).

16

EMOTIONAL DAMAGE

During the last ten years or so a whole industry has been built up around people's concern for their health. Almost every issue of every women's magazine carries at least one article about healthy cooking, weight loss, exercise, or the importance of vitamins and minerals. The food industry spends billions of pounds each year persuading us, the consumer, that one product is better for our health than the next one. Low calorie, high fibre, no additives: all are part of today's advertising language.

However, a book on optimum health would be incomplete if we just stopped there, since physical factors are only part of what it takes to make a healthy and whole person. Without doubt, physical problems can damage emotional health. Over the years, I have talked to a lot of people about the importance of good nutrition, exercise, and natural light, to both physical and emotional health. I have seen some be quite dramatically transformed by dealing with underlying conditions such as nutritional deficiencies, allergies, candida or hypoglycaemia.

It has also become very clear over the years, however, that all these things can do only a limited amount of good for people who are habitually worried, stressed, bitter, angry, obsessed or excessively ambitious for either status or possessions. There have been times in my life when I have harboured such feelings, only to find that the lifestyle that had once maintained my health, was inadequate to counter the effects of such damaging emotions.

Hormones and the mind

So let's take a look at some of the physical effects of our reactions and emotions. A friend of mine, Suzie, is a clinical biochemist, with a BSc in Biochemistry and a PhD in Clinical Biochemistry. She did her post doctoral research in endocrinology. I went to visit her to talk about the relationship between emotions and the endocrine glands.

The hypothalamus (situated in the brain), the pituitary (situated at the base of the brain and connected to the brain) and the endocrine glands are all linked. They function as one unit. The hypothalamus stimulates the pituitary gland to secrete hormones which stimulate the other endocrine glands to release their hormones. This controls growth, development, metabolism and reproduction.

Normally the whole system is balanced because circulating hormones exert a feedback mechanism, and when the correct level of a hormone is released, the feedback system indicates that it is time to stop production. 'This keeps us well, happy and perfectly balanced with everything "ticking over" nicely,' said Suzie.

However, a variety of factors, both physical and emotional, can interrupt this balanced circle of hormone production. 'As well as receiving information from the feedback mechanism,' explained Suzie, 'the hypothalamus also responds to both physical and mental stress, and to emotional status.'

An example of the way that stress affects the endocrine system, Suzie told me, is the way in which it is more or less impossible to take a measurement of the normal level of one of the pituitary hormones, known as ACTH. This is because in most people, the very sight of a needle approaching the vein in order to take blood is enough to push up the level of ACTH to an abnormal level!

I asked Suzie to talk about the causes and the effects of constantly elevated levels of ACTH. 'These elevated levels affect the adrenal glands,' explained Suzie, 'and adrenal dysfunction can occur for a number of different reasons, physical as well as emotional.' She explained that this may result in lethargy, tiredness, lack of vitality and obesity.

'To effectively treat this condition,' Suzie pointed out, 'it is important to be able to distinguish the cause. The elevated levels of ACTH found in severe depression, for example, may be due to either physical or emotional factors, or even both.'

Having established that mental stress affects the function of the endocrine system, we went on to talk about the 'other side of the coin'. 'What is also apparent,' said Suzie, 'is the way in which abnormalities of the endocrine system can affect how we behave.' She gave an example of this. Patients with an overactive thyroid gland tend to be anxious, overly energetic, and underweight, whereas those with an underactive thyroid are usually depressed, sluggish, and overweight.

'But there are also some beneficial effects between our mental state and the endocrine system,' Suzie pointed out. 'In very painful situations such as childbirth, substances called endorphins are released in large quantities and these act as natural painkillers.' Another positive effect of endorphins is the 'high' they give you when you are exercising physically. This makes you feel good, and gives you the impetus to carry on. Suzie summed it all up by saying, 'To achieve a normal, well balanced, properly functioning endocrine system, so vital to good health, it is important to overcome any prolonged anxiety, stress or emotional problems.'

Stress can cause illness

Now let's look at the effects of emotions on another area of health. Nutritionist Michael Weiner, PhD, in his book *Maximum Immunity*,[1] summed up one of the recurring themes of the book. 'Sometimes', he wrote, 'we need to come the long way around to rediscover ancient folk wisdom.' How true! He was particularly concerned there with the relationship between emotional health and the immune system.

'Our great-grandmothers', he pointed out, 'would not have been the least bit surprised to learn that depression, or a stressful life, could lead to illness.' He went on to point out that our great-grandmothers were right, and that it is now evident that attitudes, beliefs and emotions can influence immunity.

The effect of the emotions on the immune system, however, is less widely accepted than is the effect of emotions on the endocrine system. The subject is still controversial. Nevertheless there is an increasing awareness that confidence, friendships, a sense of belonging, and the ability to let go of negative feelings are important factors in immunity.

The hypothalamus, as we saw earlier, responds to stress by triggering the pituitary gland to secrete hormones which stimulate the other endocrine glands. As a result of this stimulation, the adrenal glands release the hormone adrenalin and also a group of hormones called corticosteroids. Cortisol, one hormone from the group, can suppress the function of the immune system, and a wide range of diseases are associated with constantly elevated levels of this hormone.

Michael Weiner includes depression, cancer, hypertension, ulcers, heart attack, diabetes, infections, alcoholism, obesity, arthritis, stroke, psychoses of the ageing, skin diseases, Parkinson's disease, multiple sclerosis, and myasthenia gravis in the list of stress-related diseases.

It might be worth remembering at this point, however, that adrenal dysfunction can occur for a number of different reasons, physical as well as emotional. To successfully treat the condition it is, as we saw earlier, important to be able to distinguish the cause.

Healthy attitudes

Peace of mind, stable relationships, right attitudes and a good perspective on life are just as important to health as physical considerations. There's nothing new about such observations, of course. In chapter 7 we looked at the work of the Pioneer Health Centre among the families of the London suburb of Peckham. The Peckham doctors warned that the physical nature of an illness should be studied before a psychological cause is sought. Nevertheless they were fully aware of the vital importance of attitudes and relationships.

The physical health of each member of the Pioneer Health Centre was regularly monitored through medical examinations and laboratory tests. However, the relaxed and informal atmosphere of the centre enabled the Peckham doctors to observe the members' habits and reactions. They could watch the way in which an individual behaved within their family circle, and how they related to their partner, children and others in their immediate social circle. They also took note of a person's attitude to work.[2]

In their report[3] on the work of the centre they wrote that they had become more and more aware that the major cause of ill health lay in a person's attitudes and relationships. One of the basic questions that the Peckham experiment was designed to investigate was, 'What determines how we act?' This is a question we still need to ask ourselves if we really want to achieve optimum health.

Writing later about the Peckham experiment, Dr Kenneth Barlow said that from the beginning, the Pioneer Health Centre doctors realised that health was derived, not from what was done *to* a person, but from their environment, and the *responses* of the individual to his or her social relationships. The ability of a person to integrate socially, the doctors observed, played an important part in their physical as well as their emotional health. So, it seems that it's not just a question of how we *act*, but of how we *react* and of how we *relate*.

Healthy relationships

Dr Barlow's first book, *Discipline of Peace*[4] was written and published during World War Two. It was republished in 1971 as one of a series called *Classics of Human Ecology*. In the preface to the new edition, the writer commented that it was, 'written for a future that is now emerging'. In his book Dr Barlow examined the complex interrelationships between the soil, the plant, the animal and the human, a subject which, all these years later, is now being addressed by ecologists and nutritionists.

Dr Barlow went further, however, and examined the effects of the attitudes and actions of individuals towards each other. He believed that a view of life that was purely materialistic tended to underestimate the need for personal responsibility, and led to the exploitation both of other people and of nature. Our view of life is a major factor in determining how we act. 'At present our way of life is still manipulative and irresponsible,' wrote Dr Barlow. 'Until the people are set alight with new convictions, that way of life will persist.'

There are many theories today about what determines how we act, and psychology seeks the answer in how we were brought up, our relationships, or our suppressed emotions. So often, it seems, circumstances and other people have made us what we are, and determined how we act. Rarely is any emphasis placed on personal responsibility. The idea that our actions should come under the check of an organisation greater than mankind is, for many people today, an anathema.

Yet, Dr Barlow maintained, it is the manipulative philosophies of modern society that have released us from checks and responsibilities. 'Man's initiative did not come under the check of any organization greater than himself,' he wrote, pointing out that as science grew, traditional convictions were undermined. 'In the old days this was a situation in which the prophets cried out that man had forgotten his God,' he wrote. 'Today we go back to the perplexities of social development and say nothing.'

Wholeness

'The awareness of design in nature came to our early forefathers from a faculty of reverence which is, in our society, atrophied,' Dr Barlow wrote. These people worshipped God, and Dr Barlow noted that, 'We cannot help but see that their life had a wholeness which ours lacks.'

Today we hear a lot about 'wholeness' with regard to individual health. The concept of 'holistic health', which is becoming more popular, involves physical, emotional and spiritual aspects of health, yet the concept of personal responsibility still seems to be lacking. Great emphasis seems to be put on self awareness, but the only emphasis on self discipline seems to relate to diet and exercise.

Dr Barlow wrote, 'Man has an inward spiritual life in which the problem of personal discipline is evident. Out of this discipline are born the questions of good faith and good will, of the responsibility of man towards man, and of the community of men towards the least amongst them.'

Holistic health

Does the modern concept of 'holistic health' through nutrition, exercise and self awareness really enhance how we act and relate to others, or is it an illusion? Can focusing on ourselves make us less selfish, and less manipulative towards each other? Can it really help us to develop the fulfilling relationships that are so important to our health and the health of our families? And can concentrating on self lessen the materialism which has damaged our environment and our health? Can self awareness really set us alight with new convictions?

'The primary issue is not how we are to treat materials, but how men are to treat each other, and the life of the earth which endows them,' Dr Barlow wrote, going on to point out that man's health must be understood on many levels, 'ranging from nutrition to reverent contemplation'.

Is reverent contemplation, as Dr Barlow understood it, the same thing as the type of meditation that is becoming increasingly popular today? Does modern spirituality acknowledge the checks and controls of an organisation greater than mankind? Or does it blame past experiences or even past lives for what we are? Does our modern concept of wholeness encompass a truly effective form of spirituality?

Dr Barlow, looking forward to the end of the war, concluded his book with the exhortation, 'We must return in humility to ask what is greater than man in order that, admitting this, we may know the discipline to which the gift of liberty compels our obedience.' 'Humility' and 'obedience' are not words that are frequently found in the spirituality of 'holistic health' circles.

So do we still need to ask the question, 'What is greater than man?' Do we still need to discover what determines how we act? We have seen that our actions and reactions, our attitudes and social relationships can affect our physical health. If we establish what is greater than mankind, may we also find the answer to what determines how we react and relate to others?

Poisons of the mind

'Every generation that has preceded us has helped to make this world the place it is. Right now we are affecting the environment for ourselves and for those who will come after us. And much of what we are doing is destructive.' Those words were written by a friend of mine, J John, in 1989. He went on to explain, 'I am not talking about the chemical poisons we inject into the air, the water and the earth, but the poisons we inject into one another when our behaviour is destructive.'

His words sound familiar. 'As human beings we interact with one another and as we do so we affect one another. We condition one another's thinking, feeling and behaviour, sometimes in ways we are unable to reverse.' My friend certainly believes in the importance of attitudes and relationships. It seemed that in his book,[5] published almost fifty years after Dr Barlow's book, he was expressing sentiments that were very similar. 'The problems in the world will not be sorted out until we deal with the main problem,' he wrote. 'And the main problem is and always has been us.'

J John certainly thinks that we need to address the problem of what determines how we act. He even seems to have the same view as Dr Barlow when it comes to families. In another book published in 1990 he wrote, 'Good families make a healthy society, this is a very important truth, particularly at times when some people have said, and continue to say, that the family is not very important.'[6]

Yearning for something more in life

Not long ago, over a leisurely meal in a quiet restaurant, a friend and I were discussing life, and our aims and ambitions. My friend has a very good job, a company car and an excellent salary. She told me, however, that she didn't want to work full time for too many more years, and thought that she might eventually do some voluntary work. 'It's strange,' she said, 'I felt that I wasn't fulfilled, so I changed my job. But, do you know, the feeling's still there. I still don't feel fulfilled.'

I asked her to tell me a little more about the feeling. 'Where do you feel it?' I asked, and she looked a little puzzled for a moment. Then, putting her hand to her stomach, she said, 'It's not a thought that's in my head. It's a sort of gut feeling.' 'Is it a sort of yearning?' I asked her, and she replied, 'Yes – that's it exactly!' 'That feeling', I suggested, 'may not be the sort of feeling that can ever be satisfied by a new job.'

Perhaps I should give her one of J John's books to read. 'We talk about what we want from life – to graduate successfully, to get a good job, to fall in love, to marry and to have a family,' he wrote. 'But there is something missing. We remain empty. It's as if there is some gap or void in our lives that needs to be filled with the right thing.' We try to fill it with things that just don't fit. So what will fill that gap?

It seems that a lot of people are seeking the answer to that question nowadays. Disillusioned by what they see as the materialism, ambition and ruthlessness of the eighties, they are looking for an alternative for the nineties. Some recognise that people became so selfish in the eighties that they ended up with a series of unfulfilled relationships with friends, partners and families. Others, like my friend, realise that promotion cannot satisfy that yearning.

Typically, these people are well off, idealistic, well educated and intellectually curious. They feel that there is another dimension to life and are searching for the spiritual. This has resulted in a massive explosion of interest in alternative religions and philosophies. Of course many people in different times and countries have claimed to have found God. Others who can't accept that God exists think that such people are simply suffering from a delusion.

So is God a delusion? Is there a spiritual dimension to health? And is there a design and a purpose to life?

Psychologists like Freud tell us that our actions are the result of various repressed sexual tendencies. Sociologists like B F Skinner argue that our choices are determined by social conditioning, and that our freedom is an illusion. Biologists like Francis Crick regard man as just an electro-chemical machine. If these answers are right, we are nothing but a miscarriage of nature, thrust into a purposeless universe to live a purposeless life.

'Modern scientific attitudes, because of science's effectiveness rather than any conspiracy by scientists, destroy purpose in life, reduce us all to a condition of blank, adolescent nihilism,' wrote Bryan Appleyard in *The Times*. He went on:

> The open-endedness, the valuelessness, the apparent objectivity and effectiveness of science have progressively stripped away any reason to value one way of life, one system, above another. It is as pointless trying to find God in the quantum or in chaos theory as it was to find him in the Newtonian cosmos. Science will move on, and where will God be then?[7]

Neither ambition nor science can fulfil that yearning that my friend was experiencing, nor answer the longing of the heart for something more. 'Nothing about our lived experience ever corresponded to Newton's laws of motion, and nothing in Hawking's[8] equations will ever resemble what our natures demand of the mind of God,' wrote Appleyard. 'Our experience and our history are more real than either. We know this to be true, but science has done terrible damage to our faith. It is time to start making repairs.'

Science cannot tell us everything about life, and never will. And if we limit our understanding of life and health to the physical and the emotional we'll never really discover what determines how we act and relate to others, or satisfy the yearning deep inside.

Effective spirituality

We hear a great deal nowadays, of course, about the spiritual or the paranormal – and perhaps nowhere more so than in alternative medicine. Here the concept of 'holistic health' recognises the relationship between the physical, the emotional and the spiritual.

The subject is controversial. Some alternative practitioners propose a purely scientific definition of their methodology, while others suggest there is a spiritual or paranormal dimension to their work. So, since we are concerned with optimum health, let's take a look at some of these very different theories and therapies.

Let's see if we can find there a truly effective form of spirituality, and rediscover the wholeness that is lacking in the materialistic view of life. Let's see if we can find out what determines how we act and if we can be set alight with new convictions. And let's see if there is anything there that can satisfy that yearning deep inside of us.

17

UNMEASURABLE ENERGY

The alternative health scene encompasses a vast range of therapies, from the purely physical to the clearly spiritual. In between, however, are practices and therapies that are claimed by some to be scientific, but by others to be paranormal. Let's examine some fairly commonly used techniques. We'll begin with two diagnostic practices, kinesiology and radionics.

Applied kinesiology

Kinesiology is a relatively new technique and it is most controversial in its claims to diagnose allergies, nutrient deficiencies and other medical problems by testing the resistance of the muscles. For example, a small amount of the suspected allergen may be placed between the patient's lips, or somewhere else on the surface of the body, or held in one hand. The free arm is then placed in a particular position and the patient is asked to hold the arm steady while the practitioner exerts gentle pressure for two or three seconds.

If the muscle holds tight and the patient is able to resist the pressure and keep the arm firm and steady then, it is concluded, there is no allergy to that particular substance. However, if the muscles become weak and the arm 'gives', a probable allergy is said to have been identified. This same muscle weakness under gentle pressure can, it is claimed, pick up nutrient deficiencies even before they manifest themselves. Kinesiology may be used to diagnose specific illnesses and to give information about the function of the various organs of the body.[1]

There is no satisfactory explanation of how kinesiology works, but a variety of theories have been put forward. The body is thought to recognise and react instantly to nutrients and chemicals, and these reactions affect the muscles as a result of changes in the body's electrical field. This field cannot be measured scientifically, but it is claimed that there are many levels or planes of energy which lie beyond the measurable electromagnetic field.

Radiesthesia

Radionics, psionic medicine and dowsing have been grouped together under the collective heading, 'radiesthesia'. These therapies may be used in the presence of the patient, or from a distance, using what is known as the radiesthetic faculty, which is a form of extrasensory perception. Divining is another practice that comes under the heading radiesthesis and here a forked twig is usually used to detect underground water sources or minerals. In fact, all radiesthesia is basically divination.

In radionics either a radionic diagnostic instrument or a pendulum is used in diagnosis or treatment. There are a variety of radionic instruments. One of these, a machine rather like a wireless set, is tuned into the vibrations which, it is claimed, emanate from each organ of the body. The patient's own energy pattern is monitored, with each organ being given a radionic number, depending on the strength of its vibrations. Treatment consists of directing the vibrations of healthy organs through the machine into the vibrations of organs that are not functioning properly.

The most commonly used instrument takes the form of a box covered by a panel. On the panel is a set of dials which are calibrated from o to 10, or o to 44, depending on which system is used. There is normally a metal plate upon which is placed either a spot of the patient's blood, or a snippet of his or her hair. This is called a 'witness', and is said to provide the link between the practitioner, the instrument and the patient. However, Stephen Fulder pointed out that the instruments do not in themselves have any intrinsic value, and it is thought that connects the practitioner to the patient. 'Radionics is in fact a form of mental healing,' he wrote. 'When a practitioner tunes into the patient, he literally brings that patient "to mind" and on that plane of consciousness, distance does not exist.'[2]

The pendulum consists of an object dangled on the end of a cord, and its use is known as dowsing. Some practitioners believe that the pendulum responds to the different vibrations given off by the various organs of the body, enabling a diagnosis to be made of the health or function of each organ. Other practitioners, having tuned their mind to the patient, ask a series of either mental or audible questions of either the radionic instrument or the pendulum. The pendulum will swing, as a rule, from a simple oscillation to a clockwise movement to give a 'yes'. Or, if a stick pad is built into the instrument, consisting of a rubber diaphragm, the practitioner's fingers will literally stick to the pad instead of sliding easily across as he mentally asks questions, giving a 'yes' in this way.

It is claimed that these methods identify the cause of specific symptoms, allergies or deficiencies and that they can detect residual toxins. When healing from a distance, some practitioners put a phial of a particular homeopathic remedy on the plate next to the patient witness, with the intention of modifying the energy directed to the absent patient. Many practitioners use colour as a therapeutic agent in their practices and this, they claim, can be 'broadcast' to patients at a distance in the same way that homeopathic remedies can. Often remedies such as biochemic tissue salts or Bach flower remedies are recommended to the patient as an adjunct to radionic treatment.

Parapsychological phenomena

As with kinesiology, radionics, by its very nature, cannot be proved scientifically. Research which demonstrates parapsychological phenomena in general is more appropriate to the understanding of the methodology of this group of therapies. The paranormal nature of radiesthesia can be recognised in the warning which is given that practitioners should never make a radionic analysis on an individual without his express permission. To do so, it is generally accepted, would be to psychically invade that person against his or her will. This warning is given by advocates of the practice, not just by opponents.[3]

Apparently beneficial results from the treatment of animals are claimed to demonstrate the effectiveness of radionic treatment, and most of the debate about the validity of the practice centres on examples of their effectiveness. The question, however, should not be *do* such practices work, but *how* do they work? And we need to consider the possibility of psychic invasion even when a person's permission is given.

Some practitioners of radionics use a photograph of the patient, or a letter written by the patient, in order to diagnose or treat from a distance, just as some practitioners of divination will use a map to detect the presence of underground water or minerals. This rather strains the theory that radionics works through an energy field, but it does add weight to the suggestion that extra-sensory faculties may be being used.

This is further strengthened by the observation that the radionic box, like the pendulum and the hazel twig, may only give convincing results when operated by particular individuals. Clearly there is more to this sort of activity than science and skill. We are talking here about a paranormal ability, and we need to be careful of what we are getting involved in.

Energy fields

Basic to radionic theory and practice is the concept that all life forms, including man, are submerged in and interpenetrated by a common field of energy.[4] At the lowest level, this field registers as the electromagnetic spectrum. In radionics, however, as in kinesiology, it is claimed that there are many levels or planes of energy which cannot be detected by scientific instrumentation, since they lie beyond the measurable electromagnetic field.

Early radionic practitioners diagnosed and treated in medical and clinical terms, and saw the body basically in orthodox anatomical and physiological terms. Today many practitioners have adopted a model of the body directly drawn from theosophical and Eastern teachings. Such concepts fit in more easily with the idea of man as energy. So here we are talking, not about scientifically measurable energy, but about the type of energy described in spiritual teachings.

The concept of a vital energy flowing through the body is basic to Oriental medicine, acupuncture, acupressure, reflexology, yoga and t'ai chi. Practitioners claim that these therapies encourage the free flow of this energy. Some practitioners reject the Taoist philosophy underpinning these therapies, but modern Taoist philosopher George Oshsawa, the founder of macrobiotics, insists that Oriental medicine cannot be separated from its philosophical underpinnings. Here is another example of the difference of opinion between these practitioners who insist that their work is scientific, and those who see a spiritual explanation for such therapies.

Man, it is claimed by some, not only has a physical body but an 'astral' body, as described in yoga literature. The astral, or celestial body, is also sometimes called the etheric body, or the divine or godly body. The energy that is believed to flow into the etheric body has been called 'prana' in India, 'chi' and 'tao' in China and 'the vital force' in Europe. It is also sometimes referred to as 'karma' and 'yin and yang'. This vital force, it is suggested, permeates the whole universe, including man.

Pulse diagnosis, an analytical tool used in Oriental medicine, enables the practitioner, it is claimed, to feel the vibrations of the patient's cosmic energy and to discern the flow of chi. Some advocates of Oriental therapies admit that no theory for their practices has yet been found wholly acceptable, and that the possibility still remains that some as yet unexplained force is involved.

What about homeopathy?

Many people think of homeopathy simply as 'like cures like', and the Society of Homoeopaths explains that the remedies are prescribed under what they call the Law of Similars.[5] This law, they claim, states that, 'What makes you sick shall heal'. They believe that the symptoms which are caused by an overdose of a substance are the symptoms which can also be cured by a very small dose of that same substance.

The remedies, which are derived from plants, minerals, metals or poisons, are prepared by dilution and violent shaking in a solution of alcohol and water. This process is described as potentisation and is done from three or four, to many thousands of times.

Frequently, the dilution is so great that no chemical trace of the original substance remains, and these high dilutions are regarded by homeopaths as their most potent remedies. This is where homeopathy differs from vaccination, in which a small amount of a virus or bacterium is introduced into the body to enable the immune system to recognise and to respond to any future infection by the same agent.

The Society of Homoeopaths believes that there is abundant proof that homeopathic remedies *do* work, but they say that scientists have yet to agree on *how* they work. Their explanation is similar to the theory of kinesiology and radionics, since they believe that the answer to how homeopathy works is to be found in the field of as yet unmeasurable electromagnetism. The process of dilution and violent shaking, it is claimed, apparently imprints the characteristic energy pattern of the original substance on to the liquid in which it is diluted. Homeopathic remedies, the society claims, act as a signal which energises or stimulates the body's self-healing powers, working on the mental, emotional and physical dimensions of the body.

Homeopathy, therefore, is believed to work by energising the self-healing power of the body, and the Homoeopathic Society believes that this healing power or energy has been recognised for many years in various cultures. Homeopaths in general practice according to the rules that Samuel Hahnemann, the founder of homeopathy as it is known today, laid down,[6] though not all agree with his views.

He believed that this vital healing energy is spiritual, and that illness comes about as a result of a derangement of this spiritual vital force. He claimed that this cosmic vital force was transferred to the homeopathic solution by the violent shaking. In his book *The Handbook of Complementary Medicine*, Stephen Fulder explains that homeopathic remedies do not transmit chemicals, but information. 'At high potencies,' he suggests, 'homeopathy may take off into the realm of healing, whether the homeopath recognises it or not.'[7]

Bach flower remedies

A variation of homeopathy was developed by Dr Edward Bach, a homeopath. His flower remedies were potentised solutions or extracts of flowers or twigs, obtained by means of a gentle serial dilution rather than by violent shaking. Bach was guided by intuition in the selection of his remedies, and implicit in his work were links with homeopathy, radiesthesia and healing. He believed that his remedies could draw down spiritual power. Bach's work continued after his death. Today the flowers are left for several hours in a bowl of water in the sun and this concentrate is used for the Bach flower remedies which are sent all over the world.

These remedies, it is claimed, may be used as treatment for the subtle psychological roots of disease. At least one of the thirty-eight remedies that Dr Bach discovered is believed to correspond to each negative state of mind, personality trait, mood or temperament known to man. When peace and harmony are restored, it is claimed, health and strength will return to the body.

Rather than having a physical effect, the remedies are claimed to relieve the negative states of mind which might precede an ailment. 'They work on a more spiritual level, helping balance one's link with a higher force,' said Judy Howard, one of the directors and custodians of the Bach Flower Centre in an article in the *Daily Mail*.[8]

Alternative medicine

There is often a great deal of cross-fertilisation between the different areas of alternative medicine. This makes it very difficult to draw a clear line between purely manipulative therapies such as osteopathy, and those practices which claim to work by manipulating some sort of unmeasurable energy. This can make it very difficult, at times, to tell what is being offered, and whether or not any extrasensory faculties are being used by the practitioner.

Chiropractic is a good example of this. Its nineteenth-century founder, David Daniel Palmer, from Iowa, was both an osteopath and a healer. The energy which he believed flowed through the body, he described as 'innate intelligence', which was centred on the brain and influenced by a universal intelligence.

The first and second vertebrae of the spine, he claimed, were the 'vital intermediate space between brain and body', where misalignment or obstruction was most likely to occur. This, he believed, by restricting nervous impulses, produced 'starvation of vital forces or energies' and could be corrected by spinal adjustment. He called the misalignment of the spinal vertebrae 'subluxation' and believed it to be the cause of virtually all disease.

Palmer's concept of an innate intelligence is now considered by many practitioners to be out of date, and even the subluxation itself is considered by some to be outmoded. The difference between osteopathy and chiropractic has in fact become much less marked in recent years, with many practitioners of both therapies using techniques from either discipline.

Some osteopaths and chiropractors, however, use reflexology, another form of ancient Chinese medicine, where pressure points in the foot are massaged. This again is believed to stimulate the healing forces present in the body. It is used to treat a wide range of disorders and is also employed as a method of diagnosis. As the cross-fertilisation of therapies increases, it is becoming much more difficult to distinguish between simple manipulation or massage, and the involvement of some form of unmeasurable energy.

Herbalism

Herbs can be therapeutic. In fact some drugs such as digitalis and morphine have been extracted from plants. The health-promoting properties of evening primrose and garlic, as we have seen, are now widely recognised. The roots of herbs such as comfrey reach right down to the subsoil, extracting valuable trace elements. Herbs contain a variety of medicinal qualities that can cleanse, stimulate or soothe.

Some herbalists, however, believe that plants have a vitalistic energy which can have an effect on the energy field of the patient, and they match the herbal remedy to the disharmony which they believe has caused the illness. Some, though by no means all, practitioners suggest that plants have psychic power, and information about the selection of herbal remedies is sometimes received during altered states of consciousness.

It has been suggested that our recent understanding of the effect of lunar cycles on plant growth, together with research into biorhythms, explains the occult beliefs of some herbalists. Kirlian photography is sometimes used to support claims of an energy field, which is claimed to permeate all life including herbs.

Kirlian photography

In 1939 a Soviet electrician and parapsychologist, Kirlian, discovered a photographic technique, named after him, which is supposed to show this energy field or 'aura'. If a person's hand is photographed by this method, the fingertips appear to radiate tiny bluish and reddish light effects. An aura or energy field round plants, herbs, leaves and seeds is also said to have been detected by this method.[9] Even acupuncture points have been photographed by Kirlian photography[10] and shown to change after acupuncture treatment and during disease. Changes in the aura have also been detected after yoga exercise.

Some scientists explain the phenomenon as an electrical one. But parapsychologists and some alternative practitioners are using Kirlian photographs to support their claims of the vital force postulated by Chinese and Hindu Scriptures. They claim that this proves that man has not just a physical body, but also an 'astral body'.

Auras are normally visible only in certain circumstances, and to people with psychic powers such as mediums, and it is widely believed that Kirlian photography is itself a paranormal technique. It is sometimes used to diagnose illness, though it is not very reliable. The procedure is very similar to palmistry, except that a hand print is obtained by the Kirlian photography. The photograph is then interpreted in order that a diagnosis can be made, and psychic abilities are sometimes used in the interpretation. The practitioner may then recommend another therapy such as acupuncture, or homeopathy.

Again we see differing opinions about the nature of Kirlian photography. Some explain it as a natural electromagnetic phenomenon, while others suggest that there is a paranormal element to it.

Does it matter if it works for you?

There are many more alternative therapies, too many to deal with in one chapter. Whatever explanation is given, a belief in some sort of vital energy or power that cannot be measured is held by at least some practitioners in most areas of alternative medicine, though there is considerable difference of opinion about the nature of the energy. But does it matter what the energy is, or where it comes from, so long as it is effective?

Therapies that are very clearly spiritual are becoming popular in holistic health circles, and a spiritual dimension to life is certainly recognised by many people seeking health and wholeness. So can we find a truly effective form of spirituality, fulfilment, and the answer to what determines how we act and relate to others, in the realm of the spiritual? Does it matter what area of the spiritual we choose? And are there subtle but dangerous spiritual influences that can determine how we act?

RECOMMENDED READING

Healing At Any Price by Samuel Pfeifer, MD, (Word Publishing) 1988.

18

INFLUENCES

Good nutrition, as we have seen, helps to build not only a healthy body, but also a healthy, resilient mind, since the brain, nerves and endocrine glands are nourished by the same food, water and air as the rest of the body. Our emotional reactions and our ability to relate to other people, as we have also seen, can have a direct bearing on our physical health by way of the hypothalamus, which is situated in the brain and is very responsive to emotions. In order to complete the circle of health we must consider what determines how we act and relate.

Making choices that build good health

Poor nutrition can affect the brain as well as the body. Destructive emotional states can damage the body as well as the mind. Does the same principle apply to the area of spiritual health? In other words, is there a spiritual version of junk food? We know that it's important to choose the right food. The right reactions and relationships are beneficial to health. Do we have to make a similar choice when we come to consider the spiritual?

There are still plenty of people who refuse to believe that there is such a thing as junk food. Will that protect them from the effect of low nutrient levels or food additives in their diet? Many people refuse to believe that their emotions can affect their physical health. Will that protect them from the physical effects of constant stress, bitterness or anger? Lots of people either refuse to believe that the spiritual exists at all, or won't accept the possibility of a harmful side to the spiritual. Will that protect them from any harmful spiritual effects?

As we saw in the last chapter, there are many alternative therapies that are believed by some to be spiritual in nature, and by others to be scientific, even if not yet demonstrably so. Other alternative therapies are widely accepted as having a psychic or spiritual explanation for their effectiveness. We are hearing a great many claims for the health benefits of hypnosis, trance states, mind control techniques, and the discovery of the inner self.

Pyramids and crystals are claimed to have healing properties. Then there's spiritual, pyschic or faith healing, inner healing, and healing of the emotions. We hear about regression into early or past life experiences, and the use of tarot cards or fortune telling for counselling and character assessment. Some healers go into altered states of consciousness in order to channel spirits through their own bodies so that they can be guided and empowered by these spiritual beings.

The alternative spectrum is broad. It stretches from simple manipulation and massage to mind control and spiritism. In between lie a vast array of therapies of disputed interpretation. Alan, a friend of mine, used to run training courses on massage. Working in the alternative sector brought him into contact with many other therapies and the people who practised them. 'There's nothing wrong with massage,' he told me. 'It's what some people overlay it with that causes the problem.'

Alternative medicine – not what it seems

It was this overlaying, or cross-fertilisation, of therapies among his colleagues, that caused Alan to begin to question what was happening to many of them. 'It seemed to me that they were chasing "the pot of gold at the end of the rainbow",' he explained. 'Always seeking peace and wholeness but never actually finding it. Everyone seemed to be messed up in some way. They talked about experiencing "enlightenment", yet it was so obvious that they weren't really happy at all.'

Alan told me that the initial stages of many therapies or practices seemed harmless but that people were inevitably drawn into some sort of mysticism. 'You see, a lot of these things *do* work enough of the time to convince people that they must be right,' he explained.

'Most of the people I came into contact with in those days, though rather gullible, were well-intentioned.'

Alan began to question the practices he was seeing all around him when he watched things going badly wrong. 'At a therapy workshop I once attended,' he told me, 'one man completely "flipped" and, from that time on, began to act more and more irrationally. He began to speak in tongues, to dress up in strange clothes and once used a stick to try to hold up a local cafe.'

Though Alan didn't fully appreciate what was happening around him, he recognised that overlaying many of the alternative therapies, there was a spiritual element that was harmful. Now, however, he understands the underlying nature of many of the practices he came into contact with in those days. 'People were messing around with forces that they thought they understood,' he explained, 'but in fact they didn't understand them at all.'

Experimenting with the paranormal

I had to agree with Alan, because I too have messed around with things that I was only to fully comprehend many years later. I suppose I first began to realise that I had some sort of unusual skill when I was in my late teens and discovered the art of dowsing. This is a variation on divining, when an object attached to the end of a cord is used to give answers to the practitioner's questions.

As with divining, which is often used to search for underground water sources, dowsing is dependent on the skill of the operator. I quickly discovered that I was very good at it. There was no mistaking the marked change in the direction of the pendulum when I used it. From an aimless swing, it would immediately change to a circular or a swinging movement depending on the answer to my question. I didn't give too much thought to how or why this could happen. It was fascinating, and seemed harmless enough.

I can't quite remember when I first used a ouija board, but from time to time over the years, the opportunity would crop up as I met people who were also interested in such things. Again, I didn't give a great deal of thought to it, nor pursue it with any fervour. But there was no mistaking the movement of the glass on the table or the credibility of the information given. Several of my friends were into these things, and I became more fascinated. We would have long discussions about the meaning of life and the possibility of something more.

I can clearly remember the day I bought a friend a pack of tarot cards. Our fascination with the supernatural had led us to the windswept hills of Lancashire and to Pendle, once the haunt of the witches of that area. A little stone shop stood alone on the top of a hill and was crammed with occult paraphernalia and replicas of witches riding their broomsticks. My friend had said that you should never buy your own tarot cards so I bought them for her. She was much more experienced and knowledgeable, and I admired her open-mindedness and her enquiring mind. As well as having made a study of the occult, she had also experimented with astral travel.

I had been freelancing as a photographer, and my friend had been working with me a couple of days a week. Even now, in my mind's eye, I can see us sitting in the tall grass under a brilliant blue sky, feel the warmth of the sunshine on my arms, and hear our animated discussions during the leisurely lunch breaks of that long hot summer. Neither of us had any time for religion. In fact we were both pretty scathing about what we saw as the indoctrination, narrow-mindedness, and bigotry of the Church. But we could never be atheists. We had both experienced too much of the supernatural. Whatever the explanation, there had to be more to life than the visible, the logical, the provable.

A dangerous obsession

In my unquestioning acceptance of the paranormal, it never dawned on me that I was opening my mind to spiritual forces that would alter my perceptions and opinions, influence my actions, and change my character. I saw no connection between my psychic activities, and the thoughts and emotions I then experienced. Anyway, I didn't do those things all that often. Most of the time I just got on with living my life and being myself. It all seemed so real, so right, so liberated, so modern. It was other people, I believed, who were dull, narrow-minded, restricted, old-fashioned.

Looking back now, it's difficult to understand how I could have been so blind when I thought I was anything but. There were odd times when I could see that I had changed. I was much more self centred than I'd once been; less tolerant of others, vain and rather obsessive and avaricious. But I put it down to the normal process of maturing and growing in self confidence. Life revolved mainly around me, my rights, my opinions and my plans. It was all self.

Not long ago, I talked to the friend I'd bought the tarot cards for all those years ago. She told me about her own tarot reading. 'The last card that is turned up', she said, 'is the one that is supposed to sum up the whole of your life.' Her last card had been 'The Fool'. With the benefit of hindsight, she can now see what had been the effects on her mind and emotions of dabbling with forces she hadn't understood.

'The only word I can use', she said, 'is obsession. That, I would say, is the word that sums it all up. I would get so obsessed that I couldn't concentrate on anything else.' That obsession, she was able to see with hindsight, had influenced her actions, and damaged her health for quite a few years. 'That card turned out to be so true,' she told me. 'What a fool I was.'

I asked her what she would say to anyone who was involved in any paranormal practice, either knowingly or unwittingly. She would be frightened for them, she told me, because they were going into the unknown. 'We don't realise what we are getting into,' she said. 'We don't know enough about it. We think that we are clever, but we are in fact dealing with spirits that are very, very clever indeed. They can even mimic God.'

But where's the harm?

A pendulum can be just a wooden ball or other object attached to the end of a cord, or sometimes a needle dangling at the end of threaded cotton. Of themselves these things are harmless. A ouija board is simply a board with letters on it and a needle to point to the letters, or an upturned drinking glass on a table and a circle of pieces of paper with letters on them. There's nothing wrong with a board, a table, a glass or pieces of paper with letters on them.

A pack of tarot cards is just a number of plastic-covered pieces of cardboard with pictures on them. How can any of these things be harmful? What could be wrong with a plastic triangle or a beautiful crystal? Intrinsically, there's *nothing* wrong with them. Neither is there anything wrong with flowers, aromatic oils or tablets that contain only infinitesimal amounts of the original substance. There's nothing wrong with exercise, manipulation or massage. But that's not the point.

As Alan warned, it's what some people overlay these things with that can cause the problem. What matters is what these things are used for, by whom and on whom. The objects themselves can distract attention from the real question that needs to be addressed. We shouldn't be asking *do* these things work? We should be asking *how* do these things work? And the place to look for the answer is not in the object itself, but at the forces that either practitioner or patient may be unwittingly unleashing.

It is a mistake to try to evaluate any practice or therapy simply on the basis of whether or not it appears to work. When you are dealing with that which cannot be explained scientifically, you need to use other criteria in order to evaluate it. Of course there must be many things that science will one day be able to measure or discover. But that doesn't mean everything that at present is claimed to be scientific will eventually be proven to have been so.

Unhealthy influences

C S Lewis wrote in 1942: 'There are two equal and opposite errors into which our race can fall about the devils. One is to disbelieve in their existence. The other is to believe, and to feel an excessive and unhealthy interest in them. They themselves are equally pleased by both errors and hail a materialist and a magician with the same delight.'[1]

The fact that there is a spiritual as well as a material realm can't be altered by a refusal to believe in it. It is there whether we believe in it or not. Spiritual forces exist and can influence us, whether or not we are aware of it. The problem we are facing today is that having gone through a period of materialism for many years, few people now understand the need for caution. Either they don't realise there's anything spiritual to be cautious about, or they unquestioningly accept anything spiritual so long as it appears to work.

When we ask what determines how we act, we must take into account spiritual as well as nutritional and environmental factors. Spiritual influences can affect how we act, how we react, and how we relate to others. The problem is that, at least to begin with, the effects are subtle and not easily recognised. Even when things begin to go wrong, the last explanation that is usually considered is a spiritual one.

Some people are more vulnerable than others. Psychic abilities may be inherited from previous generations, as many healers know. These people may be more easily affected by contact with either obvious or unrecognised spiritual practices. Those who are ill, or are already suffering from emotional problems may also be more vulnerable to psychic influences. Yet those times of emotional or physical health are often the very times that people seek such help. Sadly, any resulting increase in emotional problems may not be recognised as having been caused by psychic influences, and the same remedy may be sought again and again with a corresponding increase in symptoms.

The Oxford Dictionary definition of 'occult' is, 'involving the supernatural, mystical, magical; beyond the range of ordinary knowledge; not obvious on inspection'. To make detection even more difficult, the occult or psychic influences themselves can blind the mind to the true cause of mental symptoms, destructive emotional states, damaging reactions, inappropriate behaviour, or a deterioration in relationships. Thoughts and opinions can be influenced, as well as feelings about other people.

Tragic consequences

People who commit terrible crimes sometimes talk about 'voices' in their head that made them do these things. These people are invariably classed as schizophrenic, and the possibility that the person may have been affected by spiritual experiences is rarely considered. Yet psychic or spiritual influences can produce very compelling thoughts or, in extreme cases, can seem just like 'voices' in the mind, and these can have tragic consequences.

Recently I read a tragic report in a newspaper, about a fifty-two-year-old mother and her twenty-five-year-old daughter who had hurled themselves to their deaths from a Sussex headland. They were both spiritualists, and the inquest into their deaths revealed that they were convinced they were stepping into the afterlife. Notes found indicated that their deaths were planned. The mother's estranged husband was reported to have said, 'She was so confused by spiritualism.'[2]

Confusion is so often a hallmark of harmful spiritual influences, and your mind becomes your greatest enemy. You may become stressed, bitter, obsessed or compulsive. You either make a thousand excuses for your actions and emotions, or you begin to despair of yourself. And all the time, destructive emotions are damaging your health and your life.

These days we are reading a great deal about famous personalities who hit the headlines as a result of strange pronouncements or inappropriate behaviour. Newspaper and magazine articles simultaneously speculate critically on the reasons for such conduct, while running stories about these famous personalities' involvement with spiritism of one sort or another. So much condemnation and so little understanding!

Only those who know the subtle but compulsive nature of such harmful spiritual influences can make the connection, and empathise with the confusion and mental turmoil that drives people to act inappropriately. Unwary individuals who involve themselves in spiritism can become a pawn in a much wider spiritual strategy, and health problems, broken relationships, 'bad luck', and a downturn in personal circumstances often follow.

Beware of spiritual junk food

Yes, there is such a thing as 'spiritual junk food'. But, just as it has taken many, many years for our society to recognise the damage that refined foods can do to health, so the harm that certain spiritual practices can do has yet to be fully realised. One of the greatest barriers to the recognition of the harmful effects of white bread and sugar has been the fact that they are so commonplace. In the same way, the more widespread that astrology, fortune telling, and some alternative health therapies become, the harder it is to see any harm in them.

In chapter 16, I mentioned that I have talked to a lot of people about the importance of good nutrition, exercise, and natural light, to both physical and emotional health. And I have seen some make quite dramatic differences to their health by dealing with underlying conditions such as nutritional deficiencies, allergies, candida, or hypoglycaemia.

I also mentioned that it has become very clear over the years that all these things can do only a limited amount of good for people who are habitually worried, stressed, bitter, angry, obsessed, excessively ambitious or avaricious. It is worthwhile beginning by dealing with things like diet and lifestyle, in order to eliminate any physical causes of mental stress. But, if our attitudes themselves are the cause of the problem, they will continue to damage our health until they are dealt with.

For people who are suffering the emotional effects of harmful spiritual influences, improvements in diet or lifestyle rarely bring any health benefits until the spiritual problems are resolved. If we want to achieve optimum health, we not only need to deal with our diet and lifestyle, but also with the spiritual aspect of health.

We cannot go on struggling with the perplexities of social development without considering the spiritual side of human nature. Faced with ever increasing violent crime in our own country, we should investigate the possibility of a spiritual as well as a physical or emotional root to human behaviour. Surely we cannot go on watching man's inhumanity to man, graphically portrayed on our television screens, without coming to the conclusion that something is very wrong in the world.

The search for new convictions

As we saw in the last chapter, my friend J John wrote in 1989 that as human beings we interact with one another, and as we do so, we affect one another and condition one another's thinking, feeling and behaviour. He pointed out that each generation makes the world the place it is.

The health or ill health of the spiritual side of our nature affects our view of life, and is a major factor in determining the way we act.

Improved spiritual health can set us alight with new convictions, and enable us to recognise harmful spiritual practices and therapies. So how can we escape from the vicious circle of the subtle influences that affect us emotionally and physically, and improve our spiritual health?

RECOMMENDED READING

Healing At Any Price by Samuel Pfeifer, MD, (Word Publishing 1988).

19

A WAY OF ESCAPE

Anxiety, stress, bitterness, obsession, excessive ambition or avarice can damage emotional and physical health, and ruin relationships. People who are driven in this way may make a thousand excuses for their attitudes, or they may come to despair of themselves. Neither response can solve the problem and provide an escape from such damaging emotional states. So what really is the cause of our wrong motives and selfish actions? Basically, the problem is and always has been us.

As human beings we interact with one another and, as we do so, we affect each other's thinking, feeling and behaviour. So how can we become more loving towards others, and build healthy relationships? For our own sakes, and for the sake of our loved ones, we need, not only to know what determines how we act and relate, but also to know what we can do about it. If the problem is basically us, then it's ourselves that need to be changed. But how?

Do we need to have new convictions, a new view of life, or new beliefs? How can we do this? And how can we satisfy that yearning inside that leaves us feeling unfulfilled, in spite of relationships, promotion or possessions?

J John has travelled, not only in Britain, but all around the world talking about what determines how we act and how we can be set alight with new convictions. He is quick to point out that many people try to live good lives and that by and large they succeed. Though we regularly hear of marriage breakdown, many marriages (the ones we don't read about in the newspapers) hold fast with honour, faithfulness and love. 'We still have enough "health" left in us', he says, 'to perceive that we are not truly healthy.'

True health in every area of life

So what's stopping us from being truly healthy? What's preventing us from having peace of mind? And why can't we avoid or deal with the stresses in our lives? 'The problem is that many people have forgotten God,' J John explains. 'The more we choose to place ourselves at the centre of life, the lower we place humanity. True humanism lies where God, and not man, is at the centre of all.' That's all very well, but how can we place God at the centre of our lives unless we believe in him?

With words that seem to echo Dr Barlow's, written nearly fifty years ago, J John wrote in 1989: 'Some people are so busy enjoying God's creation that they forget to acknowledge that there is a God behind it.'[1] Some atheists maintain that the evidence of science proves that there is no God. Some agnostics want proof before they will accept that God exists. But how can we find out whether or not there really is a God?

There is the story of a group of people who were discussing faith. 'I was raised on the scientific method,' said one, 'and no one has ever been able to prove to me scientifically that God exists.' Another of the group responded, 'I have a similar problem. I was raised on the theological method and no one has ever been able to prove to me theologically that an atom exists.' 'But who ever heard of finding an atom by theology?' exclaimed the sceptic. 'Exactly,' the other replied.

Faith in God, is based on evidence just as surely as science is. The difference is in the kind of evidence on which each is based. We cannot define God in scientific terms. To tackle the issue of God's existence purely scientifically or mathematically just doesn't work. We must have another way of approaching the issue. God is not just a mechanical life force. God is personal.

Some people insist that they cannot possibly believe in God for a variety of reasons, or they want to know all the answers before they will even consider the possibility. They want someone to first satisfy all their questions, before they are prepared to believe in God. 'That is proud and arrogant,' J John insists. 'Mankind is not the centre of the universe with God on trial. God is at the centre of the universe with mankind on trial. And mankind, frankly speaking, has made a real mess of things.'

How can we know?

So how can we know for certain that God exists? And how will that enable us to change ourselves and relationships? Let me tell you what happened to me at the end of the seventies. By the time I'd reached my thirties I suppose I'd become an agnostic. I didn't know whether God existed or not and, to tell the truth, I really didn't care. Even my supernatural experiences had left me with no great need for a belief in God. For the previous five years I had been becoming more and more interested in the relationship between nutrition and health, spending a lot of time reading and writing on the subject.

Marge was one of those people to whom I preached my 'gospel of good grub'. But while I was preaching my gospel to her, she was preaching another gospel to me, and I didn't like it. I'd long since stopped believing in what she was talking about and, to me, she sounded naive and old-fashioned. Did she really believe that God had sent his son to die so that our sins could be forgiven, and that Jesus would one day come again, I asked her?

Could she possibly expect me to believe that she had the truth about eternal life? For that matter, how could she be so sure that there was life after death? I wasn't an atheist. I certainly believed in some sort of 'other' world after my experiences with the paranormal. I had no doubt that the supernatural existed, and I'd considered all sorts of possibilities, but the only thing I felt sure of was that there definitely was something more.

But, whatever else there might be, I wasn't looking for the sort of religion that Marge kept on talking about. My children would soon both be at school and I had plans. I was looking forward to having a little time to myself and resuming my career. I wanted to 'do my own thing', and the last thing I needed to hear was that I couldn't just 'do my own thing' if I wanted to have eternal life. I out-argued Marge every time I saw her. I was sarcastic, cynical and, at times, downright rude.

Time to make up our minds

She annoyed me with her old-fashioned beliefs and her blind faith. I even began to doubt her sanity when she told me that God guided her, and I resolved to do everything in my power to convince her that she was being brainwashed. What on earth was a woman of her age doing believing those ridiculous notions? I'd had the sense to throw them out in my teens and I certainly wasn't going to be taken in now by a seemingly neurotic woman who believed that a religious history book was the word of God and, as such, should be obeyed.

After about six months of unsuccessful reasoning with her, I decided that the best policy would be to avoid her altogether. I was getting nowhere. She wouldn't be shaken and, anyway, it was embarrassing hearing her talk about religion all the time. I'd done everything in my power to make her see sense but now it was time to give up.

For some reason, however, I just couldn't keep away, and I'd find myself walking round to her house. We'd have an argument that I invariably won, and I'd storm off thinking, 'that sorted her out'. But a few days later I'd be back again, going over the same old arguments. Why didn't I stay away? What was it that drove me back time and time again? And why was it that the more I tried to convince her, the more I found it was myself I was trying to convince?

By the time twelve months had passed I was getting desperate. All I wanted was to get on with my own life and my own plans. The last thing I needed was to have to be answerable to someone other than myself. But what if there really was a God? 'If Marge is wrong and there is no judgment after death,' I reasoned, 'then she'll never know she's wrong. But if Marge is right and I'm wrong, that could be a very different matter! And what if there is a God, and my plans are not his plans?'

There are enough problems to cope with in life, I thought, without going against God, if he existed. In fact, I decided that if God did exist and I was going against him, I really didn't fancy my chances. Could Marge possibly be right? God wouldn't really guide her, would he? I still wasn't prepared to believe what Marge told me, nor anyone else for that matter, but if somehow I could know for myself that God existed, then I'd have to believe, wouldn't I?

Discovering spiritual reality

A more reluctant 'seeker' would be hard to find. My motives were far from noble, based more on self preservation, and the fact that I was never one to 'bury my head in the sand'. I had to know. If something was true, I couldn't make it untrue by refusing to believe it. I'd rather find out in this life that I was mistaken, than find out in the next.

Somehow I knew that it was no use expecting God to reveal himself in order that I should do whatever he wanted me to do. Rather, I had to try to do whatever I felt that he, if he existed, would want me to do, in order that he would make his presence felt. I didn't understand how or why I knew this, but somehow I definitely did know it. That little bit of inspiration proved to be the key that opened the door to understanding.

I told Marge that I would go to church with her, read the Bible, and try to do what I felt that God, if he existed, would want me to do. One month I would give it, I insisted, and if nothing happened, she could shut up and leave me alone so that I could get on with my life. Just in case there really was a God, though, I said a little prayer and promised that if he would reveal himself to me, I would do whatever he asked of me for the rest of my life. Though I have to admit that I didn't think that there was much danger of my having to keep that promise, nevertheless I really meant that prayer.

Oh what I'd have given for that month to pass uneventfully! Before long, however, I began to be aware that God was very near. I didn't know why or how I knew this – I just knew it. I began to understand things I hadn't been able to understand before. I found that things that were happening to me were described in the Bible. It was uncanny, and though I still fought against believing that Marge had been right all along, it became more and more difficult to rationalise away what was happening to me.

I didn't know it at the time, but in fact I was experiencing what Jesus meant when he said, *'My teaching is not my own. It comes from him who sent me. If anyone chooses to do God's will, he will find out whether my teaching comes from God or whether I speak on my own.'*[2] Before long, I realised that my life would never be the same again, and I shall be grateful to Marge forever for her prayers and her perseverance.

Take a healthy look at yourself

In his book *Life Means What?*,[3] J John wrote, 'There is no such thing as seeking the truth and then finding Christ. Christ is the truth.' J John explains that all you have to do is to start looking for him quietly through the pages of the Bible where he is shown as a living God, reaching out to people in history and today. But he also wrote, 'Anyone who wants to be in touch with this creative, living God has to let go of the conventional values that prize power, profits and pride of intellect.'

Our worldly motives, attitudes and reactions make it difficult for us to believe in God. But, not believing in God, it can be difficult to see what is wrong with our motives, attitudes and reactions. A 'Catch 22' situation! It's like the man in court, pleading innocence, who listens for several hours to the court proceedings and then shouts, 'I'm guilty!' The judge turns to him and says, 'Why didn't you say that several hours ago?' 'Well,' replies the man, 'I didn't realise I was guilty till I heard all the evidence!'

I was rather like the man in the courtroom when I rather arrogantly gave God a month to reveal himself to me. Even though I realised that I ought to do what I thought that God would want me to do, I didn't feel that I had any real faults. For me the process of learning about myself was gradual, but without it, I could never have known real, lasting happiness. To begin with, it can be painful to come to the realisation that your attitudes and actions are wrong. But forgiveness is healing, and the very real experience of knowing God's forgiving love gradually changes the way we see things.

That love calms the anxious mind and fills the lonely heart. It brings meaning and purpose to the life that seems to be going nowhere. It determines how we act, and sets us alight with new convictions. And it enables us to be more loving towards others. The process of change is gradual and must continue for a lifetime. There *is* a time for regret, but it's not the destructive emotion that eats away at us, rather a constructive regret that enables us to learn lessons from our mistakes. There's no instant perfection or easy answers, but instead a growing desire to be changed by God into the person you were always meant to become.

Liberating laws of life

In 1942, in his book *Discipline of Peace*,[4] Dr Barlow was dismissive of the concept that man in his natural state was perfectible in his own right. He didn't accept that man would know what is best for himself and that, knowing his own good, he required no conditioning. And he warned against philosophies that attempted to free man from the checks and controls of any organisation greater than himself.

In 1990, in his book *Ten Steps to the Good Life*,[5] J John wrote: 'Law is at the heart of liberty. Laws do not restrict us — they free us to live in order and harmony.' Of the ten commandments listed in the Bible, he said, 'They were not made for any particular period in history. They were based on human nature and therefore are commandments for all seasons, for all centuries, as universal and perpetual as honour and truth.'

Imagine what would happen if all the millions of commuters read the Bible instead of their daily newspaper. Would our nation not change? John Henry Newman once said, 'I read the newspaper to see what people are doing, and I read the Bible to know what people ought to do.'

'How much of what we call "competitiveness",' J John asks, 'is really envy or greed?' He points out that there are tendencies and drives in us that have become self-destructive compulsions through the influence of countless words and actions of other people. He is right, isn't he? We are so often influenced by other people. In contrast, how refreshing it is to be with people who don't evaluate us by who we are or what we own, but simply care about us. Imagine a world full of such people!

We can sometimes be very adept at justifying the self-destructive compulsions that drive us beyond what is good for our health and our relationships. We may project those compulsions on to others, or we may find ourselves being manipulated by others. It's good to have our self-destructive motives, attitudes and reactions altered, and to be set alight with new convictions. And the simple words, 'I'm so sorry', can often heal relationships.

The checks and controls of a being greater and wiser than ourselves can free us to live life to the full. We may spend many years searching for health and happiness in the wrong place, only to discover that

God knows better than we do about what is best for us. We don't possess possessions. They possess us. They rob us of precious time and lock us into a way of life and a philosophy that is able to tell us so little about everything that is of importance.

Where to begin

What can we do when we feel trapped in a lifestyle that isn't conducive to personal or family health? What can we do when harmful attitudes are damaging our emotional and physical health? What can we do? We can begin. We can begin by ensuring that underlying health problems aren't affecting our emotional health, by returning to the simple unprocessed foods that nature provides for our health.

We can begin, as Dr Barlow suggested nearly fifty years ago, by returning in humility to ask what is greater than ourselves in order that we may know 'the discipline to which the gift of life and liberty compels our obedience'. And we can begin by starting to look quietly through the pages of the Bible for the answer to that question.

But we need to remember that anyone who wants to be in touch with the creative, living God found in the pages of the Bible, must start by letting go of the conventional values that prize power, profits and pride of intellect above all else. We can begin by asking ourselves what motives determine how we, personally, act. And we can begin by being set alight with new convictions as the realisation of God's love and infinite wisdom inspires our hearts and minds.

A gateway to freedom

But there is a very specific gateway through which we must pass, if we want to find the way of escape from the harmful attitudes, emotions, and influences that determine our actions and our ability to build healthy relationships. Everyone must pass through this gateway in order to experience peace of mind and eternal happiness. The gateway is called repentance, and it is healing and restorative. Without it there can be no enduring faith, no way to make peace with God, and no escape from harmful spiritual influences.

No matter how compulsive those attitudes, emotions, or spiritual influences may have been, the basic problem is and always has been us. Whether we make a thousand excuses for our actions, or we despair of ourselves, we can never save ourselves from ourselves. Repentance is not simply an acknowledgment that we have been wrong, though that's a good start. No, it's a change of heart that cannot be manufactured, only prayed for. True repentance is God-given and it's painful. But, once experienced, there is no mistaking its life-changing effects.

I hadn't really understood this properly when I first realised that God really does exist, and I promised to do whatever he asked of me for the rest of my life. I knew immediately that my life would never be the same again, and acknowledged that I was sinful. I even expressed sorrow for all the things I'd done wrong in my life. But I continued to justify myself. It's so easy, isn't it, to blame your circumstances or other people for your own actions.

By doing so, however, I stopped short of passing through that important gateway, and escaping from the attitudes, emotions and spiritual influences that had driven me for so many years. I remained vulnerable, and impotent to really change myself. And, though I began to experience new convictions, I missed out on so many of the benefits of real spiritual health.

A few years passed by before I was blessed with the experience of true repentance that finally swept away the blindness that had caused me to consistently justify myself, and to be unable to see things as they really were. Only then was I able to experience the God-given power that makes enduring change possible. Up till then my faith had been based on a shallow enthusiasm that so often burned out, leaving me to relapse into long-held attitudes and old ways.

Entering wholeness – optimum health

But my experience of deep repentance changed all that and at last I could know forgiveness, peace of mind, and a completely different outlook on life. At last that yearning inside could be satisfied, and I was able to understand that, all along, it had been the yearning to worship God, which is implanted in us by

God himself. For many years I had been trying to fill that gap with things that didn't fit. Now at last I could begin to experience the benefits of all round optimum health: physical, emotional and spiritual.

Many years ago, in the village where I used to live, there practised an old doctor. Often he would tell his patients that they could find the answer to their problems if they would only look in the Bible. That wise old doctor has been dead for many years now, but I'll never forget the advice he used to give. He knew the importance to our emotional and our physical health of the spiritual aspect of our nature.

There's a lot more truth in the Bible than first meets the eye. My favourite example of this is the passage of Scripture, 'And the Lord God formed man from the dust of the ground and breathed into his nostrils the breath of life, and man became a living being.'[6]

Taken superficially, this passage paints a rather comical scene. However, as I began to learn about the vital role of minerals in every function, organ and structure of the body, that passage of Scripture took on a whole new depth of meaning. Calcium, magnesium, zinc, chromium and all the other vitally important minerals are, after all, nothing more than the dust of the ground!

In chapter 16 I quoted from Dr Barlow's book, *Discipline of Peace*: 'The awareness of design in nature came to our early forefathers from a faculty of reverence which is, in our society, atrophied.' These people worshipped God, Dr Barlow noted, and 'we cannot help but see that their life had a wholeness which ours lacks'.[7]

Pinned above my desk is a little saying, 'The person who fails in prayer, fails in everything.' This is a useful reminder for me when life gets hectic, and it's tempting to rush into the day without taking the time to pray. Prayer reduces stress and brings peace of mind. It satisfies that longing deep inside, and opens the door to God's love. Prayer is the key to the gateway of repentance, and the pathway to spiritual understanding.

When evaluating new concepts in every area of health, it's good to balance old, long-held ideas against new ones – from the pioneer nutritionists and doctors who recognised the relationship between physical and emotional health, to our early spiritual forefathers whose lives displayed such wholeness.

But whether we are looking at the old or the new, we still need to be able to distinguish the helpful from the harmful, and nowhere more so than in the area of the spiritual.

RECOMMENDED READING

Dead Sure? by J John (IVP/Frameworks 1989).
Life Means What? by J John (Hodder and Stoughton 1990).
Ten Steps to the Good Life by J John (Hodder and Stoughton 1990).

20

SPIRITUAL IMMUNE SYSTEM

I'd got the impression that, by becoming a Christian, I would be automatically transformed into the person I knew I ought to be. Instead I became much more aware of my faults. I began to wonder what on earth had gone wrong for me, and spent my first few years as a Christian thinking that somewhere, if only I could find it, there had to be an experience that would make that dramatic difference in me.

I received prayer for the filling of the Holy Spirit, spoke in tongues, and practised meditation and visualisation. Christian counselling was recommended in order to heal earlier traumatic experiences and memories. Both I and my house were prayed over to deal with the effects of my past occult practices. It was suggested that I should receive prayer for what was described as a 'new heart experience'. Messages and prophecies were given to me by Christians who experienced inner voices and revelations. And I myself began to receive supernatural knowledge, prophecies and other phenomena. But little improved.

But though I tried everything that was suggested or that I read about, nothing really seemed to be able to make the change that, deep down in my heart, I'd begun to long for so much. If only I'd realised at the very beginning that the longing itself is the very best possible assurance a person can have that God is working in their life. Instead I just thought that I was a complete failure.

In desperation I went into a Christian bookshop in the centre of Liverpool in the hope that I might find a book that would tell me what to do. There was an elderly lady serving in the shop that day. I must have said something to her, I can't remember, but I can clearly recall that she had a lovely kind face and, very gently, she suggested that I should be careful to check everything that I read, and everything that I was told, by reading the Bible for myself. I'll never forget that moment. Something inside me seemed to respond to her words and I knew immediately that I had to act upon her advice.

I made a decision there and then to try to put out of my mind all the explanations I'd ever read or heard about what the Bible says on this or that, and to start all over again. That I would read the Bible afresh, but this time with an open mind. And, most important of all, I would pray for help and understanding. By now I'd got so heartily fed up of being unable to change myself that nothing seemed to matter more than that I should know what Jesus himself said about the Christian life.

Willing to try

Soon I began to comprehend things that have been known by Christians for centuries, but which I'd never before understood. Later, as I began to read some of the work of Christians of previous centuries, I discovered in their writing the very things that I'd started to learn for myself.

They described the longing to be different, the hunger for truth, and the deep desire to do whatever God asks. They also described the battle to be what you know you should be, and to do what you know you ought to do. Those Christian men of old offered no instant answers, no one-off spiritual experience, and no immediate perfection. But their realistic words made so much sense and offered so much hope. They confirmed what I'd begun to learn for myself, as I'd prayed for understanding and read the Bible afresh.

I learned that 'obedience' doesn't mean being perfect, but *trying*. That a Christian can't immediately get everything right, but only needs to *begin*. And I learned that the place to begin is with whatever is, right now, 'pricking your conscience'. One of those early Christian writers, George MacDonald, put it this way: 'We must learn to obey him in everything, and so just begin somewhere; let it be at once, and in the very next thing that lies at the door of your conscience.'[1]

Eventually I realised that, if I was willing to try, then I would be opening the door to God to begin to transform me. It wouldn't be me who changed myself, but God who changed me gradually throughout the rest of my life. All I had to do was to try, and to keep on trying, to 'show willing'. After all those years of searching for that one experience that would make the difference, I found that all I ever have to think about is that one thing that is 'knocking at the door of my conscience'.

As I began to read the Bible with the express intention of finding out what God wanted me to do and to be, I would become aware of a particular fault in me that needed dealing with. Something would come 'knocking at the door'. Let me use a parallel from nutrition to explain.

Just as years of eating the wrong sort of foods can result in a jaded palate, the conscience that is ignored becomes dulled. As you begin to eat the right foods, you start to re-educate your palate and to enjoy healthy foods. Similarly, when you start to respond to what your conscience is telling you, it becomes sharper.

Once you've got used to a better diet, you notice the difference if you go back to your old ways, and the lure of optimum health draws you back to a healthy diet. And once you've got used to responding to your conscience, it becomes much harder to go against it until, in the end, it becomes easier to respond than to ignore it. Gradually, your perspectives, your feelings and your actions change, imperceptibly at first. It's only really as you look back over the years that you can see just how much God has changed you.

It can be hard at first to accept the fact that simple, unsophisticated, natural foods could be so important to physical health. So too in my search for instant spiritual solutions I had missed the simple answer. In fact its very simplicity can make it hard to accept that to just try to do what your conscience is telling you can have such a profound effect on your physical, your emotional and your spiritual health, on your actions, your reactions and your relationships.

A lack of understanding of the vital importance of that deep longing to be changed, which is the clearest evidence that the work of God has begun in a person's life, can make the new Christian vulnerable to distorted doctrines. Any teaching which gives the impression that there's nothing more to be done in a Christian's life, can give a false sense of security. And any insistence that every Christian should be miraculously healed, and that the absence of healing is due to a lack of faith, can cause incredible distress.

Spiritual immune system

Reading the Bible prayerfully, and responding to your conscience, however, brings another, very important benefit. I'll use another analogy. The more physically healthy a person is, the better their immune system is able to recognise and reject pathogens, the agents capable of damaging physical health. Similarly, the more spiritually healthy a person is, the more easily their 'spiritual immune system' can recognise and reject 'spiritual pathogens' capable of damaging spiritual health. At the end of the last century, the Bishop of Liverpool, J C Ryle, wrote:

> There is a spiritual instinct in most true believers which generally enables them to distinguish between true and false teaching. When they hear unsound religious instruction, there is something within them which says, 'This is wrong.' When they hear the real truth as it is in Jesus, there is something in their hearts which responds, 'This is right.' The careless man of the world may see no difference whatever between minister and minister, sermon and sermon. The poorest sheep of Christ, as a general rule, will 'distinguish things that differ', though he may be unable to explain why. Let us beware of despising this spiritual instinct. Whatever a sneering world may please to say, it is one of the peculiar marks of the indwelling of the Holy Ghost.[2]

That spiritual instinct is an uncomfortable feeling, deep down inside, which will warn you that some explanation, therapy, or practice is not from God. The normal processes of the mind can then translate into words what that feeling is telling you. 'I don't feel comfortable about this,' you might say. 'Something feels wrong, somewhere.'

This is very important when it comes to spiritual matters. That instinct which, like the conscience, is felt deep down inside, and which can be translated into words by the normal processes of the mind, is the way that God warns and guides us.

I can clearly remember experiencing that uncomfortable feeling when, as a teenager, I first started to use occult practices but, sadly, I ignored it. Eventually I didn't feel it any more. As I ignored what my 'spiritual immune system' had been telling me, it became dulled like my conscience. God communicates with us in a way that is very similar to the way that our conscience works.

We need to be aware of the difference between the way that God pricks our conscience, warns us about danger, or guides us, and the way that harmful spiritual influences affect the mind as a result of occult practices. These spiritual influences may come as ready-formed words and sentences, that 'pop' into the mind. No matter what explanation is given for a paranormal practice or therapy, no matter how certain the practitioner is that it must be scientific, or that it must come from God, never ignore that uncomfortable instinctive feeling if you experience it.

In the area of alternative medicine it is impossible to generalise about what is safe and what isn't. As we saw earlier, there is so much cross-fertilisation now, and so many harmful practices may be overlaid on beneficial therapies such as massage, manipulation and herbalism, that we need another way of knowing what is involved. When you come up against the supernatural, whether it's obvious or not, you need a healthy 'spiritual immune system' to guide you.

Trusting your spiritual instinct

The youngest Christian, as much as the maturest, will at times experience that uncomfortable feeling. But the young Christian may not have the self confidence to trust their spiritual instinct. They may be intimidated by either scientific or spiritual explanations. On the other hand, no matter how many years a person has been a Christian, if they have not been aware of the need to check everything, they may as a result, have unwittingly been involved in harmful spiritual experiences or practices. Or they may not have fully recognised the need to co-operate with God in the changes that must be made in them. In either case, their spiritual instinct will have been dulled.

New Christians, in their desire to be 'Christian' in all their dealings, may be intimidated by the assertions of older Christians that certain supernatural practices must be from God. The strange attitudes or behaviour of some Christians may worry these new Christians. But their lack of confidence, and fear of being judgmental, can cause them to override the God-given warning that they are experiencing. Yet the Bible says, 'Test everything. Hold on to the good.'[3]

During the first couple of years after I'd decided to become a Christian, in my search for instant answers, and my genuine desire to please God, I accepted too much, too easily. I experienced for myself the effects of becoming involved in supernatural practices that were not from God, and yet were being done by Christians.

I didn't have enough confidence, to begin with, in the uncomfortable instinctive feeling, warning me that something was wrong. But the eventual realisation of what had actually been happening, though painful at the time, has helped me over the years to understand what can make some Christians behave in ways that the ordinary 'man in the street' can see straight through.

False spirits

Spirits can mimic God, and this can result in faulty perceptions about what is and what isn't from God. The Holy Spirit most certainly does inspire, guide and lift Christians, but not everything supernatural that happens in Christian circles is necessarily the work of the Holy Spirit.

Unfortunately a lack of understanding about this can result in people accepting and practising such things. They can then come under the influence of the harmful spiritual forces they are unwittingly messing around with. And, as a result, they may become so convinced they must be right that it can be impossible to reason with them.

This is much more than 'blind faith'. It's much more than hysteria, and it's a problem that needs to be faced. Christians can either fall into the error of refusing to believe that such spiritual influences exist, or they can fall into the error of having an excessive, unhealthy interest in them. The person who sees demons on every corner has probably missed the most relevant demonic influence of all – the one that has convinced them they need to cast demons out of everything that moves!

Standing against what people around you think is from God can be lonely. You may be accused of narrow-mindedness or lack of spirituality. But there *is* a spiritual equivalent of junk food, even within some Christian churches and groups. We can be harmed by such 'spiritual junk food'; what we need is 'spiritual wholefood'. There are plenty of Christians who refuse to believe that harmful spiritual practices could possibly happen in Christian circles, but that won't protect them from their effects.

Transformed lives, not supernatural experiences, are the evidence that God is at work. And, though that transformation must continue for the rest of our lives, we are particularly vulnerable until it has become absolutely clear that the process has begun. Crucial to that beginning is the God-given heart experience of repentance. It is the gateway to a mature, committed and enduring faith, and the prerequisite for a healthy 'spiritual immune system'.

Truth is your guide

Many today believe that truth is relative. 'That's your truth,' they say, convinced that whatever you believe is fine so long as it suits you. But more important than what we *choose* to believe, is God's revealed truth. Truth *is* absolute and God alone can impart it. But he will only do so to the one who 'returns in humility to ask what is greater than man, and is willing to accept the need for discipline and obedience'.

Then and only then, can we really call ourselves Christians. In these days of Christian liberalism and fundamentalism, the need for balanced Christian truth is as vital as it has ever been. We must be constantly vigilant about what we involve ourselves in, if we want to retain the benefits of improved spiritual health.

> In matters of faith and science I am more impressed by one evident reason or by one authoritative passage of Holy Writ correctly understood than by the chorus of mankind. I am not ashamed to be convinced of truth. In fact, to have truth victorious over me I estimate the most useful thing for me. But I never want to be defeated by the multitude. It may, indeed, be read in the sacred utterances that the multitude, as a rule, errs, and that very often one solitary man may put all the rest to flight.
>
> William of Ockham, Proem VI, 1349

In the areas of health and ecology, brave and far-sighted individuals have, in the past, spoken out against the majority view, and the passing of time has vindicated them. We each have just one body, one mind and one soul. If we want to achieve optimum health, we mustn't allow ourselves to be defeated by the multitude. We should take into account the warnings of those today who claim that, in some areas of health, the majority have still got it wrong.

In the area of the spiritual, many paranormal practices are accepted by the majority, so let's not be defeated by the majority here either. Instead, let's remember our God and seek his truth in humility and obedience. We have more to think about than just this life. There is eternity to consider, and the healthiest person on this earth must one day depart it.

'For dust you are, and to dust you will return.'[4]

APPENDIX 1

MENUS

As a general guide, the ideal daily diet should consist of:
10%–20% protein foods (meat, fish, eggs, milk, cheese, pulses, nuts).
45%–65% vegetables, salads, and fresh fruits.
20%–40% potatoes and natural whole grains (in bread, crispbread, muesli, baked products and cereals like rice).

General basic menu

The following daily menu is a basic guide to get you started. It can be built upon and varied according to individual tastes, appetite, and needs (such as food sensitivities). Specific ingredients can be chosen to compensate for any particular nutrients known to be deficient (see appendix 3), and many recipes, both English and foreign, can be adapted to use wholefood ingredients (see appendix 2).

On waking
molasses and the juice of half a lemon in hot water (see appendix 2)
– or the juice of half a lemon in carbonated or plain spring water
– or natural fruit juice diluted with carbonated or plain spring water
– or herb tea made with spring water

Breakfast
natural yoghurt and wheat germ
– or organic porridge (see appendix 2)

– or muesli with milk, yoghurt, or fruit juice (see recipe in appendix 2)
– and/or fresh fruit
– and/or egg(s) (preferably free range) boiled, poached or scrambled with wholemeal toast
– or fresh fish, grilled, steamed or poached

Mid-morning
milk (if tolerated)
– or herb tea
– or spring water
– or fruit juice diluted with carbonated or plain spring water
– if needed a piece of fruit
– or a few seeds or shelled nuts
– or wholemeal sandwich or crispbread

Lunch
home-made soup
large fresh salad, sprinkled with nuts, seeds or sprouted beans
– or wholemeal salad sandwiches, or jacket potato
– or crudités (raw vegetable sticks and florets, usually eaten with a dip)
fresh fruit, or natural yoghurt or junket for dessert

Mid-afternoon
as mid-morning

Main meal
protein with a side salad or a leafy green vegetable and a root vegetable (lightly cooked – steamed if possible), potatoes, baked or steamed in their skins, or whole grain cereal such as rice
– and raw fresh fruit, or fruit salad with natural yoghurt, or apple with celery and wholemeal crispbread and cheese, or a wholefood dessert

Mid-evening
as mid-morning

For non-vegetarians
fish at least twice a week
organ meat once or twice a week
muscle meats up to three or four times a week (avoid serving meat
more than once a day)

Note: Use simple salad dressing on salads (see appendix 2 for
recipe).

Elimination menu

This is for the detection of masked allergies to milk, eggs, wheat,
chocolate. It is also suitable for candida and hypoglycaemia.

Note: People are often addicted to the foods they are allergic to
and so may suffer from withdrawal symptoms such as a headache or
craving. They will pass.

WEEK ONE

Avoid milk, cheese, eggs, wheat, chocolate, and sugar in any form.
Also avoid tea, coffee and alcohol.

On waking
the juice of half a lemon in carbonated or plain spring water
– or herb tea made with spring water

Breakfast
fresh fruit and freshly shelled nuts
– or organic porridge, made and eaten without milk
– or home-made muesli (see appendix 2) and chopped fruit with fruit
    juice
– and/or fresh fish, grilled, steamed or poached

Mid-morning
herb tea
— or spring water
— or fruit juice, well diluted with carbonated or plain spring water
— if needed a few seeds or shelled nuts and/or raw vegetable sticks
or florets
— or rye crispbread with lettuce, sliced cucumber, pepper, tomato

Lunch
large fresh salad, sprinkled with nuts, seeds or sprouted beans
— or crudités (raw vegetable sticks and florets)
— and/or wholemeal rye crispbread with lettuce, sliced cucumber or
   tomato
— and/or jacket potato
one piece of fresh fruit for dessert

Mid-afternoon
as mid-morning

Main meal
protein with a side salad or a leafy green vegetable and a root
vegetable (lightly cooked – steamed if possible), potatoes, baked
or steamed in their skins, or whole grain rice
and raw fresh fruit, or fruit salad

Mid-evening
as mid-morning

For non-vegetarians
fish at least twice a week
organ meat once or twice a week
muscle meats up to three or four times a week (avoid serving meat
more than once a day if possible)

Note: Use simple salad dressing on salads (see appendix 2 for
recipe).

At this point you can begin to test for reactions to the eliminated foods, one at a time. I have set out the next steps weekly to give plenty of time for reactions to show. If you have a reaction to a food, cut it out immediately and go back to the previous menu for the rest of that week. You can speed the process up if you wish by using the week two menu for only half of the week, then going on to the week three menu for the rest of the week, and so on.

WEEK TWO

This week is the same as week one except for the addition of junket (see appendix 2 for the recipe – eat as much as you like every day). Since junket is made with milk, you will react to the junket if you are allergic to milk. However, if you are simply unable to digest milk, you should not react to the junket since the rennet with which it is made pre-digests the milk.

(See appendix 6 for common symptoms of food sensitivity.)

Note: If you react to the junket, cut it out again for the rest of the week, then move straight to week four.

WEEK THREE

This week is the same as week one and week two if you have had no reaction to the junket, except that this week you will add milk. Now you can drink milk and have it with your porridge or home-made muesli. You can also eat natural yoghurt as well as drinking milk itself. Watch for any reactions. (See appendix 6 for common symptoms of food allergies.)

Note: If you react to the milk, cut it out again for the rest of the week, then move to week four.

WEEK FOUR

If you reacted to the milk, then leave both the milk and the junket out for the moment (you can try the junket again when you have finished the elimination course). If you had no reaction to either junket or milk, then leave them both in this week's menu.

This week stick to the basic menu, with the addition of milk and junket if you've had no reaction to them, introduce eggs and eat one every day. Watch for any reactions. (See appendix 6 for common symptoms of food allergies.)

Note: If you react to the eggs, cut them out again for the rest of the week, then move to week five.

WEEK FIVE

This week stick to the basic menu, with the addition of any of the foods introduced which have caused no problems, add wheat to the menu and eat it every day. Watch for any reactions. (See appendix 6 for common symptoms of food allergies.)

Note: If you react to the wheat, cut it out again for the rest of the week.

You can now test chocolate if you wish, but even if you don't react immediately to it, it could still be a problem if there is candida or hypoglycaemia. If you have noticed a marked improvement in your health over the past few weeks, it may well also be due to cutting out sugar and refined carbohydrates. This would improve either or both candida and hypoglycaemia. If you suspect that you have suffered from candida, avoid bread and any other foods that contain yeast (and see chapter 8). If you suspect hypoglycaemia, keep fruit and fruit juices to a minimum (and see chapter 9).

If you have had no reaction to any of the foods, then you can switch to the General Basic Menu. However, if you have reacted to any of the foods, leave them out of your diet for a few months then try them again cautiously. You may find that you are able to eat them occasionally in the future, so long as you don't overdo them. If you reacted to milk but not junket, include junket in your menu. You may even be able to tolerate natural yoghurt since it is partly digested.

Milk, whole wheat and eggs are valuable foods. If they must be eliminated from the diet, great care must be taken to substitute equally valuable foods such as natural yoghurt and/or junket (if tolerated), raw and lightly cooked vegetables, fruit, nuts, seeds, pulses, sprouted pulses, fish, and meat. If the diet is inadequate, the immediate improvement felt as a result of the elimination of these foods could be followed by a long, slow decline in health.

If you suffered reactions to any of the foods which were introduced, and you didn't feel any improvement, you may have other allergies too, or you may have candida which can take up to six months to bring under control. Try just cutting the problem foods out of your diet for a few months and avoiding all forms of sugar and yeast in order to deal with any candida and hypoglycaemia. This could take the strain off your immune system, improve your health, and eliminate any other food sensitivities.

If there is still no improvement, you can continue to test other foods by eliminating them in the same way.

Once you have dealt with allergies, candida or hypoglycaemia for a few months, you can afford to relax a little, but stick mainly to a diet high in raw and lightly cooked vegetables, fruit, whole grains, pulses, nuts and seeds to maintain your health. Fish and organ meats are good sources of vital nutrients. Natural yoghurt supplies the friendly bacteria so important to good intestinal health. Wheat germ is an inexpensive valuable food supplement and can often be tolerated by people who cannot tolerate wheat itself.

APPENDIX 2

RECIPES

It would take another book to adequately cover the recipes for delicious, healthy meals that can be prepared with the minimum effort. Space, however, only allows me to give a few very basic tips and starter recipes. These are simple, inexpensive, healthy dishes and, once you've mastered the basic tomato sauce, you can use it with either pasta or pulses. You can add meat to it to make a bolognese sauce for spaghetti or lasagna, or vegetables to make vegetarian versions of both.

Although the quantities are for four people, they can easily be adapted for one or two people. And if a freezer is available, the full quantity can be prepared and some frozen for later. For example, half of the basic tomato sauce can be used to make today's spicy bean casserole and the rest popped in the fridge for tomorrow's lasagna.

I've included either fresh, dried or tinned ingredients so that the student, for instance, who hasn't enough time to shop daily can keep in tinned tomatoes, chick peas and butter beans. Remember though, that dried pulses are even cheaper, much better for you and, with a little forethought, not nearly as difficult to prepare as you might think (see chart). Also keep in packets of wholemeal pasta shapes, spaghetti and lasagna sheets. Splash out a little if you possibly can, however, on cold-pressed olive oil both for health and taste, and try to find a health shop that sells the really nutty organic rice. It's well worth the extra time it takes to cook.

I've kept the varieties of herbs and spices to a minimum, so that the kitchen cupboard need only contain cumin and dried oregano, though chilli and curry spice would be useful for the variations I've suggested. The fruit and vegetables, such as lemons, garlic, onion, carrots and celery store well, can be bought weekly, and can be used both in the salads and the cooked dishes. But for that special meal, try making the basic tomato sauce with fresh tomatoes and oregano leaves.

Planning is the key to preparing inexpensive healthy meals using dried pulses and whole grain cereals. You don't need to spend a great deal of time actually working in the kitchen, but it is worth devising a weekly menu and being fairly organised. There are also certain basic kitchen utensils and gadgets that can make life a great deal easier. I rely most heavily on my three-in-one set. This consists of a pan base with a porridger and a steamer that can both sit on top of the base.

The porridger is invaluable, not only for turning organically grown oats into delicious porridge but also for cooking whole grain rice, millet and other cereals. It can be left to cook perfectly, without sticking, while you prepare the rest of the meal. My student son, Mark, decided he couldn't live without a three-in-one, and informed me that he would take my old one back to his lodgings and I could buy a new one! He'd been managing with a little folding steamer that fits inside any pan, but had been finding that his favourite brown rice and morning porridge were too much trouble in a pan.

Traditional meals of meat or fish, vegetables and potatoes can also be very healthy of course, provided they are cooked carefully. In fact potatoes are rarely a problem for people with allergies whereas bread and pastry can often cause reactions. The steamer cooks surprisingly quickly since steam is hotter than boiling water, and potatoes steamed in their skins, and vegetables very lightly steamed, retain all their flavour and nutrients. Try steaming vegetables for shorter and shorter times until you get used to eating them fairly crisp. It is also ideal for steaming fish or reheating cooked, frozen rice or pulses.

My electric crockpot or slow cooker, now about fourteen years old, must have saved me a fortune in electricity since it uses so little. Once pulses have been boiled rapidly for ten minutes to destroy their natural toxins, they can be transferred to the slow cooker and left to cook until tender.

It also produces the most delicious casseroles and stews with the minimum effort, and cooking is so much more enjoyable when it can be done well in advance. There's nothing worse than having to think about what to do for the evening meal when you are tired after a long day at the office, or trying to soothe a fretful, teething baby.

I do have an electric food processor but I must admit that, unless I am doing large quantities, I tend to use a box-shaped metal grater and a sharp knife more often. It may take two minutes longer, but the knife and the grater are easier to rinse through. I've tried all sorts of expensive chef's knives, but my favourites are inexpensive wooden-handled steak knives that I buy at my local market and sharpen every day.

Again, I've tried all sorts of knife sharpeners but I keep coming back to the one I had when I was first married. It's now over twenty years old, and looks so awful that I have it screwed to the wall in the garage out of sight! But I draw the knife through it three times and it slices raw vegetables like a dream.

You don't need a lot of expensive gadgets to prepare healthy meals, but the steamer/porridger, the knife and sharpener, and the sharp grater really do make life much easier. Less essential, but also very useful, is my stainless steel pressure cooker. It reduces the cooking time for potatoes, meat, and pulses in particular, quite dramatically.

Again, not crucial, but helpful is my sprouting set for pulses. Soak a handful of dried mung beans, green lentils, or chick peas for example, overnight, then rinse thoroughly the next morning. Place them in one of the trays and rinse morning and evening. In a few days that handful of pulses has grown into a tray full of highly nutritious sprouted beans costing just a few pence. (Sprouting also destroys the natural toxins in beans.)

Dried pulses

High in fibre, pulses are not only inexpensive, the food of generations of peasants, but they are very nutritious indeed. More and more tinned varieties are to be found in the local supermarket these days. These are handy for the student or the person who lives alone and they can be used in stews, casseroles, chilli, vegetable curry, salads, falafels, and vegetable burgers. However, it's worth considering soaking and cooking a double batch of dried pulses and keeping some in the fridge for a couple of days for another meal.

You can even soak, cook and then freeze pulses, moving them around during the early stages of freezing to keep them separate. That way you can simply grab a handful or two when you need them and pop them straight into a casserole, chilli or salad. It's also the easiest way to combine several varieties of beans in one casserole or salad.

Preparation

Spread out the pulses and check for any little stones before rinsing. Mung beans and lentils need no soaking, but larger beans can either be soaked overnight in plenty of cold water, or boiled for five minutes then the heat turned off and the beans left to soak for one hour. The beans will swell so make sure that you use plenty of water. After soaking, drain off and throw away the soaking water, and rinse the beans under a running tap.

Cover with plenty of fresh water and bring to the boil. All pulses must then be boiled rapidly for ten minutes to destroy their natural toxins. The heat can then be turned down and the beans can be simmered for the remainder of their cooking time, or they can be transferred to the slow cooker. Alternatively, the beans can be cooked in much less time in a pressure cooker, and the high temperature involved does away with the need to first boil the beans rapidly for ten minutes.

Cooking times

The crockpot cooking times may seem long but it can be an advantage to have meals prepared and cooking well in advance.

Beans	Crockpot (low)	Crockpot (high)	Pan (simmering)	Pressure Cooker
aduki	8 hrs	4 hrs	40–45 mins	5 mins
black eyed	8–10 hrs	4–5 hrs	40–45 mins	10 mins
butter	8–10 hrs	4–5 hrs	45 mins–1 hr	15 mins
red kidney	8–10 hrs	4–5 hrs	45–50 mins	10 mins
soya	10 hrs	5 hrs	2 hrs	25 mins
flageolet	8 hrs	4 hrs	1–1¼ hrs	5 mins
haricot	8–10 hrs	4–5 hrs	45 mins (small) 1 hr (large)	10 mins (small) 15 mins (large)
mung	8 hrs	4 hrs	30–45 mins	bring to boil in closed cooker
split lentils	4 hrs	2 hrs	15–20 mins	bring to boil in closed cooker
whole lentils	8 hrs	4 hrs	40–45 mins	3 mins

Peas	Crockpot (low)	Crockpot (high)	Pan (simmering)	Pressure Cooker
chick	8–10 hrs	4–5 hrs	1–2 hrs	20 mins
marrowfat	8–10 hrs	4–5 hrs	1–2 hrs	20 mins
split	8 hrs	4 hrs	0–45 mins	3 mins

Cereals

Buy organic, whole grain cereals if possible (usually from health shops). The following quantities are designed to allow the cereal to absorb all the liquid so that none of the nutrients are lost. They are best cooked in a porridger or, if not, a non-stick pan with a tight-fitting lid.

	Quantity	Water (boiling)	Time
rice	225g (8oz)	400ml (15 fl oz)	30 mins
buckwheat	225g (8oz)	570ml (20 fl oz)	10 mins
millet	225g (8oz)	570ml (20 fl oz)	30 mins
porridge oats	175g (6oz)	1 ltr (35 fl oz)	20 mins

Use rice as a base for casseroles, chilli, curry, bolognese sauce, or in cold rice salad. Buckwheat or millet can be used in the same way. Millet can also be cooked in milk instead of water and sweetened with honey to make a pudding. Porridge can be served with a little cold milk, and dribbled with runny honey if sweetening is desired.

These quantities are enough to serve four people. Use half ingredients for two people or a quarter for one person. The rice can be frozen, moving occasionally during freezing to keep separate.

Pasta

225g (8oz) wholemeal dried pasta shapes or wholemeal spaghetti.

Bring about 4 pints of water to the boil in a large saucepan. Add pasta, stirring gently until water returns to the boil. Boil for 10 minutes, stirring occasionally. Drain immediately. Use with basic tomato sauce, bolognese sauce (or vegetable variation).

This quantity is enough to serve four people. Use half ingredients for two people or a quarter for one person.

Basic Tomato Sauce

This is a basic sauce which may be used to coat pasta. It can be turned into a bolognese sauce by the addition of meat, or a vegetarian sauce by the addition of vegetables (see bolognese sauce recipe).

1–2 tablespoons olive oil
6 medium-sized tomatoes, peeled and coarsely chopped (to peel easily, stick a fork in each and immerse tomatoes in boiling water for one minute) or 1 tin tomatoes
1 medium onion, finely chopped
2–4 cloves garlic, crushed
6–8 fresh leaves of oregano (or ½ teaspoon dried oregano)
1 tablespoon tomato purée
salt and black pepper to taste
Optional: ½ glass red wine or 1 teaspoon balsamic vinegar

In a medium saucepan, over moderately high heat, heat the oil, add the garlic and onion. Soften for 2–3 minutes, stirring frequently. Add the tomatoes, oregano, tomato purée, and wine or vinegar. Reduce the heat and simmer for 10 minutes. Add salt and pepper.

This quantity is enough to coat 225g (8oz) of pasta (4 servings). Alternatively, use part now and freeze the remainder, to be used either with pasta or pulses, or to be added to meat to make bolognese sauce for spaghetti or lasagna (see recipes).

Bolognese Sauce

For use either in lasagna (see recipe), with wholemeal spaghetti, or with whole grain rice.

Prepare the basic tomato sauce but add 500g (1lb) of lean minced lamb or beef and simmer for 20 minutes. (This sauce can be thickened, by adding 3 teaspoonfuls of cornflour, mixed to a smooth paste with a little cold water, for the last minute of cooking time.)

To vary: Instead of meat, add a grated carrot, chopped celery, sliced courgettes, or any spare vegetables you have in at the time, to make a vegetarian version.

To vary: The meat or vegetable sauce can be spread on the bottom of a baking dish, then topped with mashed potatoes and baked in a hot oven or grilled until brown on top.

Very Simple Lasagna

Lasagna is usually made with cheese sauce, but try using grated cheese instead. It's very quick and tasty.

Soak lasagna pasta for a few minutes in warm water. In a shallow square or oblong baking dish, place a layer of bolognese sauce (or vegetable variation), sheets of lasagna pasta, and a layer of grated cheese. Repeat these three layers once more.

Bake for 30 to 40 minutes at 180°C (350°F or Gas Mark 4).

Serve with a green salad (serves 4–6 people).

To vary: Cut thin, lengthways slices off a marrow and use instead of lasagna sheets (this is really delicious, and very much more digestible than ordinary lasagna).

NB: The bolognese sauce must be thickened when marrow is used instead of pasta sheets.

Spicy Bean Casserole

110g (4oz) dried haricot, red kidney, or butter beans (or chick peas, which are particularly nice in this recipe!) (or use 225g [8oz] of beans you've already cooked and frozen, or 2 × 430g tins of beans)

Basic tomato sauce (see recipe)

1–2 teaspoons of ground cumin

Optional: ½–1 teaspoon ground chilli powder (for those who like it hot!)

If using dried pulses, soak and cook (see chart). Make the basic tomato sauce, adding the cumin (chilli) and the cooked pulses for the last 10 minutes' simmering time.

Serve with a green salad (serves 4–6 people).

To vary: Use red kidney beans to make a vegetarian chilli, or make a vegetarian curry by substituting 2–3 teaspoonfuls of curry powder for the cumin and chilli powder.

Paola's Insalata di Tonno e Fagioli (Butter Bean and Tuna Salad)

450g (1lb) *cooked* butter beans (weight after cooking), or 2 × 430g tins, drained
1 small or ½ medium onion, finely sliced
1 tin of tuna, flaked
1 tablespoon cold-pressed olive oil
2 teaspoons of balsamic vinegar (or wine, or ordinary vinegar or lemon juice)
salt and black pepper to taste

Place the ingredients in a salad bowl, toss gently then chill (keeps well in the fridge and tastes even better the next day).

This serves 4 people.

Paola's Capresse Salad (from the Isle of Capri)

2 large or 3–4 small tomatoes, sliced
125g (4oz) of mozzarella cheese (or any hard cheese), cut into small cubes
4–6 leaves of fresh oregano (or ½ teaspoon dried oregano)
1 tablespoon cold-pressed olive oil
2 teaspoons of balsamic vinegar (or wine, or ordinary vinegar or lemon juice)
salt and black pepper to taste

Place the ingredients in a salad bowl, toss gently then chill.

To vary: Instead of mozzarella cheese, add ½ a small onion, thinly sliced and a small tin of tuna, flaked.

Simple Salad Dressing

Mix the juice of half a lemon with 200ml (7 fl oz) of extra virgin cold-pressed olive oil. Add black pepper to taste. Pour into a salad dressing bottle (or any small bottle). Do not keep in the fridge or the olive oil will solidify. Shake before pouring.

To vary: Use 1-2 tablespoonfuls of balsamic or wine vinegar instead of the lemon juice.

Easy Bean Salad

225g (8oz) cooked beans (weight after cooking), either one variety or mixed (or use tinned)
225g (8oz) chopped or sliced raw vegetables (any mixture of carrot, celery, pepper, leek, cauliflower, broccoli, etc)
4 tablespoons of 'simple salad dressing' (see recipe)
salt and black pepper

Toss the beans and raw vegetables in the salad dressing. Add salt and pepper to taste. Serves 4.

Cold Rice Salad

225g (8oz) cooked, cold rice (weight after cooking)
110g (4oz) chopped or sliced raw vegetables (any mixture of carrot, celery, pepper, leek, cauliflower, broccoli, etc)
110g (4oz) nuts (one or any mixture of hazelnuts, walnuts, brazil nuts)
4 tablespoons of simple 'salad dressing' (see recipe)
salt and black pepper

Toss the rice, raw vegetables and nuts in the salad dressing. Add salt and pepper to taste. Serves 4.
  To vary: Use cooked millet or buckwheat instead of rice.

Wholemeal Garlic Bread

1 wholemeal baguette, cut in half lengthways and buttered
2–4 cloves of garlic, crushed (wholemeal bread tends to need more garlic than white bread)
1 tablespoon of chopped fresh parsley
salt and black pepper to taste

Spread the crushed garlic on the buttered bread, sprinkle with
chopped parsley and season with salt and black pepper. Put the
two halves back together again, and bake for 20 minutes without
wrapping in tin foil, at 180°C (350°F or Gas Mark 4).

Falafels

*These savoury balls are best made with chick peas you have already soaked
and prepared in advance, since they are a little more trouble to prepare
than the other recipes. They are very tasty, however, as a starter or with
a salad, and they are ideal for children.*

110g (4oz) (uncooked weight) of dried chick peas (soaked and cooked
– see chart)
1 medium onion, chopped very fine or minced
1–2 cloves of garlic, crushed
1 tablespoon of fresh, chopped parsley (or ½ teaspoon dried oregano)
salt and black pepper to taste

To flavour:
1 teaspoon of ground cumin (mildest for children)
– or 1 teaspoon of curry powder
– or 1 teaspoon of caraway seed
– or 1 teaspoon of aniseed
– or ½ teaspoon of aniseed and ½ teaspoon caraway seed

To coat:
1 egg white
oatmeal or breadcrumbs

Mince, grind or process the chick peas. Mix together in a bowl, the
ground chick peas, onion, garlic, herbs, and flavouring. Add a little
water to form a stiff paste then form into 8 small balls. Dip each
ball in egg white then coat in oatmeal or breadcrumbs. Traditionally
falafels are fried in either deep or shallow oil but I feel that they are
healthier placed on a well-oiled tray and baked for 20 minutes at
220°C (425°F or Gas Mark 7). Serves 2–4 people.

Junket

This is the most easily digested way of taking milk.

1 pint of full cream milk (milk from Jersey cows makes the nicest junket of all)
1 teaspoon of rennet essence (from health shops and some supermarkets)
Optional: ½ to 1 tablespoon of honey

Gently warm the honey (if using) in the bottom of a pan. Add the milk and rennet essence, stirring constantly. *Gently* bring the milk to blood heat (the temperature is vital – it must feel neither hot nor cold to the touch). Pour into 4 *warmed* bowls. Leave *undisturbed*, at room temperature, for 15 to 20 minutes to set, then chill.

Serve as it is, or topped with chopped fresh fruit.

Note: This is a really simple recipe, so long as the temperature is correct. Any failure to set will be due to the milk getting either too hot or too cold.

Muesli

The following amounts are a rough guide. Vary them to taste.

450g (1lb) organic jumbo oats
225g (8oz) any crunchy whole oat cereal
  50g (2oz) bran (if needed)
225g (8oz) sunflower seeds
225g (8oz) seedless raisins or currants

Mix the ingredients together in a large bowl.

Any of the following ingredients can be added to the basic mixture to provide extra goodness and taste:
desiccated coconut
any shelled nuts
any dried fruit such as chopped dates or figs, etc

This makes a very large amount. Keep in an airtight container.
Just before serving add:
fresh fruit such as sliced banana or chopped apple
a teaspoon or two of raw unstabilised wheat germ or a tablespoon
of linseed
milk, natural yoghurt, or fruit juice
if sweetening is necessary, dribble a little runny honey over it.

Wheat germ and yoghurt

I find this the most palatable way to take wheat germ.

Mix one or two teaspoons of raw, unstabilised wheat germ into a
small bowl of natural yoghurt. If sweetening is necessary, dribble
a little runny honey over.

Molasses drink

*This is an inexpensive and very rich source of vitamins and minerals and
can be used daily as a general food supplement. It is particularly rich in
those nutrients which are used up when there is stress. Used regularly, it
can help inability to relax or insomnia.*

Take 1 jar Blackstrap Molasses (from health shop). Pour half of the
molasses into an empty jar and add hot water to top up, stirring
until well mixed. This will make the molasses runny so that it will
be easier to pour out later. Keep this mixture in the fridge and it
can then be used in one of the following ways:
Either: add one or two dessertspoonfuls to a glass of milk and
drink it with 3 brewer's yeast tablets
Or: squeeze half a lemon and top up with hot water and add 1 or
2 dessertspoonfuls of the molasses mixture. Drink with 3 brewer's
yeast tablets. (This makes a good first drink in the morning.)
    Build up to 3 drinks a day and take for one month, then find
your own 'maintenance dose' (usually 1 or 2 drinks a day). Stay on
that amount.
    NB: Brewer's yeast powder is much cheaper than tablets. Add
powder (½ teaspoonful or to taste) to molasses milk drink and whip

to mix well. This can be done with a fork, or in a blender or food processor.

Note: It doesn't taste too wonderful with the brewer's yeast powder, but it is much less expensive.

To get rid of a 'tummy bug'

This isn't exactly a recipe, but it usually works like a dream!

Avoid all food and sip only boiled spring water, cooled.

Once you can keep them down, take 3 garlic tablets (from the health shop) every hour for about six hours.

Then take 1 acidophilus tablet (also from the health shop) every two hours for about six hours (not through the night unless you are awake anyway).

Repeat the next day if necessary.

(The garlic is naturally anti-bacterial, and the acidophilus replaces the friendly intestinal bacteria.)

GLOSSARY OF CONDITIONS

The following list of nutrients associated with specific conditions is not intended as a substitute for medical diagnosis or treatment. However, optimum nutrition can alleviate symptoms, prevent illness or accelerate recovery. Discuss any nutritional changes you plan to make with your doctor.

AIDS

See chapter 8.
See also 'Immune system' (below).

Alcoholism

Ensure diet contains adequate amounts of all nutrients, but in particular the following:

    vitamins: A, B complex, C, E (see appendices 3 and 4)

    minerals: calcium, magnesium, selenium, zinc (see appendices 3 and 4)

    essential fatty acids (see chapter 10 and appendices 3 and 4)

    protein

    raw fruit and vegetables

    fibre (whole grains, seeds)

Cut down on excessive saturated fat, refined carbohydrates, salt, coffee, tea.

Avoid alcohol, hydrogenated fats (see chapter 10), cigarettes.

Consider possibility of sugar-handling problems (see chapter 9).

Consider possibility of food sensitivity, eg chocolate, milk, wheat, eggs (see chapter 8, appendix 1 and appendix 6).

Consider possibility of yeast overgrowth (see chapter 8).

Allergies

Ensure diet contains adequate amounts of all nutrients, but in particular the following:

    vitamins: B complex, C, E (see appendices 3 and 4)

    minerals: magnesium, zinc (see appendices 3 and 4)

    essential fatty acids (see chapter 10 and appendix 3)

    fibre (whole grains, seeds, vegetables, fruit)

Cut down on excessive saturated fat, refined carbohydrates, salt, coffee, tea, alcohol.

Avoid hydrogenated fats (see chapter 10), cigarettes.

Consider possibility of food sensitivity, eg chocolate, milk, wheat, eggs (see chapter 8, appendix 1 and appendix 6).

Consider possibility of yeast overgrowth (see chapter 8).

Consider possibility of sugar-handling problems (see chapter 9).

Anaemia

Ensure diet contains adequate amounts of all nutrients, but in particular the following:

    vitamins: B complex, C, E (see appendices 3 and 4)

    minerals: magnesium, copper, iron, zinc (see appendices 3 and 4)

    essential fatty acids (see chapter 10 and appendix 3)

    fibre (whole grains, seeds, vegetables, fruit)

Cut down on excessive saturated fat, refined carbohydrates, salt, coffee, tea, alcohol.

Avoid hydrogenated fats (see chapter 10), cigarettes.

Consider possibility of food sensitivity, eg chocolate, milk, wheat, eggs (see chapter 8, appendix 1 and appendix 6).

Consider possibility of yeast overgrowth (see chapter 8).

Asthma

Ensure diet contains adequate amounts of all nutrients, but in particular the following:

   vitamins: B complex, C (see appendices 3 and 4)
   minerals: magnesium, zinc (see appendices 3 and 4)
   essential fatty acids (see chapter 10 and appendix 3)
   fibre (whole grains, seeds, vegetables, fruit)

Cut down on excessive saturated fat, refined carbohydrates, salt, coffee, tea, alcohol.

Avoid hydrogenated fats (see chapter 10), cigarettes.

Consider possibility of food sensitivity, eg chocolate, milk, wheat, eggs (see chapter 8, appendix 1 and appendix 6).

Consider possibility of yeast overgrowth (see chapter 8).

Cancer prevention

Ensure diet contains adequate amounts of all nutrients, but in particular the following:

   vitamins: A, B complex, C, D, E (see appendices 3 and 4)
   minerals: calcium, iodine, magnesium, selenium, zinc (see appendices 3 and 4)
   essential fatty acids (see chapter 10 and appendix 3)
   fibre (whole grains, seeds, vegetables, fruit)
   garlic and onion
   lactobacillus acidophilus (the friendly bacteria in yoghurt)

Cut down on excessive saturated fat, refined carbohydrates, salt, coffee, tea, alcohol.

Avoid hydrogenated fats (see chapter 10), cigarettes, smoked/pickled/salt-cured foods.

Consider possibility of food sensitivity, eg chocolate, milk, wheat, eggs (see chapter 8, appendix 1 and appendix 6).

Consider possibility of yeast overgrowth (see chapter 8).

Cholesterol/vascular/heart (see also chapter 11)

Ensure diet contains adequate amounts of all nutrients, but in particular the following:

> vitamins: A, B complex, C, D, E (see appendices 3 and 4)
> minerals: calcium, magnesium, manganese, potassium, zinc, chromium (see appendices 3 and 4)
> essential fatty acids (see chapter 10 and appendix 3)
> fibre (whole grains, seeds, vegetables, fruit)
> lecithin (see appendix 4)

Cut down on excessive saturated fat, refined carbohydrates, salt, coffee, tea, alcohol.

Avoid hydrogenated fats (see chapter 10), cigarettes.

Consider possibility of food sensitivity, eg chocolate, milk, wheat, eggs (see chapter 8, appendix 1 and appendix 6).

Consider possibility of yeast overgrowth (see chapter 8).

Diabetes

See chapter 9.

Ear complaints

Ensure diet contains adequate amounts of all nutrients, but in particular the following:

> vitamins: A, B complex, C, D, E (see appendices 3 and 4)
> minerals: calcium, iron, magnesium, manganese, zinc (see appendices 3 and 4)
> essential fatty acids (see chapter 10 and appendix 3)
> fibre (whole grains, seeds, vegetables, fruit)

Cut down on excessive saturated fat, refined carbohydrates, salt, coffee, tea, alcohol.

Avoid hydrogenated fats (see chapter 10), cigarettes.

Check for toxic metals, aluminium and lead in particular (see appendix 6).

High cholesterol can cause ear problems (see chapter 11).

Consider possibility of food sensitivity, eg chocolate, milk, wheat, eggs (see chapter 8, appendix 1 and appendix 6).
Consider possibility of yeast overgrowth (see chapter 8).

Eye complaints

Ensure diet contains adequate amounts of all nutrients, but in particular the following:

> vitamins: A, B complex, C, E, bioflavoids (see appendices 3 and 4)
> minerals: selenium, zinc (see appendices 3 and 4)
> essential fatty acids (see chapter 10 and appendix 3)
> fibre (whole grains, seeds, vegetables, fruit)

Cut down on excessive saturated fat, refined carbohydrates, salt, coffee, tea, alcohol.
Avoid hydrogenated fats (see chapter 10), cigarettes.
Consider possibility of food sensitivity, eg chocolate, milk, wheat, eggs (see chapter 8, appendix 1 and appendix 6).
Consider possibility of yeast overgrowth (see chapter 8).
Consider possibility of sugar-handling problems (see chapter 9).

Fatigue (chronic)

See chapters 7 and 8.

Gall bladder

Ensure diet contains adequate amounts of all nutrients, but in particular the following:

> vitamins: A, C, B complex, E (see appendices 3 and 4)
> minerals: magnesium, chromium, manganese, potassium, zinc (see appendices 3 and 4)
> essential fatty acids (see chapter 10 and appendix 3)
> fibre (whole grains, seeds, vegetables, fruit)
> lecithin (see appendix 4)

See also chapter 11 on cholesterol problems.
Cut down on *excessive* saturated fat, refined carbohydrates, salt, coffee, tea, alcohol.

Avoid hydrogenated fats (see chapter 10), *excessive* polyunsaturated fats, overweight, cigarettes.

Note: Too little fat inhibits the absorption of fat-soluble vitamins, causing deficiencies which can have serious effects.

Consider possibility of food sensitivity, eg chocolate, milk, wheat, eggs (see chapter 8, appendix 1 and appendix 6).

Consider possibility of yeast overgrowth (see chapter 8).

Gastrointestinal

Ensure diet contains adequate amounts of all nutrients, but in particular the following:

    vitamins: A, B complex, C, D, E (see appendices 3 and 4)
    minerals: calcium, iron, magnesium, zinc, potassium (see appendices 3 and 4)
    essential fatty acids (see chapter 10 and appendix 3)
    fibre (whole grains, seeds, vegetables, fruit)
    lactobacillus acidophilus (the friendly bacteria in yoghurt)

Cut down on excessive saturated fat, refined carbohydrates, salt, coffee, tea, alcohol.

Avoid sugar, hydrogenated fats (see chapter 10), cigarettes.

Consider possibility of food sensitivity, eg chocolate, milk, wheat, eggs (see chapter 8, appendix 1 and appendix 6).

Consider possibility of yeast overgrowth (see chapter 8).

Consider possibility of hypoglycaemia (see chapter 9).

Hypoglycaemia

See chapter 9.

Immune system/infection/inflammation

(Infection resistance and auto-immune problems)

Ensure diet contains adequate amounts of all nutrients, but in particular the following:

    vitamins: A, B complex, C, D, E (see appendices 3 and 4)
    minerals: copper, iron, magnesium, manganese, selenium, zinc (see appendices 3 and 4)

essential fatty acids (see chapter 10 and appendix 3)
fibre (whole grains, seeds, vegetables, fruit)
garlic
lactobacillus acidophilus (the friendly bacteria in yoghurt)

Cut down on excessive saturated fat, refined carbohydrates, salt, coffee, tea, alcohol.

Avoid hydrogenated fats (see chapter 10), cigarettes.

In the case of recurrent infections, consider possibility of food sensitivity, eg chocolate, milk, wheat, eggs (see chapter 8, appendix 1 and appendix 6).

In the case of allergies or recurrent infections, consider possibility of yeast overgrowth (see chapter 8).

Insomnia

Ensure diet contains adequate amounts of all nutrients, but in particular the following:

vitamins: B complex, choline (see appendices 3 and 4)
minerals: calcium, magnesium, zinc (see appendices 3 and 4)
essential fatty acids (see chapter 10 and appendix 3)
fibre (whole grains, seeds, vegetables, fruit)

Cut down on excessive saturated fat, refined carbohydrates, salt.

Avoid hydrogenated fats (see chapter 10), cigarettes, coffee, tea, alcohol.

Consider possibility of hypoglycaemia (see chapter 9).

Kidney problems

Ensure diet contains adequate amounts of all nutrients, but in particular the following:

vitamins: A, B complex, C, E, choline (see appendices 3 and 4)
minerals: magnesium, potassium (see appendices 3 and 4)
essential fatty acids (see chapter 10 and appendix 3)
fibre (whole grains, seeds, vegetables, fruit)
lecithin (see appendix 4)

See also chapter 11 on cholesterol problems.

Cut down on excessive saturated fat, refined carbohydrates, salt, coffee, tea, alcohol.

Avoid hydrogenated fats (see chapter 10), cigarettes.
Consider possibility of food sensitivity, eg chocolate, milk, wheat, eggs (see chapter 8, appendix 1 and appendix 6).
Consider possibility of yeast overgrowth (see chapter 8).

Liver problems

Ensure diet contains adequate amounts of all nutrients, but in particular the following:

> vitamins: A, B complex, C, E, choline (see appendices 3 and 4)
> minerals: calcium, magnesium, iodine (see appendices 3 and 4)
> essential fatty acids (see chapter 10 and appendix 3)
> fibre (whole grains, seeds, vegetables, fruit)
> protein (yoghurt, milk, cheese, eggs, fish, meat, wheatgerm, pulses)

Cut down on excessive saturated fat, refined carbohydrates, coffee, tea, alcohol.
Avoid hydrogenated fats (see chapter 10), cigarettes.
Consider possibility of food sensitivity, eg chocolate, milk, wheat, eggs (see chapter 8, appendix 1 and appendix 6).
Consider possibility of yeast overgrowth (see chapter 8).

Myalgic encephalomyelitis (ME)

See chapter 8.

Men's problems

Eg Prostate, infertility, impotence

Ensure diet contains adequate amounts of all nutrients, but in particular the following:

> vitamins: A, B complex, C, E (see appendices 3 and 4)
> minerals: chromium, manganese, potassium, selenium, zinc (see appendices 3 and 4)
> essential fatty acids (see chapter 10 and appendix 3)
> fibre (whole grains, seeds, vegetables, fruit)
> lecithin (see appendix 4)

Cut down on excessive saturated fat, refined carbohydrates, salt, coffee, tea, alcohol.

Avoid hydrogenated fats (see chapter 10), cigarettes.

Consider possibility of food sensitivity, eg chocolate, milk, wheat, eggs (see chapter 8, appendix 1 and appendix 6).

Consider possibility of yeast overgrowth (see chapter 8).

Mental/emotional/behavioural problems

Ensure diet contains adequate amounts of all nutrients, but in particular the following:

vitamins: A, B complex, C, E, choline (see appendices 3 and 4)

minerals: calcium, iron, magnesium, manganese,* potassium, selenium, zinc (see appendices 3 and 4)

essential fatty acids (see chapter 10 and appendix 3)

fibre (whole grains, seeds, vegetables, fruit)

Cut down on excessive saturated fat, refined carbohydrates, salt, coffee, tea, alcohol.

Avoid hydrogenated fats (see chapter 10), cigarettes.

Check for toxic metals, aluminium, lead, cadmium, arsenic, mercury, excess copper (see appendix 6).

Consider possibility of food sensitivity, eg chocolate, milk, wheat, eggs (see chapter 8, appendix 1 and appendix 6).

Consider possibility of yeast overgrowth (see chapter 8).

Consider possibility of hypoglycaemia (see chapter 9).

Muscle/joint/bone problems

Ensure diet contains adequate amounts of all nutrients, but in particular the following:

vitamins: A, B complex, C, D, E, K, choline (see appendices 3 and 4)

minerals: calcium, magnesium, manganese, potassium, copper, iron, selenium, sulphur, zinc (see appendices 3 and 4)

essential fatty acids (see chapter 10 and appendix 3)

---

* Note: Excessively high levels of manganese have also been associated with mental problems (see appendix 6 for methods of testing).

fibre (whole grains, seeds, vegetables, fruit)

Cut down on excessive saturated fat, refined carbohydrates, salt, coffee, tea, alcohol.

Avoid hydrogenated fats (see chapter 10), cigarettes.

Consider possibility of food sensitivity, eg chocolate, milk, wheat, eggs (see chapter 8, appendix 1 and appendix 6).

Consider possibility of yeast overgrowth (see chapter 8).

Periodontal disease (Gum Disease)

Ensure diet contains adequate amounts of all nutrients, but in particular the following:

    vitamins: A, C, D, E, K (see appendices 3 and 4)

    minerals: calcium, magnesium, zinc (see appendices 3 and 4)

    essential fatty acids (see chapter 10 and appendix 3)

    fibre (whole grains, seeds, vegetables, fruit)

Cut down on excessive saturated fat, refined carbohydrates, salt, coffee, tea, alcohol.

Avoid sugar, hydrogenated fats (see chapter 10), cigarettes.

Consider possibility of yeast overgrowth (see chapter 8).

Skin conditions

Eg Dryness, acne, eczema, psoriasis, poor wound healing, ulcers

Ensure diet contains adequate amounts of all nutrients, but in particular the following:

    vitamins: B complex, A, C, E (see appendices 3 and 4)

    minerals: zinc, magnesium, selenium, chromium (see appendices 3 and 4)

    essential fatty acids (see chapter 10 and appendix 3)

    fibre (whole grains, seeds, vegetables, fruit)

Cut down on excessive saturated fat, refined carbohydrates, alcohol.

Avoid hydrogenated fats (see chapter 10).

Consider possibility of food sensitivity, eg chocolate, milk, wheat, eggs (see chapter 8, appendix 1 and appendix 6).

Consider possibility of yeast overgrowth, particularly when there is a fungal skin condition (see chapter 8).

Weight problems

See chapter 12.

Women's problems

Eg Premenstrual or menopausal symptoms, infertility

Ensure diet contains adequate amounts of all nutrients, but in particular the following:

vitamins: A, B complex, C, D, E, K (see appendices 3 and 4)

minerals: calcium, iron, iodine, magnesium, manganese, selenium, zinc (see appendices 3 and 4)

essential fatty acids (see chapter 10 and appendix 3)

fibre (whole grains, seeds, vegetables, fruit)

Cut down on excessive saturated fat, refined carbohydrates, salt, coffee, tea, alcohol.

Avoid hydrogenated fats (see chapter 10), cigarettes.

Consider possibility of food sensitivity, eg chocolate, milk, wheat, eggs (see chapter 8, appendix 1 and appendix 6).

Consider possibility of yeast overgrowth (see chapter 8).

Consider possibility of hypoglycaemia (see chapter 9).

Note: The contraceptive pill can increase vitamin A to an undesirably high level, cause deficiencies of the B vitamins and vitamins C and E. It can increase copper to an undesirably high level, and reduce zinc, iron and possibly magnesium and manganese.

APPENDIX 3

NUTRIENTS: ROLE AND FOOD SOURCE

You will see from the food sources of each nutrient that the inclusion of molasses, brewer's yeast, wheat germ, kelp tablets or powder and cod liver oil in the diet would supply every nutrient except vitamin C, bioflavonoids and vitamin K. These can be obtained by the inclusion in the diet of fresh fruit and green leafy vegetables. There is also sodium, but we generally get more than enough salt in our diet.

The food sources of nutrients are dependent upon the quality of the soil in which the crop is grown. Organically grown foods may be more reliable.

1. Minerals

Calcium
What it does: bone and tooth formation, blood clotting, heart rhythm, nerve tranquillisation, nerve transmission, muscle growth and contraction.
Bodily parts affected: blood, bones, heart, skin, muscles, soft tissue, nervous system, teeth.
Deficiency symptoms: insomnia, nervousness, irritability, joint pains, muscle cramps, PMT, constipation, arthritis, heart palpitations, tooth decay, osteoporosis, osteomalacia (softening of the bones and teeth), brittle fingernails.
Antagonists: lack of exercise, magnesium or vitamin D deficiency, stress, excessive saturated fat.

Food sources: kelp tablets or powder, brewer's yeast, molasses, milk, cheese, yoghurt, broccoli, peas and beans, pulses, green leafy vegetables, nuts, seeds.

Chromium
What it does: regulates blood sugar level, glucose metabolism (energy), synthesis of fatty acids, cholesterol metabolism.
Bodily parts affected: blood, eyes, circulatory system, sperm formation.
Deficiency symptoms: atherosclerosis, insulin irregularities, reduced effectiveness of insulin, opaqueness of cornea, depressed sperm formation.
Antagonists: refined carbohydrates, iron.
Food sources: molasses, brewer's yeast, wheat germ, whole grains, cheese, black pepper, vegetables.
Note: Brewer's yeast contains the most active and easily utilised form of chromium, known as chromium GTF (glucose tolerance factor).

Copper
What it does: bone formation, hair and skin colour, healing processes of body, haemoglobin and red blood cell formation, production of RNA.
Bodily parts affected: blood, bones, circulatory system, hair, skin, brain function.
Deficiency symptoms: general weakness, anaemia, nerve problems, immune deficiency, skin sores, loss of hair, skeletal defects, reproductive problems, demyelination, cardiovascular conditions.
Antagonists: zinc, vitamin C, calcium (high intakes), mercury, lead.
Food sources: molasses, peas and beans, green vegetables, nuts (particularly brazil nuts), organ meats, seafood, dried fruit, pulses.
Note 1: The contraceptive pill and pregnancy increase copper levels, and can produce zinc deficiency, causing depression.
Note 2: Excessive copper, particularly combined with zinc and/or manganese deficiency has been associated with mental illness such as schizophrenia.

Iodine
What it does: production of thyroid hormones, energy production, metabolism (excess weight), physical and mental development.
Bodily parts affected: hair, nails, skin, thyroid gland.
Deficiency symptoms: cold hands and feet, fatigue, lethargy, dry hair, irritability, nervousness, low blood pressure, high cholesterol levels, heart disease, slow pulse, retarded development of sex organs, obesity, loss of interest in sex, goitre, cancer of the thyroid.
Antagonists: none known.
Food sources: seafood, kelp tablets or powder, salt (iodised), dark green leafy vegetables, onions, eggs, whole grains, milk and milk products, meat.

Iron
What it does: haemoglobin production, stress and disease resistance, growth in children.
Bodily parts affected: blood, bones, nails, skin, teeth.
Deficiency symptoms: breathing difficulties, brittle nails, iron deficiency anaemia (pale skin, fatigue), headache, depression, poor memory, mental confusion, constipation, lack of stomach acid. In children: lack of appetite, reduced growth, poor immunity, learning and behavioural difficulties.
Antagonists: coffee, tea, excess phosphorus, zinc (excessive intake), manganese.
Food sources: molasses, brewer's yeast, wheat germ, whole grains, kelp (tablets or powder), eggs, fish, organ meats, peas and beans, parsley, vegetables, muscle meats, poultry, nuts.

Magnesium
What it does: acid/alkaline balance, blood sugar metabolism, energy production, muscle contraction, nerve function, enzyme production, protein structuring (RNA/DNA), lecithin production.
Bodily parts affected: arteries, bones, heart, muscles, nerves, pancreas, teeth.
Deficiency symptoms: fatigue, apathy, insomnia, inability to cope, poor memory, impaired learning ability, clouded or irrational thinking, confusion, disorientation, depression, nervousness,

apprehension, irritability, easily aroused anger, personality changes, hyperactivity, convulsions, epilepsy.

Weakness, tingling, trembling, tremors, twitches, jerkiness, cramps, shaking hands, quivering lip, eye tic, bladder weakness, abnormal cardiac rhythms.

Loss of appetite, nausea, diarrhoea or constipation, hair loss, premenstrual symptoms, hypoglycaemia, pancreatic insufficiency, osteoporosis, osteomalacia (softening of the bones and teeth), bedwetting, low birthweight babies.
Antagonists: excessive calcium, vitamin D, protein, sugar, saturated fat or fluid intake, bran, alcohol, oral contraceptives, diuretics, antibiotics, fluoride, stress.
Food sources: molasses, kelp (tablets or powder), wheat germ, whole grains, dark leafy vegetables, nuts, seeds, bran, eggs, seafood, spinach, tuna fish.
Note: Since vitamins B1 and B6 are dependent upon magnesium, some of the symptoms may actually be those of vitamin B1 or B6 deficiency, due to a lack of available magnesium.

Manganese
What it does: enzyme activation, reproduction and growth, sex hormone production, nerve function, tissue respiration, vitamins B1 and E utilisation, metabolism of fat and sugar.
Bodily parts affected: bones, tissues, brain, pituitary gland, liver, kidneys, mammary glands, muscles, nerves.
Deficiency symptoms: ataxia (muscle co-ordination failure), dizziness, middle ear imbalances, loss of hearing, disc and cartilage problems, glucose intolerance, growth retardation, lack of fertility, reduced brain function.
Antagonists: excessive calcium, phosphorus or iron, choline deficiency, insecticides.
Food sources: brewer's yeast, seeds, whole grains, green leafy vegetables, parsley, bananas, pineapple, egg yolks, peas and beans, liver, nuts.

Phosphorus
What it does: bone and tooth formation, cell growth and repair, digestion, energy production, heart muscle contraction, kidney function, metabolism of fats, protein, carbohydrates, nerve and muscle activity, vitamin utilisation.
Bodily parts affected: bones, brain, nerves, teeth.
Deficiency symptoms: appetite loss, fatigue, irregular breathing, nervous disorders, overweight, weight loss.
Antagonists: aluminium, iron, magnesium (excessive intake), white sugar (excessive).
Food sources: brewer's yeast, whole grains, seeds, nuts, eggs, fish, meat, poultry, cheese, milk, yoghurt.
Note: Phosphorus is usually plentiful in the average diet.

Potassium
What it does: heartbeat, muscle contraction, growth, nerve tranquillisation, utilisation of enzymes, maintenance of normal blood glucose levels.
Bodily parts affected: blood, heart, kidneys, muscles, nerves, skin.
Deficiency symptoms: headaches, acne, continuous thirst, poor appetite, dry skin, constipation, general weakness, fatigue, apathy, depression, insomnia, muscle cramps, joint pain, weak peristalsis, nervousness, irritability, irregular heartbeat, high blood pressure, oedema (tissue swelling).
Antagonists: alcohol, coffee, cortisone, diuretics, laxatives, excessive salt or sugar, stress.
Food sources: molasses, brewer's yeast, wheat germ, whole grains, fruit, vegetables, nuts.

Selenium
What it does: protects cells against oxidative damage, preserves tissue elasticity, pancreatic function.
Bodily parts affected: cells, blood, muscles, glands, pancreas.
Deficiency symptoms: hair loss, premature ageing, ageing pigment, loss of sensation in hands and feet, 'pins and needles', poor appetite, gastrointestinal disturbances, weight loss, increased risk of cancer and birth defects.
Antagonists: lack of vitamin E, cadmium, sulphates.

Food sources: brewer's yeast, wheat germ, whole grains, fish, eggs, nuts (particularly brazil nuts), liver, garlic.

Sodium

What it does: normal cellular fluid level, proper muscle contraction.
Bodily parts affected: blood, lymph system, muscles, nerves.
Deficiency symptoms: appetite loss, nausea, vomiting, weight loss, intestinal gas, muscle cramps, exhaustion, apathy, low blood pressure.
Antagonists: excessive sweating.
Food sources: salt, milk, cheese, seafood.
Note: Sodium is normally plentiful in the average diet, and excessive sodium can increase blood pressure.

Zinc

What it does: burn and wound healing, enzyme function, brain development and function, carbohydrate digestion, bone growth, prostate gland function, maintenance of hormone levels, growth and maturity of sex organs, vitamin B1, phosphorus, protein and essential fatty acid metabolism, mobilisation of vitamin A from the liver.
Bodily parts affected: blood, muscles, arteries, heart, lungs, liver, kidneys, pancreas, thyroid, pituitary and adrenal glands, spleen, intestinal lining, prostate gland, testes.
Deficiency symptoms: lethargy, apathy, poor concentration, depression, irritability, aggression, unwillingness to learn, dyslexia, behavioural problems.

Loss of sense of taste, loss of sense of smell, night blindness, painful joints, cold extremities, immune deficiency (allergies and infections), retarded growth, muscle weakness, diarrhoea, fatigue, poor appetite, anorexia, flatulence, impaired glucose tolerance.

Prolonged wound healing, sores on mucous membranes of mouth and throat, white flecks on nails, stretch marks on the skin, acne, dermatitis, psoriasis, boils, poor hair health, dandruff, loss of hair, hardening of the arteries, high cholesterol.

Delayed sexual development, immaturity of sexual organs, retarded onset of menstruation, infertility, prostate problems, low sperm count, lack of sperm motility, impotence, increased risk of miscarriage or congenital malformations.

Antagonists: alcohol, tea, coffee, bran, stress, pancreatic insufficiency, malabsorption, contraceptive pill, diuretics, steroids, penicillamine, excessive calcium, iron, or copper, lead, cadmium, lack of phosphorus.

Food sources: Muscle and organ meats, poultry, egg yolk, seafood, wheat germ, brewer's yeast, sunflower seeds, nuts, whole grains, pulses, fruit, vegetables.

Note: Zinc is much better absorbed from meat than vegetable sources; breast milk is high in easily absorbable zinc.

Toxic metals

(The presence of these is usually detected by a hair mineral test. See appendix 6.)

Aluminium

Sources in environment: aluminium cooking utensils, antacids, aluminium foil, anti-perspirants, aluminium-containing baking powders, processed food containing aluminium, soft water.

Interferes with bodily functions: irritating to the gut, affects bone formation, brain convulses (in high concentrations).

Bodily parts affected: stomach, bones, brain.

Toxicity symptoms: gastrointestinal irritation, colic, rickets, convulsions.

Protective nutrients: none known.

Nutritional treatment: garlic, eggs, vitamin C, high sulphur amino acid supplements.

Arsenic

Sources in environment: coal burning, pesticides, insecticides, herbicides, defoliants, metal smelting, manufacture of glass.

Interferes with bodily functions: metabolic inhibitor (reduces efficiency of energy production), cellular and enzyme poison.

Bodily parts affected: cells (cellular metabolism).

Toxicity symptoms: fatigue, low vitality, listlessness, loss of pain sensation, loss of body hair, skin colour changes (dark spots), gastroenteritis.

Protective nutrients: iodine, selenium, calcium, zinc, vitamin C, sulphur amino acids.

Nutritional treatment: garlic, eggs, beans, vitamin C, adequate levels of iodine and selenium, sulphur amino acid supplements.

Cadmium

Sources in environment: cigarette smoke, oxide dusts, contaminated drinking water, galvanised pipes, paints, welding, pigments, contaminated shellfish from industrialised seashores.

Interferes with bodily functions: heart and blood vessel structure (hypertension), kidney damage, loss of sense of smell, decreased appetite (cadmium can reduce levels of zinc).

Bodily parts affected: renal cortex of kidney, heart and blood vessels, brain.

Toxicity symptoms: hypertension, hypotension, kidney damage, loss of sense of smell, loss of appetite.

Protective nutrients: zinc, calcium, vitamin C, sulphur amino acids.

Nutritional treatment: garlic, eggs, beans, vitamin C, adequate levels of calcium, sulphur amino acid supplements.

Lead

Sources in environment: polluted air from leaded petrol exhaust fumes, lead-based paint, newsprint, hair dyes and rinses, leaded glass, pewter ware, pencils, pesticides, fertilisers, tobacco smoke.

Interferes with bodily functions: enzyme poison, osteoblast production (cells producing the intercellular bone matrix), blood formation, blocks enzymes at cell level.

Bodily parts affected: bone, liver, kidneys, pancreas, heart, brain, nervous system.

Toxicity symptoms: weakness, listlessness, fatigue, pallor, abdominal discomfort, constipation.

Protective nutrients: zinc, iron, calcium, vitamins C and E, sulphur amino acid supplements.

Nutritional treatment: garlic, eggs, beans, vitamins C and E, adequate levels of calcium and iron in the diet, sulphur amino acid supplements.

Mercury

Sources in environment: amalgams in dentistry (tooth fillings), fungicides, cosmetics, hair dyes, manufacture and delivery of petroleum products, fish caught in contaminated areas.

Interferes with bodily functions: destroys cells, blocks transport of sugar (energy at cell level).

Bodily parts affected: nervous system, appetite and pain centres, cell membranes.

Toxicity symptoms: loss of appetite and weight, severe emotional disturbances, tremors, blood changes, inflammation of gums, chewing and swallowing difficulties, loss of sense of pain, convulsions.

Protective nutrients: pectin, vitamin C, selenium, sulphur amino acid supplements.

Nutritional treatment: garlic, eggs, beans, vitamin C, selenium, sulphur amino acid supplements.

2. Vitamins

Vitamin A (retinol)

What it does: body tissue repair and maintenance, hormone production, resistance to infection, visual purple production (necessary for night vision), production of red and white blood cells, RNA synthesis, cancer prevention.

Bodily parts affected: eyes, hair, skin, mucous membranes, blood, bones, teeth.

Deficiency symptoms: allergies, appetite loss, digestive problems, gastric ulcers, skin blemishes, dry hair, fatigue, dry, itching or burning eyes, night blindness, poor vision, rough dry skin, sinus trouble, soft tooth enamel, susceptibility to infections, increased risk of congenital defects.

Antagonists: alcohol, coffee, cortisone, excessive iron, mineral oils such as liquid paraffin, vitamin D deficiency.

Food sources: fish oils, oily fish, eggs, whole milk, butter, yoghurt,

cheese, cream, organ meats, dark green, yellow and orange fruits
and vegetables.
Note: Zinc is necessary for vitamin A to be released from the liver.

Vitamin B complex
What it does: energy, metabolism of carbohydrate, fat, and
protein, muscle tone maintenance.
Bodily parts affected: eyes, gastrointestinal tract, hair, liver, mouth,
nerves, skin.
Deficiency symptoms: acne, anaemia, constipation, high cholesterol,
digestive disturbances, blood sugar problems, fatigue, hair
(dull, dry, falling), insomnia, skin (dry, rough), mental
changes.
Antagonists: alcohol, birth control pills, coffee, infections, sleeping
pills, stress, sugar (excessive), sulpha drugs.
Food sources: brewer's yeast, wheat germ, whole grains, liver (see
also other B vitamins).

Vitamin B1 (thiamine)
What it does: appetite, blood building, carbohydrate metabolism,
energy production, circulation, digestion (hydrochloric acid
production), brain function, skeletal and muscle growth and
maintenance.
Bodily parts affected: brain, ears, eyes, hair, heart, liver, kidney,
muscles, nervous system.
Deficiency symptoms: depression, irritability, nervousness, poor
concentration or memory, appetite loss, anorexia, digestive
disturbances, muscle weakness, fatigue, apathy, inflammation
of the nerves, numbness or tingling of hands and feet, pain and
noise sensitivity, abdominal or chest pains, shortness of breath,
disturbed sleep.
Antagonists: alcohol, coffee, tobacco, contraceptive pill, sugar,
stress, diuretics, surgery, fever, refined food.
Food sources: molasses, brewer's yeast, wheat germ, whole grains, seeds,
fish, meat, nuts, organ meats, poultry, milk, peas, beans, pulses.
*Note: Since vitamin B1 is dependent upon magnesium, the deficiency
symptoms of vitamin B1 may well be caused, not by a shortage of this
vitamin, but by a deficiency of magnesium.*

Vitamin B2 (riboflavin)

What it does: antibody and red blood cell formation, cell respiration, metabolism (carbohydrate, fat, protein).

Bodily parts affected: eyes, nails, hair, skin, soft body tissue.

Deficiency symptoms: mouth ulcers, cracks and sores at corners of mouth, dermatitis, dry, itching, sore, burning or bloodshot eyes, sensitivity to light, cataracts, dizziness, poor digestion, retarded growth, red sore tongue, burning feet, broken capillaries in the face, dry, wrinkled, peeling lips, increased risk of congenital defects.

Antagonists: alcohol, coffee, sugar, tobacco, contraceptive pill.

Food sources: molasses, brewer's yeast, wheat germ, whole grains, nuts, leafy green vegetables, whole milk, butter, cheese, eggs, peas and beans, pulses, organ meats, fish.

Vitamin B3 (nicotinamide, niacin, niacinamide)

What it does: aids circulation, cholesterol level reduction, growth, hydrochloric acid production, enzyme production, metabolism (protein, fat, carbohydrate), sex hormone production.

Bodily parts affected: brain, liver, sex glands, arteries, nerves, skin, soft tissue.

Deficiency symptoms: appetite loss, depression, aggression, fatigue, insomnia, nervous disorders, loss of memory, headaches, indigestion, muscular weakness, nausea, diarrhoea, halitosis (bad breath), mouth ulcers, skin complaints (such as redness, scaling, pigmentation), high cholesterol, deficiency of sex hormones.

Antagonists: alcohol, antibiotics, coffee, excessive sugar and starches, too little protein.

Food sources: molasses, brewer's yeast, wheat germ, whole grains, nuts, seafood, lean meats, whole milk, whole milk products, poultry, liver, eggs.

Vitamin B5 (pantothenic acid, calcium pantothenate)

What it does: antibody formation, carbohydrate, protein conversion (energy), cholesterol and fatty acid metabolism, growth stimulation, vitamin utilisation.

Bodily parts affected: adrenal glands, digestive tract, nerves, skin.
Deficiency symptoms: allergies, fatigue, headaches, weakness,
dizziness, restlessness, nerve problems, diarrhoea, duodenal ulcers,
eczema, hypoglycaemia, intestinal disorders, kidney trouble, loss
of hair, muscle cramps, premature ageing, respiratory infections,
low blood pressure, sore feet, nausea, vomiting.
Antagonists: alcohol, coffee.
Food sources: molasses, brewer's yeast, wheat germ, whole grains,
green vegetables, peas and beans, organ meats, salmon, eggs,
chicken.

Vitamin B6 (pyridoxine)
What it does: antibody formation, digestion (hydrochloric acid
production), fat and protein utilisation, nerves (maintains
sodium/potassium balance), essential fatty acid metabolism, zinc,
manganese and magnesium utilisation, growth and synthesis of
RNA and DNA.
Bodily parts affected: blood, muscles, nerves, skin.
Deficiency symptoms: general weakness, headaches, mental changes,
nervousness, depression, irritability, inability to concentrate,
insomnia, anaemia, loss of appetite, abdominal pain and cramps,
nausea, halitosis, skin complaints, dandruff, hair loss, poor
immunity, increased risk of fetal abnormalities.
Antagonists: magnesium deficiency,* coffee, smoking, alcohol,
excessive saturated fat, protein or carbohydrate in the diet, birth
control pill, penicillin, streptomycin, radiation (exposure).
Food sources: molasses, brewer's yeast, wheat germ, whole grains,
organ meats, green leafy vegetables, peas and beans, fish, milk,
eggs, nuts, seeds.

B12 (cyanocobalamin)
What it does: aids appetite, blood cell formation, cell longevity,
healthy nervous system, metabolism (carbohydrate, fat, protein).
Bodily parts affected: blood, nerves.

---

* Note: Since vitamin B6 is dependent upon magnesium, the deficiency symptoms of vitamin B6 may well be caused, not by a
shortage of this vitamin, but by a deficiency of magnesium.

Deficiency symptoms: general weakness, nervousness, pernicious anaemia, numbness and tingling in hands and feet, walking and speaking difficulties, mental depression, confusion.
Antagonists: alcohol, coffee, laxatives, tobacco, deficiencies of iron, calcium and B6.
Food sources: brewer's yeast, organ meats, meat, cheese, fish, milk, milk products, eggs.

Biotin (B complex vitamin)

What it does: aids cell growth, fatty acid production, carbohydrate, fat, and protein metabolism, vitamin B utilisation.
Bodily parts affected: hair, muscles, skin.
Deficiency symptoms: depression, panic attacks, fatigue, weakness, muscular pain, dry skin, scaly dermatitis, conjunctivitis, hair loss, insomnia, poor appetite, nausea, weight loss, stunted growth.
Antagonists: alcohol, coffee, raw egg white, antibiotics (antibiotics destroy the friendly bacteria which produce biotin in the intestines).
Food sources: brewer's yeast, whole grains (particularly rice), organ meats, egg yolk, nuts, milk, peas and beans.

Folic acid (B complex vitamin)

What it does: appetite, hydrochloric acid production, protein and carbohydrate metabolism, antibody production, red blood cell formation, zinc metabolism, cell growth and reproduction (important for the normal development of the fetus).
Bodily parts affected: blood, glands, liver.
Deficiency symptoms: anaemia, lethargy, tiredness, shortness of breath, digestive disturbances, greying hair, poor immunity, growth problems, depression, insomnia, increased risk of congenital defects.
Antagonists: alcohol, coffee, stress, tobacco, oral contraceptives, sulpha drugs.
Food sources: brewer's yeast, wheat germ, whole grains, green leafy vegetables, root vegetables, organ meats, milk, eggs, nuts.

Choline

What it does: lecithin formation, liver and gall bladder regulation,

metabolism (fats, cholesterol), nerve function.
Bodily parts affected: hair, kidneys, liver, thymus gland.
Deficiency symptoms: headaches, dizziness, insomnia, growth
problems, heart trouble, high blood pressure, oedema, impaired
liver, kidney and adrenal function, intolerance to fats, bleeding
stomach ulcers, visual disturbances, haemorrhage in the eye, ear
noises.
Antagonists: alcohol, coffee, sugar (excessive), insecticides.
Food sources: molasses, brewer's yeast, wheat germ, fish, peas
and beans, organ meats, soya beans, egg yolks.

Inositol
What it does: artery hardening retardation, hair growth, lecithin
formation, metabolism (fat and cholesterol).
Bodily parts affected: brain, hair, skin, heart, kidneys, bone marrow,
liver, muscles.
Deficiency symptoms: high cholesterol, constipation, eczema, eye
abnormalities, hair loss, digestive problems, irregular heartbeat.
Antagonists: alcohol, coffee.
Food sources: molasses, brewer's yeast, lecithin, whole grains, meat,
milk, eggs, nuts, citrus fruits, vegetables.

PABA para-aminobenzoic acid (B complex vitamin)
What it does: blood cell formation, skin and hair colouring,
intestinal bacteria activity, protein metabolism.
Bodily parts affected: glands, hair, intestines, skin.
Deficiency symptoms: constipation, depression, digestive disorders,
fatigue, grey hair, headaches, irritability.
Antagonists: alcohol, coffee, sulpha drugs.
Food sources: molasses, brewer's yeast, wheat germ, whole grains,
green leafy vegetables, yoghurt, organ meats.

Vitamin C (ascorbic acid)
What it does: bone and tooth formation, collagen production and
health, cholesterol metabolism, digestion, iodine conservation,
healing (burns and wounds), absorption of iron, red blood
cell formation, prevention of haemorrhaging, resistance to
infection, vitamin protection (oxidation).

Bodily parts affected: adrenal glands, blood, capillary walls, connective tissue (skin, ligaments, bones), gums, heart, teeth.
Deficiency symptoms: anaemia, swollen and bleeding gums, capillary wall ruptures, nosebleeds, tendency to bruise easily, depression, dental cavities, low resistance to infection, poor digestion.
Antagonists: antibiotics, aspirin, contraceptive pill, cortisone, high fever, stress, smoking.
Food sources: fruit, green vegetables, potatoes, cauliflower, carrots, tomatoes, parsley, sprouted alfalfa seed.

Vitamin D (calciferol)

What it does: calcium and phosphorus metabolism (bone formation and growth), heart action, nervous system maintenance, normal blood clotting, skin respiration.
Bodily parts affected: bones, heart, eyes, nerves, skin, teeth, thyroid gland.
Deficiency symptoms: burning sensation (mouth and throat), hot flushes, night sweats, diarrhoea, insomnia, myopia (short-sightedness), nervousness, poor metabolism, joint pains, osteomalacia (softening bones and teeth), osteoporosis, rickets and poor skeletal development in children.
Antagonists: mineral oils such as liquid paraffin.
Food sources: oily fish, fish liver oils, milk, butter, eggs, organ meats (also the action of sunlight on skin oils).

Vitamin E (tocopherol)

What it does: antioxidant, ageing retardation, utilisation of selenium and essential fatty acids, anti-clotting factor, blood cholesterol reduction, blood flow to heart, capillary wall strengthening, wound healing, prevention of scarring, fertility, male potency, lung protection (antipollution), muscle and nerve maintenance.
Bodily parts affected: blood vessels, heart, lungs, nerves, pituitary and prostate glands, muscles, skin.
Deficiency symptoms: dry, dull or falling hair, premature ageing, enlarged prostate gland, liver and kidney damage, gastrointestinal disease, muscular wasting, heart disease, stroke, varicose veins, phlebitis, miscarriages, impotency, sterility.

Antagonists: excessive polyunsaturated oils, birth control pills, chlorine, mineral oils such as liquid paraffin, rancid fat and oil, iron, air pollution.
Food sources: wheat germ, whole wheat, nuts, seeds, unrefined vegetable oils, dark green vegetables, eggs.

Essential fatty acids (vitamin F)

What it does: prostaglandin production, enzyme activation, artery hardening prevention, blood coagulation, blood pressure normaliser, cholesterol metabolism, glandular activity, production of sex and adrenal hormones, growth, vital organ respiration, utilisation of nutrients.
Bodily parts affected: cells, glands (adrenal, sex, thyroid, kidney, liver, pancreas), hair, mucous membranes, brain, nerves, skin.
Deficiency symptoms: excessive thirst, acne, eczema, allergies, hyperactivity, diarrhoea, dry skin, poor wound healing, membrane permeability, bronchial problems, dry brittle hair or loss of hair, gall stones, loss of muscle tone, nail problems, dry eyes, underweight, varicose veins, impaired growth, reproductive failure (particularly in men), mental disturbances, impaired cholesterol metabolism, heart and circulation abnormalities (see chapters 10 and 12).
Antagonists: see chapter 10.
Food sources: wheat germ, nuts, seeds (particularly linseed), unrefined vegetable oils, oily fish, fish oils, evening primrose oil (see chapters 10 and 12).

Bioflavonoids (vitamin P)

What it does: blood vessel wall maintenance, bruising minimisation, prevention of infection, strong capillary maintenance.
Bodily parts affected: blood, capillary walls, connective tissue (skin, gums, ligaments, bones), teeth.
Deficiency symptoms: anaemia, bleeding gums, capillary wall ruptures, bruise easily, dental cavities, low infection resistance (colds), nosebleeds, poor digestion.
Antagonists: antibiotics, aspirin, cortisone, high fever, stress, tobacco.

Food sources: fruits (skins and pulp) – apricots, cherries, grapes, grapefruit, lemons, plums, buck wheat.

Vitamin K
What it does: blood clotting.
Bodily parts affected: blood.
Deficiency symptoms: increased susceptibility to bleeding, particularly in the newborn.
Antagonists: anti-epileptic drugs.
Food sources: green vegetables, whole grains, liver.

APPENDIX 4

FOOD SUPPLEMENTS

The following food supplements may be added to the diet, in moderation, to provide a concentrated source of nutrients:

Live natural yoghurt. This is the best way to take milk, as the protein is predigested. It is useful for reintroducing the friendly bowel bacteria after the use of antibiotics and to provide a constant supply of beneficial intestinal flora.

Wheat germ (raw, fresh and unstabilised – keep refrigerated) contains the B vitamins B1, B2, B3, B5, B6, folic acid, vitamin E, phosphorus, iron, selenium and zinc.

Brewer's yeast (powder or tablets). An excellent source of the B complex vitamins, containing 17 vitamins, 16 amino acids and 14 minerals. It is one of the best sources of RNA (a nucleic acid that helps the body's immune system) (see appendix 2 for recipe).

Crude black molasses is the first extraction of sugar from sugar cane. It contains the B vitamins biotin, folic acid, inositol, B1, B2, B5 and vitamin E. It is rich in potassium, iron, copper, magnesium, phosphorus, calcium, and many trace minerals.

Liver. Rich in the B complex vitamins, including B12, vitamins A, C, and D, calcium, copper, iron and phosphorus.

Bean sprouts (especially alfalfa). These are easy to grow and rich in nearly every vitamin and mineral. They are valuable as a living food, full of enzymes and amino acids (see appendix 2).

Cod liver oil. A valuable source of vitamins A and D, and of essential fatty acids.

Sea kelp (powder or tablets). One of the best sources of iodine, it is also rich in calcium, magnesium, vitamins D, E, K, and the B complex vitamins.

Linseed/linseed oil (keep refrigerated). Linseed contains both types of essential fatty acids, linoleic and linolenic.

Sunflower seeds. Sprinkled on cereal, or as an ingredient in home-made muesli – they are packed with nutrients and an excellent source of protein.

Lecithin granules (keep refrigerated). Acts as an emulsifier to disperse fats. Useful wherever there is high cholesterol or excess weight (take straight off the spoon or sprinkle on cereal).

Acidophilus (capsules or powder). An excellent source of the friendly bacteria found, to a much lesser extent, in yoghurt.

Garlic (or garlic tablets – odourless are available). A natural antibiotic and antifungal agent, garlic is also useful for reducing cholesterol (take at a different time of the day to the acidophilus tablets and any mineral supplements).

APPENDIX 5

TAKING VITAMIN AND MINERAL TABLETS – IMPORTANT ADVICE

Although vitamin and mineral supplements can be very helpful at times, they can also cause problems. Magnesium taken alone, for example, can cause a deficiency of calcium. Another example of this is vitamin B6, often taken apart from the other members of the B complex vitamins, which can unbalance vitamin B2 levels.

Unbalanced supplements

A photographer I know highlighted this problem pretty graphically in a letter he wrote to me. He explained that, not long after he had started to take vitamin B6 tablets, he came down with influenza. Soon he became more ill than he had ever been in his life before, experiencing such severe chest pains that he began to wonder if he was heading for a heart attack. 'I later fully recovered and went on to understand how people used to die of influenza. At that point I didn't make any other connection.'

Later that year we met and talked about nutrition. He was interested in the subject and I gave him a folder of leaflets that I had produced. He glanced through them pretty quickly, he told me and, later again that year, he came across the bottle of vitamin B6 tablets. 'Why don't I take some more of these?' he thought. 'Isn't this what I read about in Eileen's leaflets?'

Five days later, he began to experience the same chest pains, which continued for a few more days before he suddenly remembered just what it was that he'd read in my leaflet. '*Supplementation with B6 alone*

will always create immediate imbalance which is detrimental to health.'
Now he began to see a possible connection between the vitamin tablets and how he was feeling. 'I have thought about it over the past few
days and I am pretty sure it was not just a coincidence,' he wrote.

He wanted to confirm the warning in my leaflets and also wrote,
'to let you know that by giving me the folder you could possibly have
saved my life. I am certain that I would have carried on taking the
tablets. They would have appeared to me to be the last thing making
me feel so rotten. Indeed there was nothing written on the tablet
bottle to suggest the danger. It was reading and suddenly remembering what you had written. From now on I will be more careful.'

Time and time again I have come across people who have run into
problems by taking unbalanced supplements. There was the friend
who started to suffer from nervous problems and, at the same time,
from recurrent chest infections that wouldn't respond to antibiotics.
I discovered that, for some months previously, she had been taking
a supplement containing just magnesium and vitamin B6.

This can lead to a shortage of calcium and vitamin B2. Since
calcium is important to the health of the nerves and vitamin B2
deficiency inhibits the production of antibodies, both the nervous
system and immunity can suffer. Within a few days of correct
supplementation, my friend was feeling markedly calmer and her
chest infection had begun to clear up.

Stopping too suddenly

I constantly see people suffering from the effects of taking supplements for a while, then stopping them suddenly or forgetting
to take them. One friend experienced violent pain in her shoulder
muscles, which was so bad that she had to go to hospital, where she
was told that the muscles had gone into spasm.

She had been taking calcium and magnesium supplements for
another health problem and had forgotten to take them for a few
weeks. I pointed out that, when you take vitamin or mineral
supplements, your body can get used to an easily absorbed supply
and get 'lazy'. It can also get into the habit of excreting any excess
and continues to do so for a while after the supplementation is
stopped. So, if you stop them suddenly, you may be worse off than

you were before you took them, becoming even more inefficient at utilising the available minerals.

My friend began taking the supplements again and the problem disappeared. She now understands the need to stop such supplements very gradually. It worries me that so many books and newspaper articles recommend this vitamin or that mineral without any of these warnings. So often they bring about an immediate improvement followed by a long slow decline in health which may not be seen to be linked to the nutritional supplement originally taken.

Vitamin and mineral tablets can be expensive, and tedious to remember to take. They can cause problems by affecting other nutrient levels, or they may simply be replacing nutrients which are being depleted by stress, smoking, alcohol, too much tea or coffee, environmental factors or the contraceptive pill.

It really is far, far better to first improve the diet and deal if possible with any factors that are depleting nutritional reserves (see appendix 3), and then see if any health problems persist. If they clear up, though you may never know which nutrients you were short of, it doesn't matter so long as you continue to eat a good diet.

There are natural food sources that can be added to the diet to give the highest possible amounts of nutrients, and these will often be all that is needed. These include foods such as wheat germ, molasses, brewer's yeast, sunflower seeds and so on (see appendix 4). Their advantages are that they are cheap and they contain a balance of nutrients which work synergistically, each making the other more effective. Their disadvantages are that they may be less convenient than tablets, and some of them cannot be used by people with allergies (brewer's yeast or wheat germ, for example).

Only answer

Nevertheless, in certain circumstances, careful supplementation can be the only way of breaking a vicious circle of health problems. Whatever the limitations or drawbacks of vitamin and mineral tablets, they can achieve dramatic results, particularly where there is an inability to utilise nutrients properly or where environmental factors are concerned. Sometimes deficiency has reduced the appetite, making it difficult to eat an adequate diet, or stress or deficiency has been so severe that the energy and motivation to prepare healthy meals are lacking.

Toxic metals in the body may need to be cleared through the use of supplements. Lead and zinc are a good example of this. A low level of zinc can make the individual more susceptible to lead pollution in the atmosphere. The lead drives the levels of zinc still lower, causing loss of appetite and emotional problems, among other symptoms. Often the only way to deal with this problem is to supplement with zinc in order to drive the lead out of the system and restore the zinc status. Consequently the appetite and motivation to prepare food returns.

Guidelines – (1) Minerals

Calcium and magnesium
Should always be taken together, usually 2 calcium to 1 magnesium. So a daily supplement of 500mg to 1,000mg of calcium would need to be taken with 250mg to 500mg of magnesium.

Chromium
Daily supplement: 50mg to 200mg.

Copper
Daily supplement: 2–4mg.
Note: Only use copper supplement if deficiency is certain. High copper levels can reduce zinc, while zinc supplementation in excess of 50mg per day can reduce copper levels.

Iodine
Iodine can be toxic in excess so kelp tablets are a safer source of iodine.

Iron
Daily supplement: 10mg to 60mg.
Note: Iron competes for absorption with zinc and potassium so it is best taken at another time of the day. Tea and coffee can inhibit the absorption of iron.

Manganese
Daily supplement: 5mg to 20mg.
Note: Excessive supplementation with manganese can reduce iron and potassium.

Potassium
Supplementation with potassium can cause problems so food sources of potassium are safer (see appendix 3).

Selenium
Daily supplement: 50mcg to 200mcg.
Note: Excessive selenium (over 200mcg) can be toxic. Brewer's yeast is a safer source, provided there is no allergy to yeast.

Zinc
Daily supplement: 20mg to 100mg.
Note: High copper levels can reduce zinc, while zinc supplementation in excess of 50mg per day can reduce copper levels.

Guidelines – (2) Vitamins

Vitamin A (retinol)
Daily supplement: 5,000 IUs (as beta carotene).
Note: Excessive doses of vitamin A (more than 10,000 IUs) over several months can be toxic. However, doses of 10,000 IUs can be taken for short periods, at the onset of infection, for example. Doses of over 10,000 IUs should not be taken by anyone who is pregnant or planning a pregnancy.

Vitamin B complex
The proportions of B vitamins are important. For every 5mg of vitamin B1, B2 and B6 there should be:
30mg to 50mg of B3 and B5
15mcg to 25mcg of B12 and biotin
50mcg to 100mcg of folic acid
15mcg to 30mcg of PABA

Choline
Best taken as lecithin (see appendix 4).

Inositol
Best taken as lecithin (see appendix 4).

Vitamin C
Daily supplement: 200mg to 500mg.
Note: Vitamin C can be taken in doses of 1,000mg to 2,000mg or more per day to treat illness or infection. Long-term use of higher doses, however, may reduce vitamin B12 levels.

Vitamin D (calciferol)
Daily supplement: 400 IUs.
Note: Vitamin D can be highly toxic and doses of more than 400 IUs should never be taken without medical supervision.

Vitamin E (tocopherol)
Daily supplement: 100 IUs to 600 IUs.
Note: Vitamin E supplementation is not recommended without medical supervision for those who are taking anticoagulants.

Bioflavonoids (vitamin P)
Usually combined with vitamin C in supplements.

Vitamin K
Rarely used as a supplement except under medical supervision.

Essential fatty acids (vitamin F)
See chapter 10 and appendix 3.

APPENDIX 6

MINERAL AND ALLERGY TESTING

Hair mineral analysis

A laboratory analysis of a sample of hair (widely used in forensic work), can be a useful guide to the mineral status of the body, *provided it is interpreted by an expert who understands the relationships between the minerals in the body.* Hair analysis has received some adverse publicity through a study which was later demonstrated to have been poorly designed and statistically incorrect. However, it would be advantageous if preparation of the hair sample techniques were standardised.

Nevertheless, research has shown that for many minerals, hair more closely reflects body mineral stores than does blood or urine, particularly in the case of toxic metal accumulations. Hair grows slowly and analysis of hair levels indicates the average levels in the body over a long period of time. Hair analysis can be a helpful indicator, but it is not a complete answer.

A sample of hair, taken from near the scalp, is analysed using spectroscopy equipment in a medical laboratory. It is often used in combination with blood and sweat analysis. These are laboratory tests and not analysis by dowsing (using a pendulum) or any other paranormal means. Here again there have been adverse reports in the media when hair was analysed by dowsing.

Hair mineral analysis may be obtained through a general or private practitioner, or from a reputable laboratory such as Biolab of London. Unfortunately it is not available on the National Health Service and the cost varies from practitioner to practitioner (see useful addresses).

Testing for food intolerance or allergy

Some common symptoms of food sensitivity:

Bloated feeling in the stomach, abdominal cramps or pains, flatulence, nausea, vomiting, diarrhoea, constipation, drowsiness after eating, headaches, migraine, dizziness, faintness, insomnia.

Wheezing, asthma, bronchial congestion, rapid pulse, runny or stuffy nose, recurrent sinusitis, catarrh, itching ear, earache, recurrent ear infections, hearing loss, itching on the roof of the mouth, mouth ulcers, sore throats, watery eyes, blurred vision, gagging, chronic cough.

Dark circles under the eyes, skin rash, hives, dermatitis, eczema, weakness, aching, chronic fatigue, muscle or joint aches or pains, swelling of hands, feet or ankles, food craving or bingeing, vaginal discharge, frequent or urgent urination.

Mental lethargy or indifference, poor concentration, excessive daydreaming, confusion, depression, anxiety, panic attacks, slurred speech, stuttering, irritability, aggression, restlessness, hyperactivity, learning disabilities.

Note: All of the symptoms are unlikely to occur together. However, a cluster of the symptoms could indicate food sensitivity. The most common problem foods are wheat, dairy products, eggs and chocolate, and the first step should be to eliminate these products from the diet and then reintroduce them (see chapter 8 and appendix 1).

Another method of detecting food sensitivities is to use fasting and raw-food regimes for a few days (see chapter 15). Often the initial adverse reactions to such regimes are due to withdrawal symptoms, experienced as foods to which the individual is both sensitive and addicted are avoided. And the sense of well-being felt after a few days is often due to the elimination of problem foods. Suspect foods should then be reintroduced one at a time so that any reactions may be monitored (see chapter 8 and appendix 1).

Cytotoxic testing

The simplest method of testing for food allergy is by cytotoxic testing, using a sample of the patient's blood. However, it is expensive and controversial, with some practitioners considering it to be of great value, while others feel that it is of little use. But it has been widely used in the USA for many years, and in Britain for several years, and results can give a guide to food allergies which can be confirmed by elimination and challenge (see appendix 1).

The cytotoxic test is based on alterations in the appearance of live white blood cells when exposed to a range of common foods. The results are then grouped into foods which cause severe, moderate, mild, and no reactions (see 'Useful Addresses' for cytotoxic testing services).

Building health

Care must be taken to ensure that nutritious foods, which must be eliminated at least for a while, are replaced by equally nutritious foods. Otherwise an immediate improvement may be followed by a long slow decline in health.

It is worth remembering that apparent reactions to foods can in fact be due to chemical additives, crop sprays, or residues of drugs used in intensive farming (meat, poultry, dairy produce). Use organically grown or reared produce whenever possible (see chapter 14).

Once food sensitivities have been detected and eliminated, the emphasis must be on building health by ensuring that all nutrients are supplied in the diet in optimum amounts (see appendices 1 to 5). Vitamin, mineral and essential fatty acid deficiencies can be the *cause* of food allergy, intolerance or malabsorption. When such deficiencies are put right, sensitivities often become much less severe or even disappear altogether. Raw foods are particularly good sources of nutrients (see chapter 15).

Where there is allergy, it is also worth considering the possibility of candidiasis (see chapter 8), and hypoglycaemia (see chapter 9). Exercise and daylight have a beneficial effect on the immune system (see chapter 15). For the person who has been suffering from the symptoms of underlying health problems, the initial effort will be repaid in increased energy, motivation, and generally improved health.

USEFUL ADDRESSES

The Chambers Clinic
29 Purser's Cross Road
Parson's Green
London SW6 4QY
Tel: 071-731 4281

Private treatment for chronic fatigue, ME, allergies, candida, eczema, hay fever, asthma, hyperactivity, preconceptual care. Cost of Alcat test (similar to cytotoxic test) at time of going to press: £105.

The clinic can arrange for hair mineral test (cost at time of going to press: £38).

ECHO (UK) Centre of Information for Oxygen Therapies
13 Albert Road
Retford
Nottinghamshire DN22 6JD

For information on hydrogen peroxide treatment for candida and related conditions. (Very inexpensive and effective.)

ECHO (US)
Department OT, PO Box 126
Delano
Minnesota 55328
USA
Tel: 612 972 2144

Food for Thought
PO Box 94
Wokingham
RG11
Berkshire

For information on Christianity, nutrition and the environment.

Foresight
28 The Paddock
Godalming
Surrey GU7 1XD
Tel: 0483 427839

For information on preconceptual care.

The Hyperactive Children's Support Group
71 Whyke Lane
Chichester
West Sussex PO19 2LD
Tel: 0903 725182 (between 10 a.m. and 3 p.m.)

Membership costs £12 per year (£8 for anyone on any sort of government benefit), includes a copy of the diet book and 3 free issues of the journal. (The diet book is available on its own, price £3.50.)

The Maternity Alliance
15 Britannia Street
London WC1X 9JP
Tel: 071-837 1265

For information on preconceptual care.

The McCarrison Society
Hackney Hospital
Homerton High Street
London E9 6BE

Nature's Best
1 Lambert's Road
PO Box 1
Tunbridge Wells
TN2 3EQ
Tel: 0892 539595

(Price of Zincatest at time of going to press: £3.25.)

Nutrition Associates
Galtres House, Lysander Close
York YO3 8XB
Tel: 0904 691591

For copies of the book *Daylight Robbery* by Dr Damian Downing
(£4.50 inc. p&p)

York Nutritional Laboratory
Tudor House, Suite 2
Lysander Close
Clifton Moor
Clifton, York YO3 4XB
Tel: 0904 690640

The laboratory will deal directly with the public but insist on the involvement of a GP or private practitioner to interpret the results and give nutritional guidance.

Cost of cytotoxic test at time of going to press: £80 for testing 72 substances.

Wholefood Books
24 Paddington Street
London W1M 4DR
Tel: 071-935 3924
In case of difficulty obtaining any of the recommended books.

NOTES

Chapter 1 Health On A Budget
1. Lobstein, T, *When parents go hungry so children can eat* (The Food Magazine July/Sept 1991).

Chapter 2 **Hard Times**
1. Hanssen, M, *E For Additives* (Thorsons 1984).
2. *Diet For A Lifetime* (Horizon BBC2 30.3.92).

Chapter 4 **Healthy Races**
1. Price, WS, *Nutrition and Physical Degeneration* (Keats Publishing 1989), p 24.
2. Wrench, G, *The Wheel of Health* (Schoken Books 1972), pp 26–7.
3. Griggs, B, *The Food Factor* (Penguin 1986).
4. McCarrison, R, *Nutrition and Health* (Westbury Press 1982).

Chapter 5 **So What's Wrong With Our Diet?**
1. Davis, A, *Let's Get Well* (Unwin 1979), p 117.
2. Davis, A, *Let's Get Well*, p 17.
3. Pfeiffer, CC, *Mental and Elemental Nutrients* (Keats 1975), p 220.
4. Passwater, RA, Cranton, EM, *Trace Elements, Hair Analysis and Nutrition* (Keats Publishing 1983), pp 22–33.
5. Passwater, RA, Cranton, EM, *Trace Elements, Hair Analysis and Nutrition*, p 70.
6. Davis, A, *Let's Get Well*, p 51.
7. Passwater, RA, Cranton, EM, *Trace Elements, Hair Analysis and Nutrition*, p 45.
8. Davies, S, Stewart, A, *Nutritional Medicine* (Pan 1987), p 137.
9. Davies, S, Stewart, A, *Nutritional Medicine*, p 121.
10. Davis, A, *Let's Get Well*, pp 40, 79.

11. Passwater, RA, Cranton, EM, *Trace Elements, Hair Analysis and Nutrition*, pp 79–85.

12. Pfeiffer, CC, *Zinc and Other Micro-Nutrients* (Keats 1978), pp 163–74.

13. Passwater, RA, Cranton, EM, *Trace Elements, Hair Analysis and Nutrition*, p 282.

14. Davies, S, Stewart, A, *Nutritional Medicine*, p 138.

15. Davies, S, Stewart, A, *Nutritional Medicine*, pp 142–3.

16. Barnes, B, Bradley, SG, *Planning for a Healthy Baby* (Edbury Press 1990), p 107.

17. Passwater, RA, & Mindell, E, *The Vitamin Robbers* (Keats Publishing 1983), p 9.

18. Passwater, RA, & Mindell, E, *The Vitamin Robbers* (Keats Publishing 1983), p 10.

19. Passwater, RA, & Mindell, E, *The Vitamin Robbers* (Keats Publishing 1983), p 8.

20. Passwater, RA, & Mindell, E, *The Vitamin Robbers* (Keats Publishing 1983), p 9.

Chapter 6 Before Life Begins

1. Price, WS, *Nutrition and Physical Degeneration* (Keats Publishing 1989), p 24.

2. Wynn, AHA, Crawford, MA, Doyle, W, Wynn, SW, 'Nutrition of women in anticipation of pregnancy', *Nutrition and Health* Vol 7 (A B Academic Publishers 1988), pp 69–88.

3. Wynn, M, Wynn, A, 'Nutrition around conception and the prevention of low birthweight', *Nutrition and Health* Vol 6 No 1 (A B Academic Publishers 1988), pp 37–52.

4. Wynn, AHA, Crawford, MA, Doyle, W, Wynn, SW, 'Nutrition of women in anticipation of pregnancy', pp 69–88.

5. Wynn, M, Wynn, A, 'Nutrition around conception and the prevention of low birthweight', pp 37–52.

6. Wynn, M, Wynn, A, *The Importance of Nutrition Around the Time of Conception in the Prevention of Handicap. Applied Nutrition: 1* EC Bateman editor, proceedings of the British Dietetic Association Study Conference, Exeter, April 1–7, 1981, John Libby, London.

7. Wynn, M, Wynn, A, *The Importance of Nutrition Around the Time of Conception in the Prevention of Handicap.*

8. Jennings, I., *Vitamins in Endocrine Metabolism* (William Heinemann, Medical Press 1972), p 140.

9. Wynn, M, Wynn, A, 'Nutrition around conception and the prevention of low birthweight', pp 37–52.

10. Wynn, AHA, Crawford, MA, Doyle, W, Wynn, SW, 'Nutrition of women in anticipation of pregnancy', pp 69–88.

11. Barnes, B, Bradley, SG, *Planning for a Healthy Baby* (Edbury Press 1990).

Chapter 7 A Physical Cause Of Mental Symptoms

1. Scott Williamson, G, Pearse, IH, *Biologists In Search Of Material* (Scottish Academic Press 1982), p 75.

2. Medawar, C, *Power and Dependence* (Social Audit 1992).

3. Passwater, RA, Cranton, EM, *Trace Elements, Hair Analysis and Nutrition* (Keats Publishing 1983), p 68.

4. Bryce-Smith, D, Hodgkinson, L, *The Zinc Solution* (Century Arrow 1986), pp 47–9.

5. *Nutrition and Health* (A B Academic Publishers).

6. Barlow, K, *Recognising Health* (The McCarrison Society 1988).

7. Griggs, B, *The Food Factor* (Penguin 1986).

Chapter 8 Underlying Problems

1. Dawes, B, Downing, D, *Why ME?* (Grafton 1989).

2. Pottenger, FM, 'The effect of heat processed foods and metabolized vitamin D milk on the dentofacial structures of experimental animals', American Journal of Orthodontics and Oral Surgery (Vol 32, No 8, 1946).

3. Beach, RS, Gershwin, ME, Hurley, LS, *Gestational Zinc Deprivation in Mice: Persistence of Immune Deficiency for Three Generations* (*Science* 1982), pp 218, 469–71.

4. Bryce-Smith, D, Hodgkinson, L, *The Zinc Solution* (Century Arrow 1986), p 47.

5. Hodgkinson, N, 'Silent virus challenges thinking on Aids' (*Sunday Times* 26.7.92).

6. Chaitow, L, *Candida Albicans* (Thorsons 1991).

7. Benjamin, H, *Everybody's Guide to Nature Cure* (Thorsons 1975).

Chapter 9 Sweet Complications

 1. Airola, P, *Hypoglycemia: A Better Approach* (Health Plus 1977).
 2. Davies, S, Stewart, A, *Nutritional Medicine* (Pan 1987), p 302.
 3. Airola, P, *Hypoglycemia: A Better Approach*, p 59.
 4. See Pfeiffer, CC, *Mental and Elemental Nutrients* (Keats 1975), pp 254, 289, Davis, A, *Let's Get Well* (Unwin 1979), pp 79, 88, 94–5, Airola, P, *Hypoglycemia: A Better Approach*, pp 68–9.
 5. Davies, S, Stewart, A, *Nutritional Medicine*, pp 302–3.
 6. Davies, S, Stewart, A, *Nutritional Medicine*, p 304.
 7. Davies, S, Stewart, A, *Nutritional Medicine*, p 305.
 8. Pfeiffer, CC, *Zinc and Other Micro-Nutrients* (Keats 1978), p 127.
 9. Airola, P, *Hypoglycemia: A Better Approach*, p 29.
10. Cleave, TL, *The Saccharine Disease* (Wright 1974).
11. Adams, R, Murray, F, *Minerals: Kill or Cure?* (Larchmont 1974), p 169.
12. Davis, A, *Let's Get Well*, p 88.
13. Davis, A, *Let's Get Well*, p 79.
14. Cleave, TL, *The Saccharine Disease*, p 89.
15. Davis, A, *Let's Get Well*, p 83.
16. See Pfeiffer, CC, *Zinc and Other Micro-Nutrients*, p 13, Adams, R, Murray, F, *Minerals: Kill or Cure?*, p 169 and Davis, A, *Let's Get Well*, p 212.

Chapter 10 Healthy Fats

 1. Davies, S, Stewart, A, *Nutritional Medicine* (Pan 1987), p 116.
 2. Graham, J, *Evening Primrose Oil* (Thorsons 1984), p 24.
 3. Graham, J, *Evening Primrose Oil*, p 48.
 4. Shreeve, C, *Fish Oil, The Life Saver* (Thorsons 1992), p 70.
 5. Graham, J, *Evening Primrose Oil*, pp 27–8.
 6. Graham, J, *Evening Primrose Oil*, p 28.
 7. Galland, L, *Allergy Prevention For Kids* (Bloomsbury 1989), p 3.
 8. Graham, J, *Evening Primrose Oil*, p 33.
 9. Galland, L, *Allergy Prevention For Kids*, p 7.
10. Shreeve, C, *Fish Oil, The Life Saver*, p 70.
11. Bryce-Smith, D, Hodgkinson, L, *The Zinc Solution* (Century Arrow 1986), p 73.
12. Graham, J, *Evening Primrose Oil*, p 29.
13. Shreeve, C, *Fish Oil, The Life Saver*, p 60.

14. Shreeve, C, *Fish Oil, The Life Saver*, p 58.

15. Graham, J, *Evening Primrose Oil*, pp 68–9.

Chapter 11 **The Cholesterol Myth**

1. Davies, S, Stewart, A, *Nutritional Medicine* (Pan 1987), pp 113–14.

2. Shreeve, C, *Fish Oil, The Life Saver* (Thorsons 1992), pp 69–70.

3. Shreeve, C, *Fish Oil, The Life Saver*, p 60.

4. Shreeve, C, *Fish Oil, The Life Saver*, p 71.

5. Moore, TJ, *The Cholesterol Myth* (*The Atlantic Monthly* September 1989), p 39.

6. Moore, TJ, *The Cholesterol Myth*, p 65.

7. Ravnskov, U, 'Cholesterol lowering trials in coronary heart disease: frequency of citation and outcome' (*British Medical Journal* 4.7.92), p 18.

8. Davis, A, *Let's Get Well* (Unwin 1979).

9. Teo, KK, Yusuf, S, Collins, R, Held, PH, Peto, R, 'Effects of intravenous magnesium in suspected myocardial infarction: overview of randomised trials' (*British Medical Journal* 14.12.91), p 1502.

10. Davis, A, *Let's Get Well*, p 37.

11. Adams, R, Murray, F, *Minerals: Kill or Cure?* (Larchmont 1974), p 58.

12. Pfeiffer, CC, *Zinc and Other Micro-Nutrients* (Keats 1978), pp 97, 105.

13. Howard, JMH, 'Magnesium deficiency in peripheral vascular disease' (*Journal of Nutritional Medicine* Vol 1, No 1 1990), p 47.

14. Davis, A, *Let's Get Well*, p 41.

15. Pfeiffer, CC, *Zinc and Other Micro-Nutrients*, p 131.

16. Adams, R, Murray, F, *Minerals: Kill or Cure?*, pp 160–6.

17. Adams, R, Murray, F, *Minerals: Kill or Cure?*, p 162.

18. Adams, R, Murray, F, *Minerals: Kill or Cure?*, p 169.

19. Passwater, RA, Cranton, EM, *Trace Elements, Hair Analysis and Nutrition*, pp 129–32.

20. Passwater, RA, Cranton, EM, *Trace Elements, Hair Analysis and Nutrition*, pp 64, 80.

21. Passwater, RA, Cranton, EM, *Trace Elements, Hair Analysis and Nutrition*, pp 81–2.

22. Passwater, RA, Cranton, EM, *Trace Elements, Hair Analysis and Nutrition*, p 80.

Chapter 12 Weight Problems

1. Davis, A, *Let's Get Well* (Unwin 1979), p 57.
2. Davis, A, *Let's Get Well*, p 129.
3. Passwater, RA, Cranton, EM, *Trace Elements, Hair Analysis and Nutrition* (Keats Publishing 1983), p 171.
4. Passwater, RA, Cranton, EM, *Trace Elements, Hair Analysis and Nutrition*, pp 64–7.
5. Davis, A, *Let's Get Well*, p 252.
6. Passwater, RA, Cranton, EM, *Trace Elements, Hair Analysis and Nutrition* pp 68, 106.
7. Davies, S, Stewart, A, *Nutritional Medicine* (Pan 1987), p 21.
8. Pfeiffer, CC, *Zinc and Other Micro-Nutrients* (Keats 1978), pp 13–14.
9. Bryce-Smith, D, Hodgkinson, L, *The Zinc Solution* (Century Arrow 1986), pp 46–7, 96.
10. Bryce-Smith, D, Hodgkinson, L, *The Zinc Solution*, p 91.
11. Passwater, RA, Cranton, EM, *Trace Elements, Hair Analysis and Nutrition*, pp 134–5.
12. Bryce-Smith, D, Hodgkinson, L, *The Zinc Solution*, p 41.
13. Adams, R, Murray, F, *Minerals: Kill or Cure?* (Larchmont 1974), p 97.
14. Davis, A, *Let's Get Well*, p 9.
15. Bryce-Smith, D, Hodgkinson, L, *The Zinc Solution*, p 41.
16. Davis, A, *Let's Get Well*, p 143.
17. Davis, A, *Let's Get Well*, p 128.
18. Bryce-Smith, D, Hodgkinson, L, *The Zinc Solution*, p 69.
19. Bryce-Smith, D, Hodgkinson, L, *The Zinc Solution*, p 69.
20. Bryce-Smith, D, Hodgkinson, L, *The Zinc Solution*, p 69.
21. Gordon, J, 'I know what bulimia is like, Di. I suffered it too' (*Today*, 10.6.92).

Chapter 14 Time To Go Back, For The Sake Of Our Future

1. Hills, LD, *Organic Gardening* (Penguin 1977).
2. Balfour, EB, *The Living Soil and The Haughley Experiment* (Universe Books 1976).

3. Griggs, B, *The Food Factor* (Penguin 1986), p 116.
4. Balfour, EB, *The Living Soil and The Haughley Experiment*, p 70.
5. Griggs, B, *The Food Factor*, p 118.
6. Griggs, B, *The Food Factor*, p 165.
7. Tyrrel, R, 'Lifeline to Chernobyl' (*The Mail on Sunday* 21.6.91).
8. Carson, R, *Silent Spring* (Pelican, 1962).
9. Bryce-Smith, D, Hodgkinson, L, *The Zinc Solution* (Century Arrow 1986), pp 118–19.
10. Carson, R, *Silent Spring*, p 173.
11. Bryce-Smith, D, Hodgkinson, L, *The Zinc Solution*, pp 20–1.

Chapter 15 The Best Things In Life Are Free!
1. Kenton, L, *10 Day Clean-up Plan* (Vermillion 1992).
2. Downing, D, *Day Light Robbery* (Arrow Books 1988), p 10.
3. Price, WS, *Nutrition and Physical Degeneration* (Keats Publishing 1989), p 291.
4. Downing, D, *Day Light Robbery*, p 114.

Chapter 16 Emotional Damage
1. Weiner, MA, *Maximum Immunity* (Gateway 1986).
2. Barlow, K, *Recognising Health* (The McCarrison Society 1988), p 62.
3. Scott Williamson, G, Pearse, IH, *Biologists In Search Of Material* (Scottish Academic Press 1982).
4. Barlow, K, *Discipline of Peace* (Charles Knight 1971).
5. John, J, *Dead Sure?* (IVP/Frameworks 1989), pp 38–9.
6. John, J, *Ten Steps to the Good Life* (Hodder and Stoughton 1990), p 47.
7. Appleyard, B, 'Science and Spirit' (*The Times* 25.4.92).
8. Reference to Prof Stephen Hawking, physicist and author of *A Brief History of Time* (Bantam Press 1988).

Chapter 17 Unmeasurable Energy
1. Fulder, S, *The Handbook of Complementary Medicine* (Coronet Books 1989).
2. Fulder, S, *The Handbook of Complementary Medicine*, p 263.
3. Fulder, S, *The Handbook of Complementary Medicine*, p 263.
4. Fulder, S, *The Handbook of Complementary Medicine*, pp 261–2.

5. *The Society of Homoeopaths Annual Report* (1991), p 1.

6. Fulder, S, *The Handbook of Complementary Medicine*, p 197.

7. Fulder, S, *The Handbook of Complementary Medicine*, p 192.

8. Olsen, C, 'Shocked? Take a Rescue Remedy and feel better immediately' (*Daily Mail* 29.10.91).

9. Kenton, L, Kenton, S, *Raw Energy* (Arrow 1987), p 74.

10. Fulder, S, *The Handbook of Complementary Medicine*, p 128.

Chapter 18 **Influences**

1. Lewis, CS, *The Screwtape Letters* (Fount Paperbacks 1952), preface.

2. 'Spiritualists death leap to afterlife' (*Today* 31.7.92).

Chapter 19 **A Way Of Escape**

1. John, J, *Dead Sure?* (IVP/Frameworks 1989), p 28.

2. Holy Bible, New International Version, *John* 7:17.

3. John, J, *Life Means What?* (Hodder and Stoughton 1990), p 39.

4. Barlow, K, *Discipline of Peace* (Charles Knight 1971), p 134.

5. John, J, *Ten Steps to the Good Life* (Hodder and Stoughton 1990).

6. Holy Bible, New International Version, *Genesis* 2:7.

7. Barlow, K, *Discipline of Peace*, p 130.

Chapter 20 **Spiritual Immune System**

1. MacDonald, G, *Unspoken Sermons* (Longmans, Green, & Co 1886), p 245.

2. Ryle, JC, *Expository Thoughts On The Gospels* (James Clark 1985), p 198.

3. Holy Bible, New International Version, *1 Thessalonians* 5:21.

4. Holy Bible, New International Version, *Genesis* 3:19.